Collection Development for a New Century in the School Library Media Center

Collection Development for a New Century in the School Library Media Center

W. BERNARD LUKENBILL

Greenwood Professional Guides in School Librarianship
Harriet Selverstone, Series Adviser

GREENWOOD PRESS
Westport, Connecticut • London

Library of Congress Cataloging-in-Publication Data

Lukenbill, W. Bernard.
    Collection development for a new century in the school library media center / W.
Bernard Lukenbill.
      p. cm.—(Greenwood professional guides in school librarianship, ISSN 1074–150X)
    Includes bibliographical references and index.
    ISBN 0–313–31295–8 (alk. paper)
      1. School libraries—Collection development—United States. 2. Instructional
materials centers—Collection development—United States. I. Title. II. Series.
Z675.S3 L8953 2002
025.2'1878—dc21   2001040563

British Library Cataloguing in Publication Data is available.

Library of Congress Catalog Card Number: 2001040563
ISBN: 0–313–31295–8
ISSN: 1074–150X

First published in 2002

Greenwood Press, 88 Post Road West, Westport, CT 06881
An imprint of Greenwood Publishing Group, Inc.
www.greenwood.com

Printed in the United States of America

The paper used in this book complies with the
Permanent Paper Standard issued by the National
Information Standards Organization (Z39.48–1984).

10 9 8 7 6 5 4 3 2

Dedicated to the life and memory of my mom and dad,
Lee Roy Lukenbill (1900–1981) and
Tommie Lee McCorkle Lukenbill (1908–1998)

Contents

Introduction

The world of the twenty-first century is a world of technology, innovation, and uncertainty. While not new to the human experience or to the school library media center, technology has become increasingly intense and pervasive. Demands are being placed on the managers of technology to improve society and education in ways that the educational environment has rarely experienced. The school library media center is one of the major players in this technological transformation. The school library movement has always been aligned with progressive education, and this historical background has laid a solid foundation for change and new development.

This book is constructed around five themes that affect collection development.

- Social and Cultural Action
- Management and Decision Making
- Creativity and the Production of Information and Literature
- Collection Development and Aesthetics
- Technology and Collection Development

COLLECTION DEVELOPMENT AS A SOCIAL AND CULTURAL ACTION

Society and culture have always been central to defining the role of the collection development process of the school library media center. Within this framework of culture and society, the collection in schools has served the curriculas and instructional needs of students, faculty, and staff; and within American and Canadian culture and society, the center's collection has always played a role in serving recreational and personal information needs as well.

In meeting these various expectations, school library media specialists have great impact on society and on the educational environment through their decisions and behaviors. Collection development can never be separated from the larger society and is subject to all of the political, social, and cultural pressures that surround it. In a democratic and open society these pressures are intense, as they represent a wide variety of values, interests, and expectations. Recognizing this, this book attempts to approach collection development from a social and cultural perspective. It offers practical guidance based on many years of professional practice and the conventional wisdom that has grown out of that practice. For that reason, references to the historical record are often made so that a continuum of professional development and evolution is evident to the reader. This is particularly true in terms of how professional organizations such as the American Library Association (ALA) through the American Association of School Librarians (AASL), the Association for Educational Communications and Technology (AECT), and the Association for Media and Technology in Education of Canada (AMTEC), as well as the historic role played by the National Education Association (NEA), have influenced the role of the school library media center and its collection. In addition, complex or vexing contemporary social issues such as sex information and family life are discussed in detail in terms of how they influence collection development decisions.

COLLECTION DEVELOPMENT AS MANAGEMENT AND DECISION MAKING

Another central theme of this book is that collection development is a decision-making and managerial process. Decisions must be made logically based on sound management principles such as cost-benefit analysis, and they must be made in the context of social and legal responsibilities within a democratic culture. Using selection aids and guides and the equitable application of selection criteria are also discussed as management and decision operations.

The many demands placed on collection development may be educational, legal and ethical, multicultural, aesthetic, technological, and political in nature. For that reason, much attention is given to policy formation and execution, censorship and legal determinants of censorship, government policy development and practice, educational theory, and free access to materials and equipment.

CREATIVITY AND THE PRODUCTION OF INFORMATION AND LITERATURE

Creativity is an integral part of the human experience. Without creativity technology could not have developed and little in human culture and society could have been realized. Certainly information and aesthetics are expressions and products of human creativity. Of course, not all works of creativity are positive, and history provides many examples of the power of negative creativity; but in the context of this book, creativity is viewed largely as a positive human experience.

Creativity is a complex process involving psychology, biology, culture, and society. Historically, some eras and geographic areas have produced more creative works than others. Society and the surrounding culture play a large role in creativity. Control and support mechanisms such as religion, economics, and political systems can either promote or stifle creativity. An individual's environmental experiences, psychology, biology, and place in history are fundamental influences on creativity. Great works of science, technology, and literature can be seen as personal and group responses to internal psychological forces as well as external social creative forces. Although not well understood, creativity is the driving force of society and culture. The information age of the twenty-first century is fundamentally defined by it. Creativity also has a place in the school library media center. Creative works are part of the collection, and making choices and managing a collection are creative processes.

COLLECTION DEVELOPMENT AND AESTHETICS

Libraries throughout history have always been associated with fine literature and aesthetic experiences. This book continues that tradition by discussing how collection development can serve aesthetics through the acquisition of fine fiction, biography, folklore, drama, poetry, and music. The book also recognizes the conflicts that often arise when aesthetics and popular needs clash and compete for public support, acceptance, and inclusion in collections.

TECHNOLOGY AND COLLECTION DEVELOPMENT

This volume attempts to place the technology that surrounds us within a historic continuum and to view current technological problems, issues, and trends in school library media center collection development within that continuum. To understand new technology and apply it intelligently we need the advice and experience of others. As a managerial approach to technology, this book offers avenues to professional and technical experiences, predictions, and guidance. Because predicting future developments in technology is difficult, library media specialists will need to seek out relevant resources, guides, and professional observations and opinions to make good decisions. Keeping this in mind, I have attempted to base my review of technology on reliable professional resources, and serious critical social commentaries. Thomas K. Glennan and Arthur Melmed were particularly helpful in assessing educational technology in their report, *Fostering the Use of Educational Technology: Elements of National Strategy* (RAND 1996). In articles appearing in *Time* June 19, 2000, Vinto Cerf, Laurel Clyde, and Michael Kaku offered valuable insight into the future of the Internet and advanced technologies that will likely influence all areas of education and communication in the future.

Collection Development as
Science and Art

.1

THE SCIENCE OF COLLECTION DEVELOPMENT

School library media collection development is both a science and an art. It is a science because it is a process that is systematically developed and carefully managed, similar to methods used in the various scientific disciplines. One definition of science is "something . . . that may be studied or learned like systematized knowledge."[1]

The scientific aspect of collection development is based on long years of practice, research, and professional observations. In 1920 and 1925 the first standards for school libraries were published. They outlined the scientific approach to school library management, recommending that all aspects of a school's library program be scientific and systematic. This included not only procedures and operations, but also collection development practices. These standards likewise emphasized the importance of the systematic and scientific development of the library's collection in the educational process.[2]

These early assumptions about the scientific nature of school library and collection management were undoubtedly influenced by the prevailing ideas about good management theory and practice. Chief among these was the scientific management school, which was introduced by Louis Brandeis in 1910 when he appeared before the U.S. Interstate Commerce Commission. This school's main influence on school library management appears to be its emphasis on maximum output with minimum effort, and the elimination of waste and inefficiency at all levels of operation.[3] Since that time other management approaches have likewise influenced school library media management and collection development. Today one of the most generally accepted theories of management is general systems theory. Its approach to overall management is well suited to collection development. It includes a variety of interests and approaches as it seeks to merge the ideas of the more classical scientific theories of management with those of the human relations movement.[4]

Among the key concepts that currently guide this approach are its emphasis on the scientific method of inquiry, its systematic use of problem-solving techniques, and its reliance on the total systems approach.[5] Throughout the years such principles of management as they apply to collection development have evolved into specific models for practice. As in any other human management endeavor, conflicts and differing points of view are found within these models.

CONFLICTING MODELS FOR COLLECTION DEVELOPMENT

Two major models of collection development and selection have evolved in American librarianship, reflecting different beliefs about the purpose of libraries. At one end of the spectrum, some believe that the major mission of libraries, especially school and public libraries, is to raise literary appreciation and awareness within the community by providing fine literature. At the other end of the spectrum are those who believe that libraries, especially public libraries, as public institutions, should provide exactly what the public wants or needs. School libraries, because they have a very specific mission of educating youth, have tended to follow the more prescriptive path in collection development.

EVOLUTION OF A COLLECTION DEVELOPMENT PARADIGM

Although support for the curriculum is the main principle of school library collection development, over the years complex theories and practices of collection development have evolved that reflect modern educational, social, and cultural thinking and philosophies. One way to understand how current ideas about collection development have evolved is to review some of the major documents that have influenced their development and contributed to the formation of a recognized scientific paradigm. Professional standards and highly regarded textbooks are two logical places to search for evidence of paradigm formation and articulation.

In viewing collection development as a scientific process, we need to consider the role of paradigm development in the sciences and whether and how this concept can apply to collection development.

Defining a Scientific Paradigm

Thomas S. Kuhn, in his influential book *The Structure of Scientific Revolutions*, defined a paradigm as an accepted model or pattern. In science a paradigm is a concept that is always subject to further articulation and specification under new or more stringent conditions. Kuhn holds that a paradigm gains and maintains its status and power because it is more successful than competing paradigms in solving immediate problems. Within a scientific framework, although there may be ambiguities, a paradigm will prevail as long as it is successful in helping to solve critical problems faced by the discipline. It will be replaced when new problems and situations are introduced into the environment that it cannot address successfully. A successful paradigm in a science builds a community of followers, and the conceptual, observational, and instrumental applications of the paradigm are revealed in standard forms of communication such as textbooks, lectures, and laboratory exercises. By studying the prevailing paradigm members of the community learn their trade.[6]

Like all well-established scientific paradigms, the current paradigm of collection development has been and continues to be repeated in textbooks, classroom lectures, discussions, and professional standards. Standards present the evolution of the thinking and ideas within a profession, and they naturally reflect the major paradigms within the discipline.

SCHOOL LIBRARY STANDARDS, 1920 TO 1999: MATERIALS, LIBRARIANS, AND TECHNOLOGY

When we look at the school library standards and their interpretations published between 1920 and 1999, several things stand out. The librarian is seen as central to the selection and management of a collection. He or she is viewed as an essential element not only in the selection of materials, but also in their use and integration into the curriculum and the lives of faculty, staff, and students. Likewise, all of these standards are progressive in that they reflect the current educational philosophies and practices of their eras. All address technology issues. They state in varying ways how educational and information technologies can be and are used in the educational process. Collectively they reflect a stability of values, practices, methodologies, and measurements necessary for consistency in school library collection development and in the continuing refinement of the prevailing collection development paradigm.

Standards of 1920 and 1925

The first national standards for school libraries, published in 1920 and 1925, were issued by the National Education Association and the North

Central Association of Colleges and Secondary Schools under the chairmanship of C.C. Certain and supported by and published through the American Library Association. The 1920 standards addressed the needs of secondary school libraries, while the 1925 standards considered elementary school library requirements. Both sets of standards gave considerable attention to collection development. Although all types of materials were considered essential, special attention was given to the role of vocational information and audiovisual items in collection development. Vocational information was considered important because at that time most students ended their formal education after finishing elementary school or high school and entered the work force. These standards clearly recognized the importance of information in the everyday lives of students and the importance of information technology in addressing such needs.

Another important aspect of these standards was their clear understanding of the role of the librarian in the educational process. The librarian is presented as active in providing bibliographic instruction for both students and faculty, developing reading guidance programs and activities, and, in cooperation with counselors, disseminating vocational information.[7,8]

Standards of 1945

The American Library Association published the next important national standards for school libraries in 1945 under the title *School Libraries for Today and Tomorrow*. These standards revealed the lasting effects of World War II and the fight to defeat fascism. One compelling aspect was the role ascribed to information in protecting freedom and American democracy. The library was described as "a laboratory for exploration and experimentation with printed and audiovisual materials." Knowing how to use the library was seen as "a proving ground for carrying out democratic responsibility."[9]

Within this laboratory context librarians were to be active in curriculum development, in planning programs, including reading programs, and in offering reference services. These standards recognized that the librarian had a responsibility to offer social guidance as well as vocational guidance.[10]

Standards of 1960

Standards for School Library Programs was published in 1960 under the sponsorship of the American Association of School Librarians. These standards were explicitly designed to address the changes in educational demands and approaches that had occurred since 1945. The library was described as a place where "boundaries can be extended immeasurably in all areas of knowledge and in all forms of creative expression, and the means provided to meet and stimulate the many interests, appreciations and curiosities of youth".[11,12]

These standards gave far more attention to educational and information technology (i.e., audiovisuals) than previous standards by recognizing technology as a powerful force in education and information dissemination. The standards took pains to explain how technology had impacted school library programs in recent years and outlined how technology could be accommodated administratively within a school, including the role the school library could play in this accommodation. Most important, the standards recognized the impact of technology by noting that the school library need not be called a library. It could appropriately be called "a materials center, an instructional materials center, an instructional resources center, or any of the equivalent terms now springing into existence."[13]

Within these centers, the librarian was expected to promote a "cross-media approach" to instruction by encouraging and supporting modern teaching strategies that used instructional materials on either a subject or a problem-centered basis. Librarians were expected to continue providing programs of reading and reading guidance; guidance in listening and viewing; reference and research services; instruction in use of materials; and personal and social guidance.[14]

Standards of 1969

Only nine years later, the American Association of School Librarians, together with the Department of Audiovisual Education of the National Education Association (now the Association for Educational Communications and Technology), issued *Standards for School Media Programs*. These updated standards were needed because "significant social changes, education developments, and technological innovations" had taken place since the 1960 standards were issued.[15]

These standards continued to emphasize the role of technology in school library collection development.[16] To reinforce the increasing importance of information technology in school library programs, these standards introduced the generic term "media" to refer to print and audiovisual forms of communication and their related technology.[17] Furthermore, "library" and "librarian" were replaced with "media specialist" and "media center." Librarians were given this advice about programs and services:

Participate actively in shaping the learning environment and design of instruction thereby [insuring] that every media facility, piece of equipment, book or material be selected, produced, and used so that the students in our schools are challenged to a dynamic participation in a free, exciting and enriched life.[18]

Standards of 1975

Published under the title *Media Programs: District and School*, the 1975 standards were perhaps the most conceptually sophisticated yet formulated.[19] Not only did they define the relationship between building-level media programs and programs at district levels, but they also presented what was felt to be a consensus among educators and information professionals regarding the conceptual relationship of librarianship, information science, and educational technology. These standards asserted that through media, students could become skilled at reading, observing, listening, and communicating ideas and could develop a spirit of inquiry, achievement, self-motivation, and discipline and a capacity for self-evaluation. In essence they saw the media program as one based on a sound scientific understanding of educational and information communication theory, emphasizing the interaction of media personnel, materials, technology, and users.[20]

Standards and Interpretations of 1988 and 1999

The 1988 standards, undoubtedly more far-reaching and educationally integrative than any previous standards, were published under the title *Information Power: Guidelines for School Library Media Programs*. They stated specifically that the mission of the school library media program— to "ensure that students and staff are effective users of ideas and information"—was to be accomplished

by providing intellectual and physical access to materials in all formats, by providing instruction to foster competence and interest in reading, viewing, and using information and ideas, [and] by working with other educators to design learning strategies to meet the needs of individual students.[21]

A further interpretation of these standards was issued as a new revision in 1998 under the title *Information Power: Building Partnerships for Learning*. Although this interpretation continued to reinforce the 1988 principles, it did emphasize an enlarged mission for school library media programs. It stated clearly that the school library media center should offer programs and services that are centered on information literacy and that are designed around active, authentic student learning as described in the information literacy standards for student learning. The goals of today's library media program point to the development of a community of learners that is centered on the student and sustained by a creative, energetic library media program.[22]

The goal was to provide access to carefully selected and systematically organized information at the local level, offering diverse learning resources representing a wide range of subjects, levels of difficulty, and formats. Other goals were establishing "systematic procedure[s] for acquiring information and materials from outside the library media center and the school through such mechanisms as electronic networks, interlibrary loan, and cooperative agreements with other information agencies" and providing "instruction in using a range of equipment for accessing local and remote information in any format."[23]

Taken together, these two documents offer a challenge to school media librarians as they face a new century filled with new technologies and demands for information skills and literacy. These new demands will test the prevailing paradigm. Will the procedures and philosophies developed over the last century be adequate to meet these new demands? What can we bring from the past that will help us develop collections suitable for an age of new technologies and social demands?

MAJOR TEXTBOOKS, 1929 TO 1999

Among the major textbooks and monographs in school librarianship published through the 1970s that discuss collection development are those by Annie T. Eaton, Martha Wilson, Hannah Logasa, Lucile F. Fargo, Ruth Davies, John T. Gillespie, and Emanuel T. Prostano and Joyce S. Prostano.[24]

Textbooks by Eaton, Logasa, and Fargo published in the 1920s and 1930s went to great lengths to explain the emerging progressive educational movement and to underscore its meaning for school librarianship. These authors stressed that this new approach to education and learning had freed students from rote textbook-centered learning. By its very nature, this progressive approach to education had moved the library into a more central place in the school and in student learning. These authors envisioned the school library and the librarian as playing a central role in meeting student needs. They suggested that the librarian was a facilitator who guided students in developing a worldview, helping them move toward self-discovery and giving them an abundance of vicarious experiences through media. The librarian's role certainly included helping students know how to use books and libraries for study as well as for leisure reading. Eaton, Logasa, and Fargo likewise recognized technology as important to this role. As early as 1923 Eaton advocated a multidimensional approach to collection development. She perceived books as well as nonprint media as being central to the mission of the library.[25]

Fargo, in her 1939 book, recognized the need for nonprint media in library collections, but she did this reluctantly, claiming that they were of less educational value than books and periodicals. By the time her fourth edition was published in 1947, however, she had become more accepting of nonprint materials, agreeing that they, too, often reflected educational principles.[26] In the late 1960s and into the 1970s Davies published other major textbooks in school librarianship. In various editions published during these years she expanded on many of the concepts presented by her predecessors, C.C. Certain, Eaton, Wilson, and Fargo. She outlined the limitations of textbook-centered teaching, spoke in favor of discovery learning, and endorsed multimedia teaching and learning. She especially promoted the librarian as being totally involved in the educational process. She saw the school librarian as an active, multifaceted teacher, fulfilling many roles such as cooperating teacher, team teacher, and master teacher. Her concept extended to include the librarian as a curriculum consultant, a media specialist, and an integral part of the guidance program.[27] Other textbooks of the period—those by Gillespie and Prostano and Prostano—reflected Davies's model of the school library media center in terms of philosophy, methodology, management, and resources.[28]

During the 1980s and 1990s authors such as Eisenberg and Berkowitz (1988), Donham (1998), Haycock (1999), Farmer and Fowler (1999), Hicks (1981), Van Orden (1982), Kuhlthau and her colleagues (1999), Wright and Davie (1999), and Yesner and Jay (1998) further consolidated ideas that both influenced the development of the 1988 and 1998 standards and were codified in them. Central to all of these writings was the idea that the school library held a cardinal place in the intellectual, social, and information makeup of any school and that the development of the collection was central to the implementation of this role.[29]

COLLECTION DEVELOPMENT AS AN ART AND A PHILOSOPHY

Although collection development embraces many aspects of scientific management, it has artistic elements as well. Webster's defines art as the conscious use of skill and creative imagination."[30] Like art, collection development is often based on individual experiences, observations, skills, and creative imagination, elements difficult to teach and to place in a schema suitable for cognitive understanding. Like art, collection development is often conditioned by personal and political judgments, intuitions, and individual and professional philosophy.

Unlike science, philosophy "searches for a general understanding of values and reality by chiefly speculative rather than observational means."[31] Because professional philosophy impacts collection development and influences the development of a personal approach to the management of a collection, it is necessary to consider the "artistic" or "quality selection" approach to collection development.

The late Helen Haines, author of *Living with Books*, is perhaps the best-known proponent of this theory.[32] She recognized that the public library in particular must respond to popular demand, but had a low opinion of it:

Mass demand . . . is more weighted by ignorance and instinct than by intelligence and reason. It is supplied and stimulated by many exploiting agencies of our machine civilization. It has enforced and established crudities and superficialities in mass education. It represents the most difficult problem in library service.[33]

She fundamentally believed that the better mission of the librarian was to select books that would enrich the lives of those who read them. She noted that this approach required librarians to have an extensive knowledge of literature, including the classics, and believed that priority must be given to books of high quality.

The editors and reviewers of *The Horn Book Magazine* held similar views on the selection of books for youth. *The Horn Book Magazine* was founded in 1924 for the express purpose of lifting the literary appreciation of children and their parents. In her interpretive study of the magazine from its founding in 1924 to 1973, Joan Olson found that it clearly reflected the classic aesthetic approach to literary criticism, emphasizing the beauty of reading. During this time period, reviews and commentaries often criticized prevailing professional theories about reading that emphasized the psychological processes over reading as an art form. Clearly the *Horn Book* sought to elevate literary taste among children and their adult caregivers through the encouragment and promotion of fine writing.[34]

CONCLUSION

Collection development as practiced in school libraries has evolved since the nineteenth century into a scientifically based system that employs modern management practices. It is a system that has a well-articulated scientific paradigm reinforced by professional standards, textbooks, and monographs. It is a paradigm that is taught and practiced widely. Although exacting in many respects, this paradigm can accommodate varying social and political views and approaches to collection management. It also allows for change and the incorporation of new ideas, formats, and technology. In the following chapters, important elements of this paradigm will be discussed and analyzed.

NOTES

1. *Merriam-Webster's Collegiate Dictionary*, 10th ed. (Springfield, MA: Merriam Webster Co., 1999), p. 1045.

2. National Education Association and North Central Association of Colleges and Secondary Schools Committee on Library Organization and Equipment, *Standard Library Organization and Equipment for Secondary Schools of Different Sizes*, C.C. Certain, chairman (Chicago: American Library Association, 1920); National Education Association of the United States, Department of Elementary School Principals, "Report of the Joint Committee on Elementary School Library Standards," in *Fourth Yearbook. The Elementary School Principalship: A Study of its Instructional and Administrative Aspects*, Arthur Gist, ed. (Washington, DC: National Education Association, 1925), pp. 326–59.

3. Robert D. Stueart and Barbara B. Moran, *Library and Information Center Management 5th ed.* (Littleton, CO: Libraries Unlimited, 1998), p. 8.

4. Ibid., pp. 21–22.

5. Ibid., p. 21.

6. Thomas S. Kuhn, *The Structure of Scientific Revolutions*, 2d ed., enlarged (Chicago: University of Chicago Press, 1970), p. 43.

7. National Education Association, *Standard Library Organization*; National Education Association, "Report of the Joint Committee."

8. W. Bernard Lukenbill, "Learning Resources and Interactive Learning Principles," *Drexel Library Quarterly* 19 (Spring 1983): 94–95.

9. American Library Association, Committee on Post-War Planning, *School Libraries for Today and Tomorrow* (Chicago: American Library Association, 1945), p. 13.

10. Lukenbill, "Learning Resources," pp. 95–96.

11. American Association of School Librarians, *Standards for School Library Programs* (Chicago: American Library Association, 1960), p. 4.

12. Lukenbill, "Learning Resources," pp. 96–97.

13. American Association of School Librarians, *Standards*, p. 13.

14. Lukenbill, "Learning Resources," pp. 96–97.

15. American Association of School Librarians and the Department of Audiovisual Instruction of the National Education Association, *Standards for School Media Programs* (Chicago: American Library Association; Washington, DC: National Education Association, 1969).

16. Lukenbill, "Learning Resources," pp. 97–98.

17. Ibid.

18. American Association of School Librarians and the Department of Audiovisual Instruction of the National Education Association, *Standards for School Media Programs*.

19. American Association of School Librarians and Association for Educational

Communications and Technology, *Media Programs: District and School* (Chicago: American Library Association; Washington, DC: Association for Educational Communications and Technology, 1975).

20. Lukenbill, "Learning Resources," pp. 98–99.

21. American Association of School Librarians and Association for Educational Communications and Technology, *Information Power: Guidelines for School Library Media Programs* (Chicago: American Library Association; Washington, DC: Association for Educational Communications and Technology, 1988), p. 1.

22. American Association of School Librarians and Association for Educational Communications and Technology, *Information Power: Building Partnerships for Learning* (Chicago: American Library Association; Washington, DC: Association for Educational Communications and Technology, 1998), p. 6.

23. Ibid., p. 7.

24. Lukenbill, "Learning Resources," pp. 102, 114. Some representative early titles include: Ruth Ann Davies, *The School Library Media Center: A Force for Educational Excellence* (New York: R. R. Bowker, 1969); Ann T. Eaton, *School Library Service* (Chicago: American Library Association, 1923); Lucile Foster Fargo, *The Library and the School* (Chicago: American Library Association, 1928); John T. Gillespie, *Creating a School Media Program* (New York: R. R. Bowker, 1973); Hannah Logasa, *The High School Library: Its Function in Education* (New York: D. Appleton, 1928); Emanuel T. Prostano and Joyce S. Prostano, *The School Library Media Center* (Englewood, CO: Libraries Unlimited, 1971); and Martha Wilson, *School Library Management* (New York: H. W. Wilson, 1919).

25. Ibid., p. 102.

26. Ibid.

27. Ibid., pp. 102–3, 114.

28. Ibid., p. 103.

29. Jean Donham, *Enhancing Teaching and Learning: A Leadership Guide for School Media Specialists* (New York: Neal-Schuman, 1998); Michael B. Eisenberg and Robert Berkowitz, *Curriculum Initiative: An Agenda and Strategy for Library Media Programs* (Norwood, NJ: Ablex, 1988); Lesley S.J. Farmer and Will Fowler, *More than Information: The Role of the Library Media Center in the Multimedia Classroom* (Worthington, OH: Linworth, 1999); Ken Haycock, ed., *Foundations for Effective School Library Media Programs* (Englewood, CO: Libraries Unlimited, 1999); Warren B. Hicks, *Managing the Building-Level School Media Program* (Chicago: American Association of School Librarians, American Library Association, 1981); Carol Collier Kuhlthau, M. Elspeth Goodin, and Mary J. McNally, eds., *The Virtual School Library: Gateway to the Information Superhighway* (Englewood, CO: Libraries Unlimited, 1999); Phyllis J. Van Orden, *The Collection Program in Elementary and Middle Schools: Concepts, Practices, and Information Sources* (Englewood, CO: Libraries Unlimited, 1982); Keith C. Wright and Judith F. Davie, *Forecasting the Future: School Media Programs in an Age of Change* (Lanham, MD: Scarecrow Press, 1999); Bernice L. Yesner and Hilda L. Jay, *Operating and Evaluating School Library Media Programs: A Handbook for Administrators and Librarians* (New York: Neal-Schuman, 1998).

30. *Merriam-Webster's Collegiate Dictionary*, p. 65.

31. Ibid., p. 873.

32. Helen Haines, *Living with Books* (New York: Columbia University Press, 1935), pp. 16–24.

33. Ibid., pp. 19–20.

34. Joah Blodgett Peterson Olson, "An Interpretive History of the *Horn Book Magazine*, 1924–1973," Ph.D. dissertation, Stanford University, 1976, cited in *Dissertations Abstracts International*, vol. 37-A, p. 2875.

Vision, Mission, and a Changing Society

.2

STRUCTURE AND ORDER IN SELECTION

Selecting materials for any collection requires structure and order. Professional standards and guidelines such as those formulated by the American Association of School Librarians (AASL) and the Association for Educational Communications and Technology (AECT) provide structure and order by explaining in detail what is expected of and wanted from school library media specialists. Standards and guidelines generally have no legal authority, but they do provide strong motivation for the library media specialist to act in an ordered and professional way in developing a collection. They are also useful for explaining to outside parties such as administrators and parents the value of a school library media collection in the overall educational process.

BUILDING COLLECTIONS WITHIN A BUREAUCRATIC STRUCTURE

Librarians select materials for a collection within an organizational and bureaucratic framework, not in a vacuum. At the local level, this bureaucratic structure directs selection and collection development processes. As in any bureaucratic organization, this structure can exert a positive or negative influence. It is useful to take a brief look at the nature of modern bureaucracy to see how it influences building library collections and selecting and weeding materials.

As industry developed during the nineteenth century, bureaucracy came into its own as a form of organizational structure. Theorists have noted that bureaucracy has both strengths and weaknesses. For one thing, it promotes *specialization or division of labor*, which in turn encourages productivity.[1] In modern organizations we see this reflected in job differentiation, position classification, and the breakdown of work into simple tasks. Past and current school library standards and guidelines certainly reflect this. Since the 1920s all national standards have reflected the specialization of the librarian within the school environment. Later formulations such as *Standards for School Media Programs*, published in 1969 by the AASL, have served to accelerate this trend.

In large organizations, the overspecialization of labor can have disastrous consequences. However, within school media centers, labor specialization has served largely to place the educational role of the librarian within a clearly defined theoretical framework. This is especially true in terms of collection development and materials selection by school media librarians. School library media specialists are seen as professionals who know how to integrate materials into the curriculum and how to incorporate information, materials, and aesthetic experiences into the lives of students.

One of the primary complaints about the division of labor within large organizations is that it confines workers to repeated and routine tasks, leading to employee boredom. It likewise does not promote the best use of workers' talents and potentials. From the school library media specialist's perspective, selecting materials and building collections is an exciting and intellectually stimulating undertaking.

Hierarchy is another aspect of bureaucracy that influences collection development activities. Hierarchy provides for authority, direction, and coordination.[2] Again, recent national library standards published by the AASL and the AECT have suggested in great detail the hierarchical structure necessary for modern school media librarianship. Collection development and management are clearly defined as major responsibilities of the school library media specialist within the framework of not only the library media center, but also within the overall administrative structure of the school environment.

Rules, regulations, and policies comprise another hallmark of formal bureaucracy. They help ensure equality, uniformity, equity, consistency, and order. They likewise make life within an organization less capricious, arbitrary, and discriminatory.[3] The collective wisdom and practice of school librarianship show that collection development must be based on clear rules, regulations, and policies. The collection development policy and its supporting manual of procedures and operations are a necessary part of school library management, acting as guideposts for consistency. If disagreements and disputes arise over the nature of the collection, they ensure that fairness and the rights of all parties will be protected. In recent years, modern national library standards as well as professional expectations have placed great emphasis on the importance of collection development policies and regulations.

Nevertheless, rules, regulations, and policies can be carried too far. One must keep in mind the reason for a rule or policy and not let it take on a life of its own. The good school library manager will also try to avoid too many rules, regulations, policies, and written directives because they can create confusion and promote indecision and dysfunctional organizational behaviors.[4] For example, a librarian not given adequate support by the school administration in a dispute over censorship of library materials might react by developing excessively detailed collection development plans and procedures that require approval at several levels of administration and teaching staff before any item can be purchased. It is easy to see how such rules and policies would soon become a burden to all parties involved.

Management by administrators is another aspect of bureaucracy. In large organizations, the bureaucracy requires an administrative generalist to manage the work done by technical experts. In theory, this ensures the smooth operation of the organization so its real work can be carried out by the technical experts.[5] Also, in theory, management by administrators is an advantage in that it sets clear lines of responsibility. School library media center management theory, as presented through various standards, guidelines, and professional statements, clearly outlines the management role of the school library media specialist. This is true not only for the management of the collection and resources, but also applies to the management of technology and the support staff necessary to ensure that high-level technological infrastructure is available within the school environment.

COLLECTION DEVELOPMENT IN A CLIMATE OF EDUCATIONAL CHANGE

In the United States, Canada, Great Britain, Australia, New Zealand, and elsewhere over the past twenty years, the educational process has become more decentralized, relying less on control from a central administrative office and more on a site-based and shared decision-making model. The model includes goal-directed, ongoing training and development as well as empowerment of others through collaborative planning and shared decision making. The principal's role is paramount in the success of this model.[6]

In education, as in other areas of society, total quality management (TQM) has been implemented as a means of improving organizational processes and productivity. W. Edwards Deming identified fourteen principles he believed to be at the heart of total quality management that would ensure success as determined by productivity through quality control and customer satisfaction.[7] Essentially, these principles were based on the assumption that the success of an enterprise such as a manufacturing company could best be realized by striving for high quality services and products. The heart of these principles was to produce a quality product or service that would satisfy and delight customers. To do this, the traditional bureaucracy of the typical workplace had to be reorganized so that all employees from top management to assembly-line workers would be free to contribute to the ongoing production of better quality products and services. In educational environments, these principles would likewise empower all employees to work toward better quality educational programs and services for students, parents, and society in general. Some research has indicated that within school environments not all of these principles are understood or endorsed by school principals. Problems seem to lie in the principals' support of empowerment of others and the need to decrease fear and break down barriers. This finding has implications for collaborative decision making, sensitivity to others, and working together to fulfill an organization's mission.[8] On the other hand, some research has indicated that principals understand and support the need for a clear vision and philosophy for the school, to support faculty experimentation and new ideas and approaches, and trust teachers to make decisions in the best interest of students. Their trust level was not as high with regard to curriculum quality control or in service planning.[9]

Bonstingl describes the new paradigm for education thus: "Teachers should be viewed as primary sources of development and implementation of new instructional methodologies and assessment techniques directed toward their students' acquisition of critical thinking and lifelong learning skills."[10] To create this kind of educational environment, traditional authoritarian leadership roles, in which commands come from the top, must be discarded in favor of a management environment where thinking and acting are encouraged at all levels.[11]

Modern paradigms of school library media management clearly reflect these ideas. In this paradigm the media center must be considered a central force within the school where learning and critical thinking are encouraged and supported. Sound collection development involving books, nonprint media, and new technologies is central to this paradigm and the development of critical thinking skills.

BUILDING COLLECTIONS WITHIN ORGANIZATIONAL CULTURES

Each organization has its own unique culture. Aspects of this culture are both material and nonmaterial and are displayed in many ways.

Dress, behavior, attitudes, values, and even speech are elements of organizational culture. It is important to understand an organization's culture because it presents its values to members of the organization as valid behavior expectations. The organization teaches its members how to perceive, think, and feel in relation to the problems it faces.[12]

The organizational structure of a school can influence the selection process by the value it places on the library and its collection. The physical placement of the library and how it is laid out and designed can be indications of the organizational climate and values and how the library has been permitted or elected to respond to those values. The role of the library media specialist is another indication of organizational culture. What are the organizational expectations for this role, and what part is the librarian allowed to play? In some schools the librarian may be given a relatively free hand to make decisions and to encourage participation by others in selection, while in other schools decisions on selection of materials may be made elsewhere by others. Although professional guidelines and policies may be in place, the individual librarian at the building level has an important role to play in defining the place of the librarian in the organizational culture of the school. The librarian also is paramount in establishing and defining the cultural role of collaborative collection development by faculty, student, staff, and parents within the local school environment.

THE PLANNING PROCESS IN COLLECTION DEVELOPMENT

A plan of operation and an approach for systematic development of the collection must be carefully worked out. The collection development plan is more than a plan of daily operation. It is also a statement of the central philosophy of the library media center about what the collection is and how it is to serve its users. In one sense developing a collection plan is simple, in that it is a clearly stated map of how the collection is to be managed and cared for over many years. Nevertheless, the process is also complex because of the variety of issues that must be taken into account, including curriculum needs, information and instructional requirements, recreational needs, and various social and cultural expectations. The planning process must likewise include issues involving various media formats—both print and electronic—and their support technologies. Cost, content, delivery systems, and appropriateness and effectiveness are only a few issues that must be considered. The role of the Internet in the delivery of information is a powerful example of how carefully media formats must be evaluated and considered. At this point the Internet forces school library media center specialists to face squarely issues of policy formation, accessibility, social expectations, educational and information needs, and legal considerations.

Planning is an integral part of collection development. Cyert and March define a plan as "a goal, indicating certain beliefs; a schedule specifying steps to be taken; a theory, considering relationships; and a precedent, established for existing decisions.[13] Stueart and Moran note that planning involves answering these questions: why, who, when, where, and how.[14] Within the context of developing a collection plan for a school library media collection, we can ask these questions:

Why and for what purposes is the collection to be developed?

Who will be involved in developing the collection?

When will the plan and its various aspects pertaining to the collection be implemented?

Where will the plan be developed and executed?

How will the plan be developed and executed?

In answering these questions, the planning process becomes a practical and theoretical undertaking designed to understand and control in positive ways both external and internal forces that influence the library environment and its collection. Planning is a collaborative effort that must involve all elements of the organization—librarians, faculty, students, staff, administrators, and parents. Planning must also lead to a written document. One of the primary written documents to come out of the collection development planning process is an official collection development policy. Generally speaking, this policy outlines in detail the following points:

Why are collection development and selection undertaken?

Who is responsible for selection decisions and who is generally involved in selection decisions?

What criteria and general guidelines are used for selection of materials?

How and when is selection carried out within the structure of the school?

What general processes have been established for review of challenged materials?

A more detailed discussion of collection development policies is presented later in this book. Stueart and Moran also provide a detailed discussion of the overall planning process within a school library media center environment.[15]

Strategic planning underpins all planning processes, and it now absorbs much of what is considered long-term planning. Begun in the 1960s amid rapid economic shifts, strategic planning was used as an effective means of identifying and reacting to rapidly changing organizational priorities. In the market economy of the late twentieth-century, strategic planning must begin with a clear understanding of what the customer wants and will buy. Business plans are not to be determined by who produces products, but rather by those who purchase products. Therefore strategic planning starts with knowing exactly what the customer wants. In terms of collection development within a school library media center, this means knowing exactly what is expected of the collection by its many user groups. Strategic planning involves "describing a vision for the organization, identifying a mission within that context, setting realistic goals, establishing obtainable goals and developing activities that are stated as policies and procedures to accomplish those goals and objectives."[16] Stueart and Moran see strategic planning as "the process of translating decisions into policies, and policies into actions."[17]

VISIONS, MISSIONS, AND POLICIES

The planning process within an organizational structure such as a school consists of a hierarchical arrangement of its vision and mission statement, and an outline and explanation of its goals, objectives, and activities. Policies and procedures are derived from a clear understanding of those elements.[18] In recent years an organizational *vision statement* has become increasingly important in this planning hierarchy. The vision statement is more imaginative and theoretical than other statements in the hierarchy. It seeks to convey in a few words the underlying philosophy of the organization and the positive attributes that invigorate it. This is the vision statement of the Cleveland Municipal School District:

Each student in the Cleveland Municipal School District will be successful in a rigorous instructional program, and our teachers, principals and administrative staff will be valued, will hold themselves responsible and accountable, and will be rewarded for their professionalism.[19]

The *mission statement*, falling just below the vision statement in this hierarchy, sets out the organization's goals, objectives, and activities. Mission statements may be very simple. For example, that of the St. Louis Public School District reads: "The district's primary mission is to improve the achievement of students in every class and in every school."[20] Most are more involved, as is that of the Denver Public Schools:

The mission of the Denver Public Schools, the center of community learning, is to guarantee that our children and youth acquire knowledge, skills, and values to become self-sufficient citizens by providing personalized learning experiences for all students in innovative partnerships with all segments of the community.[21]

Goals are general designs and aspirations, stated in operational terms, which lead to operations, strategies, activities, and policies.[22] For example, the Denver Public Schools have developed several objectives that flow from their mission statement. Two examples of their goals are given below:

Goal 1. Literacy—increase the number of students who can demonstrate a high level of proficiency in the use of language.

Goal 2. School Readiness—increase the readiness levels of children preparing to enter the Denver Public Schools.[23]

Objectives are measurable actions that can be achieved. Objectives are usually stated quantitatively: "By [2004] funding for reference materials will be increased by 25% in real dollars (adjusted for rises in costs of reference materials)."[24] In addition to being measurable, objectives must be suitable for the organization and sustainable over time.

Activities are predetermined acts constructed to help meet an objective.[25] Collectively, *operations, strategies*, and *activities* are practical means for meeting larger expectations of the organization that are carried out on a day-to-day basis. According to Stueart and Moran, to be effective they must be based on policies and procedure statements and they are generally short-term, repetitive, numerous, and measurable.[26]

Policy formation is a codified form of decision making. That is, policy is usually published and distributed, and is made available for study and review. In some organizations common policies may be unwritten, yet based on well-understood practices and traditions. Although most policy formation is formal, it should also be open for discussion and review, so that policies can be changed when needed and justified. Policy grows out of a great deal of collective discussion and thinking, and it serves as a guideline for actions. In complex organizations and procedures it helps ensure consistency and fairness.[27]

COLLECTION DEVELOPMENT POLICY

Policy making is an important part of management and administrative responsibilities. The school library media center will be involved in many aspects of policy. Writing a well-constructed collection development policy statement and manual is one of the most important and far-reaching activities with which the librarian can expect to be involved. Policies are guides to thinking and action, and they help meet the stated objectives and mission of the school. They are implemented on a daily basis, and they offer guidance to all levels in the organization. Because a collection development policy is so far-reaching it must be formulated by more than just top administrators. Ideally, policy should be formulated based on input from a variety of sources, including the library media center staff, support staff, teachers, students, and parents. Although many policies may be stated in broad, comprehensive terms, a collection development policy should be detailed and clearly written. In addition, it must be written in such a way that it can stand as a legal document representing the collective judgment of the professional community. When it is tested it must be strong enough to stand the heat of attack and even legal challenge.

SOCIETAL TRENDS AND COLLECTION DEVELOPMENT

As we have seen, management, policy formation, and collection building do not happen in a vacuum, separated from political, social, technological, and economic forces. In *School Library Media Centers in the 21st Century: Changes and Challenges* (Greenwood, 1994) Kathleen Craver discusses the most important ones. Here we will consider specifically how they affect collection development.

Technology

Technology now is in a rapid state a flux, a trend that will continue well into the future. Collection development policies and procedures must consider how to accommodate current as well as unforeseen technological advances. The wider use of fiber-optic cabling means that data can now be transferred more quickly and in greater density than was possible using only wire and telephone line transmission, giving schools a choice of well over 500 channels from which to select information and instruction resources.[28] The further realization that existing coaxial wire can carry fiber-optics information has led to a great reduction in the cost of rewiring the nation. Cable companies quickly began to market this technology to homes and businesses, and opening the school market was not far behind. Craver notes that this technology alone allows "a limitless environment for information delivery," making "the entire *Encyclopaedia Britannica* deliverable every second."[29] This delivery technology is already making itself felt at local market levels where more cable channel selections are being offered to customers along with more diverse program content. For years, many schools have had access to educational cable television through various forms of distribution such as satellite delivery, but in the future schools will have even more choices and better delivery at lower prices.

Distance learning and instruction delivered by telephone and satellite have been widely used for several decades. But with the improvement of delivery systems such as fiber-optic and other forms of technology such as integrated services digital networking (ISDN; see below), this type of instruction will undoubtedly increase. The question to ask now is how will resources be made available at the local level to support this instruction? College and university distance instruction programs as well as those serving rural and isolated areas have had to face this question already. Solutions have been varied. For colleges and universities the initial solution was to increase traditional library holdings at the site where the instruction was to be received. However, this solution was generally not found to be practical for secondary school distance education programs. For example, distance learning classes often served schools with as few as fifty students, with no library or librarians and a few other resources on hand. In resource-scarce environments such as these, distance education is coming to rely more on electronic resources that can be delivered by computer or other forms of distal transmission right to the site or even directly to individual students. Collection development policies in schools will have to be formulated to accommodate such transformations. The role of the school library media specialist will not change, but rather will be expanded to encompass identifying, evaluating, selecting, recommending, and acquiring electronically available information products so that they can be integrated into distance education programs and classes.

The trend toward digitalizing all forms of information has accelerated. Integrated services digital networking (ISDN) now allows non–fiber-optic telephone circuitry to convert analog signals to digital signals. The advantage here is that ISDN can use existing telephone circuitry to access databases of all types. Because of this technological development, simpler and more affordable hardware requirements allow schools to have greater access to electronic information. The impact of this technology in terms of collection development is significant.

What was once considered new technology is now rather commonplace in schools and in school library media collections. Such technologies include scanners, CD-ROMs, hypertext technologies, and interactive media. In the future "smart technologies" will come to play an even greater role in collection development.

Although expert learning and information systems have been available for several decades, they are now being perfected and expanded to serve larger audiences. In the past expert systems worked well in applications involving exacting fact-based situation. A good example of their early use was in medical diagnostic work. For example, in a medical expert system known facts about selected diseases were programmed into a computer, allowing physicians or other medical personnel to query the system by feeding into it data about symptoms experienced by patients. Through an expert programming system, the computer matched the symptoms stored in its memory with the disease characteristics given by the inquirer and suggested a diagnosis and possible treatment for the disease. Craver notes that library-based expert systems have also been developed to help users navigate complex online catalogs such as the National Agriculture Library.[30] Neural networking systems are a refinement of this older system. These systems are programmed to act much as the human brain works in the processing of information and decision making. Instead of relying on a lineal system of matching characteristics to existing facts, as is traditionally done in expert systems, a neural system works in a parallel fashion, recognizing patterns of information and delegating to other parts of the system tasks that can be performed there; and the system learns and remembers as it processes a problem.[31]

Along with expert systems, virtual reality information and learning systems are now becoming more commonplace. These systems are designed to "simulate three-dimensional visual and aural sensory experiences."[32] It is easy to see how virtual reality can be used to recreate historical events, laboratory experimentation, and field visits to museums and other places of interests. The selection of such systems will naturally become a part of the library media center's collection development plan. Chapter 6 discusses technology issues in more detail.

Economic Trends

In economic terms, many school library media centers did well in the 1960s. Through federal support contained in the Great Society legislation of the Johnson administration such as the Elementary and Secondary Act of 1965 and other programs, many elementary school libraries were established and numerous secondary school library collections were established and improved. Over the years this funding slowly decreased until it came to an end in the 1990s.

Although the initial impact of these federal programs was positive, over the years problems have arisen. Many federal library aid programs are intended to encourage and supplement local support, not replace it. Nevertheless, evidence shows that when federal support ends or is reduced, often local and state governments cannot or will not take up the gauntlet and build on this support base.[33] This has happened with school library collections. After federal funding for school library collections decreased, many local school districts did not move in significant ways to fill this vacuum. Consequently, over the years collections have deteriorated.[34] Research indicates that the average age of a book in a children's collection is twenty years.[35] Aging collections are especially a problem in subject categories where rapid advances have been made, such as science and technology.[36]

The economic turbulence of the 1970s and 1980s also played an important role in the failure of local school systems to meet the needs of

school library collections. In many parts of the country, the local economic base was in trouble, jobs were being lost or moved to foreign sites,
and generally the tax support base was reduced. For school systems to
survive, hard choices had to be made. Often library programs were cut,
staffs were reduced or even eliminated, and money for collection development was not made available.

At the same time, some people began to question the effectiveness of
the public school system in terms of its cost. In some parts of the country
this distrust was mobilized into active campaigns for lower taxes. California's Proposition 13, passed in 1978, is a good example of how effective an organized effort can be at reducing tax support for public
institutions.[37]

By 1999 the U.S. economic situation had greatly improved. Personal
income was up, unemployment was at a record low, and generally business and industry were thriving. Nevertheless, support for schools and
other public agencies lagged behind the upswing in the economy. Indications are that economic conditions of the early twenty-first century will
be less robust than before, and this will likely influence support for education.

At the beginning of the new century, improving education became a
national political issue. Educational issues played a significant role in the
presidential election campaign of 2000.[38] Similarly, the professional library community had made some progress in convincing the federal
government that increased support for school libraries was needed to
halt collection deterioration. In the 106th Congress House bill H.R. 543,
Elementary and Secondary School Library Media Resources Training and
Advanced Technology Assistance Act, and its related Senate bill S. 97
were submitted to address this problem. These bills were designed to
greatly improve collections by providing up-to-date school library media
resources and well-trained, professionally certified school library media
specialists for elementary and secondary schools. The need for new technology was recognized in these bills as well as other bills such as Senate
bill S. 1004, the School and Libraries Internet Access Act, which specifically addressed the need to help libraries and schools as well as other
institutions afford computers and Internet connections.

Social and Cultural Trends

Seldom can *social and cultural trends* be separated from economic developments. Craver, in tracing the impact of economic and social development on libraries, points out that the United States, Canada, and other
economically advanced countries are moving from manufacturing to
service-based economies.[39] Service economies are information-based in

that they require the use of information to solve various types of problems and to provide services related to the solving of problems. Technology is significantly associated with modern-day service economies. Increased skills are required to be successful in such an environment. With this comes a change in cultural and social expectations. For example, the length of adolescence is expanding as youth are required either to stay in school longer or to spend more time engaged in formal training to learn advanced skills.[40] With this comes an increasing demand for educational experiences that emphasize higher-level thinking, reasoning, and problem-solving skills.[41]

Although the American public school system has been remarkably successful in providing educational opportunities for its youth, serious problems must be addressed, many of them socially and culturally based. For example, illiteracy and the so-called decline in school achievement must be faced. At its basic level illiteracy is the inability to read or write; but use of the term has now expanded to include the inability to use information. The whole problem of illiteracy involves such questions as how to teach reading skills to children who learn in different ways; the influence of parenting and different approaches to parenting on fostering literacy; how poverty and the lack of environmental stimulation affect literacy; and how literacy can be encouraged by social agencies such as schools while at the same time respecting cultures that follow an oral tradition.

Declining achievement, at least as measured by national test scores, is problematic to school systems in the United States. To fairly consider this question, we must look at the historical changes in the nation's educational patterns. More students today are enrolled in the public school system than ever before, and there is greater cultural and social diversity among students. Since the 1920s in the United States, as elsewhere, social expectations as well as legal requirements have led more students to seek a high school education. In earlier decades high school was considered necessary only for a select few, and it was often criticized as being an elitist institution.[42] Admissions to the early public high schools were often based on competitive standards, and attendance was voluntary.[43]

Today, more students have opportunities for higher education than ever before in American history, and more are taking standard admission examinations for colleges and universities.[44]

Federal support for higher education for returning service persons at the end of World War II had historic consequences for American culture and society, opening higher and technical education to many who would otherwise never have had such opportunities. In addition to its far-reaching impact on higher and technical education systems in the United States, this federal action greatly influenced what society expected of public schools in preparing students for the work force and for higher education.[45] The expansion of regional colleges, the growth of the community college system, and the development of technical training schools today are examples of this expansion of educational opportunity.[46]

The decline of achievement in education must also be viewed from a larger cultural perspective. The growth of poverty-ridden ghettos within inner cities, crime, unemployment, the decline of family structures, and the drug culture that controls and/or influence many who live and work in the inner city cannot be divorced from school achievement.[47] Similarly, rural poverty, along with the cultural and social isolation and the lack of good educational opportunities often found in rural environments, plays an important role in educational achievement.[48]

Cultural Values and Conflicts

Most cultures and societies face conflicts over basic values and behaviors. The term "cultural wars" has been applied to these societal conflicts within Western society. The causes of such conflicts are many, but the fundamental conflict lies with a basic sense of need to determine within a cultural and social context what is right and wrong, what is good and bad, and what is secular and what is religious. Within these confines arise most of the questions about human society and the relationships among people and groups of people.[49]

Because education and educational systems are so fundamental to the survival and advancement of the societies and cultures they serve, it is no wonder that they are expected to play a forceful role in helping to form the values and behaviors of the young. As the structure of the family has changed, the school and the educational system have faced even greater pressures to play stronger roles in teaching and enforcing socially accepted values and behaviors. This is seen in curriculum reform movements that call for more instruction in values and morals. It is also seen in reform movements that demand more traditional approaches to teaching. Craver describes these reform movements and conflicts in detail.[50]

When the school system attempts to respond to these movements and demands, it is often faced with conflicting political, cultural, social, and religious choices. By omission of specific directives, the Constitution of the United States implies that the control of education as well as other activities are largely under state control. The idea of a centralized, federally controlled education system has never been widely accepted by the American people. Federally mandated uniform curricula, national personnel assessment and credentialing, and national testing of students have historically been rejected by the American people. Although the First Amendment to the Constitution calls for the separation of church and state, a large portion of the U.S. population claims to be religious, and religious and moral values are expected to play a role in the education of its youth. The presidential election campaign of 2000 is a good example of how the teaching of "traditional family values," faith-based public assistance programs, and the right to constitutionally protected religious observation within public life can become a part of national debate.[51]

When building collections for school library media centers we face these values, issues, and conflicts. The American Library Association (ALA) throughout the years has issued a number of directives and policy statements designed to help librarians make good choices in building collections suitable for diversified populations while at the same time honoring the value systems of many individual persons and groups. One of the most important is the Library Bill of Rights and the various documents the ALA has issued to interpret it. Any school library media center specialist will be well served by understanding and applying the principles found in the Library Bill of Rights and related documents. Library policies and procedures at the local level should be built around the principles articulated in these important guidelines. Chapter 5 discusses these documents and the roles they play in collection development at greater length.

THE DEMOGRAPHICS OF YOUTH AND SOCIAL RESPONSES

Census data clearly indicate that the twenty-first century will see racial, ethnic, and age changes in the population that will require much social adjustment. In the United States the total population is projected to be 394 million by 2050. All racial and ethnic minority group populations will increase faster than non-Hispanic whites. Hispanics will comprise the fastest growing minority group. The U.S. Census Bureau considers Hispanics to belong to several groups, some of which are racial (e.g., persons of Black and Puerto Rican descent). Because of this diversity, the Bureau allows respondents to select their own designations for census-counting purposes. The non-Hispanic white population will see negative growth rates after 2035. Because of this decrease every minority group will represent an increasing share of the population in the future. By the year 2050 the minority population is projected to surpass the non-minority, non-Hispanic white population. In terms of the youth population, by the year 2050 there will be 18 million more minority persons under age thirty-five than non-minority persons under that age. By the year 2015 it is projected that there will more elderly non-Hispanic whites than non-Hispanic youths, but the opposite is true for all minority groups.[52]

In her book Craver likewise notes that in the early part of the twenty-first century, the overall youth population will be small while the older people will be more numerous. She claims that because resources will be limited, a generational conflict will occur, with each group and its supporters vying for resources at the expense of the other.[53] This may indeed happen, but other population trends indicate that competing factors must be considered before we accept the conflict scenario. These population figures indicate that the educational system will be called upon to educate an increasingly multicultural youth population. The system must remain vibrant and inclusive. Should conflict for resources develop among age, ethnic, or racial groups, the country must find the will and the resolve to fairly allocate resources.

CONCLUSION

Resource selection must be based on a philosophy that has sound educational and instructional principles. Selection of materials is an important part of the overall management of a school library media center. As such it must fit into a suitable, positive, and rewarding bureaucracy that ensures structure, order, consistency, and fairness in how materials are selected and collections developed. Policies and procedures can then arise from this structural framework that are responsive to educational, curriculum, and individual needs. This ordered management scheme must be based on principles of quality and responsiveness to social and cultural changes and expectations.

NOTES

1. Gerald E. Caiden, "Excessive Bureaucratization: The J-Curve of Bureaucracy and Max Weber Through the Looking Glass," in *Handbook of Bureaucracy*, edited by Ali Farazmand (New York: Marcel Dekker, 1994), pp. 31–32.

2. Ibid., p. 33.

3. Ibid., pp. 34–35.

4. Ibid.

5. Ibid., p. 36.

6. Yvonne Cano, Fred H. Wood, and Jan C. Simmons, eds., *Creating High Functioning Schools: Practice and Research* (Springfield, IL: Charles C Thomas, 1998), p. 5.

7. Bonnie M. Beyer and Connie Ruhl-Smith, "Leadership Styles for Total Quality Schools," in Cano, Wood, and Simmons, *Creating High Functioning Schools*, p. 9.

8. Beyer and Ruhl-Smith, "Leadership Styles of School Administrators," cited in Beyer and Ruhl-Smith, "Leadership Styles," p. 13.

9. Ibid., pp. 15–16.

10. John Jay Bonstingl, "The Quality Revolution in Education," *Educational*

Leadership 50 (November 1992): 5–7, quoted in Beyer and Ruhl-Smith, "Leadership Styles," p. 16.

11. Peter M. Senge, "Building Learning Organizations: The Real Message of the Quality Movement," *Journal of Quality and Participation* (March 1992), quoted in Beyer and Ruhl-Smith, "Leadership Styles," p. 16. Also available as Peter M. Senge, "The Leader's New Work: Building Learning Organizations," in *Learning Organizations: Perspectives for a New Era*, edited by Gill Robinson Hickman and others (Thousand Oaks, CA: Sage Publications, 1998).

12. R. G. Issac, "Organization Culture: Some New Perspectives," in *Handbook of Organizational Behavior*, edited by T. Y. Golembiewski (New York: Marcel Dekker, 1992), pp. 92–93.

13. R. N. Cyert and J. G. March, *A Behavioral Theory of the Firm* (Englewood Cliffs, NJ: Prentice-Hall, 1963), pp. 111–12, quoted in Stueart and Moran, *Library and Information Center Management*, (Littleton, CO: Libraries Unlimited, 1998) p. 36.

14. Stueart and Moran, *Library and Information Center Management*, p. 36.

15. Ibid., pp. 31–86.

16. Ibid., p. 43.

17. Ibid., pp. 41–43.

18. Ibid., p. 57.

19. Cleveland Municipal School District, "Vision Statement," available at www.cmsdnet.net/administration/cmsdvision.htm.

20. St. Louis Public School District, "Facts, 1999–2000," available at www.dtds.slps.k12mo.us/articles/schlfact.htm.

21. Denver Public Schools, "Policies and Procedures," available at www.ed.denver.k12.co.us:8080/policy/default.html.

22. Stueart and Moran, *Library and Information Center Management*, p. 59.

23. Denver Public Schools, "Where Are We Heading?," available at www.denver.k12.co.us/districtinfo/Where_Are_We_Heading.html.

24. Stueart and Moran, *Library and Information Center Management*, p. 64.

25. Ibid., p. 63.

26. Ibid.

27. Ibid., p. 69.

28. Kathleen W. Craver, *School Library Media Centers in the 21st Century: Changes and Challenges* (Westport, CT: Greenwood Press, 1994), p. 31.

29. Ibid., p. 3., citing Philip Elmer-Dewitt, "Take a Step into the Future on the Electronic Super-highway," *Time* 141 (April 12, 1993): 53.

30. Ibid., p. 28.

31. Ibid., p. 26.

32. Ibid., p. 28.

33. Deborah A. Verstegen, "Redistributing Federal Aid to Education: Chapter 2 of the Education Consolidation and Improvement Act of 1981," *Journal of Education Finance* 10 (Spring 1985): 517–23.

34. Daniel Callison, "A Review Related to School Library Media Collections," *School Library Media Quarterly* 19 (Fall 1990): 57–61.

35. Carol Ann Doll, "Quality and Elementary School Library Collections," *School Library Media Quarterly* 25 (Winter 1997): 95–102.

36. Carol Morrison and others, "School Library Snapshots: A Brief Survey of

Illinois School Library Collections in Three Areas of Science," *Illinois Libraries* 76 (Fall 1994): 211–19.

37. Larry Picus, *California and Proposition 13: A Brief Analysis* (Portland, OR: Northwest Regional Educational Lab, n.d.). Also available as ERIC Reproduction document no. ED 225 248.

38. Adam Clymer and Janet Elder, "Poll Finds Greater Confidence in Democrats," *New York Times*, November 10, 1999, late edition—final, p. 1.

39. Craver, *School Library Media Centers*, p. 59.

40. Philip F. Rice, *The Adolescent: Development, Relationships, and Culture*, 9th ed. (Boston: Allyn and Bacon, 1999), pp. 9, 22.

41. American Association of School Librarians and Association for Educational Communications and Technology, *Information Literacy Standards for Student Learning* (Chicago: American Library Association, 1998), pp. 1–5.

42. William J. Reese, *The Origins of the American High School* (New Haven: Yale University Press, 1995).

43. William J. Reese, "Academic Excellence in an Early U.S. High School," *Social Problems* 31 (June 1984): 558–67.

44. Meg Sommerfeld, "Number of Minorities Taking A.P. Exams Continues to Go Up," *Education Week* 13 (November 10, 1993), p. 10; "Number of Students Taking A.P. Exams Doubles in a Decade," *College Board Review*, no. 180 (March 1997): 45.

45. Michael Bennett, *When Dreams Come True: The GI Bill and the Making of Modern America* (McLean, VA: Brassey's, 1999).

46. V. R. Cardozier, *American Higher Education: An International Perspective* (Aldershot, England: Avebury, 1987), pp. 5–6, 8–9, 10–11.

47. Kevin Watkins, *Education Now: Break the Cycle of Poverty. A Report.* "Poverty in the United States, Chapter 1, Box 1.6" (Washington, DC: Oxfam, 1999), available at http://www.caa.org.au/oxfam/advocacy/education/report/index.html.

48. Gary G. Huang, *Sociodemographic Changes: Promise and Problems for Rural Education*, ERIC Digest 1999-01-00 (Charleston, WV: ERIC Clearinghouse on Rural Education and Small Schools, 1999). ERIC Reproduction No. ED 435048, available at http://www.ed.gov/databases/ERIC_Digests/ed425048.html.

49. Ogley Roderick, "Theories of Conflict," in *Encyclopedia of Violence, Peace, and Conflict*, Vol. 1, edited by Lester Kurtz and Jennifer Turpin (San Diego: Academic Press, 1999), pp. 401–12; Steven Seidman, *Embattled Eros: Sexual Politics and Ethics in Contemporary America* (New York: Routledge, 1992).

50. Craver, *School Library Media Centers*, pp. 73–150.

51. Adam Clymer, "Filter Aid to Poor Through Churches, Bush Urges," *New York Times*, July 23, 1999, late edition—final p. 1.

52. U.S. Department of Commerce, The Minority Business Development Agency (MBDA), *Dynamic Diversity: Projected Changes in U.S. Race and Ethnic Composition 1995 to 2050* (Washington, DC: U.S. Department of Commerce, [ca.2000]) available at http://www.mbda.gov/Emerging_Markets/Dynamic/firstpage.html.

53. Craver, *School Library Media Centers*, p. 49.

Theories and Concepts in Collection Development

3

As the preceding two chapters have emphasized, collection development is based on order and a systematic approach to making decisions. Within schools the selection process is a natural part of positive bureaucratic structure and policy formation. It takes its direction from professional standards and guidelines and must reflect sound and wise professional judgment. Overall, collection development is the process of making good decisions in terms of a school's stated vision, missions, and goals.

THEORIES AND APPROACHES TO SELECTION

There are several approaches to collection development and the selection of materials. Taken together, the process is complex, involving literary and aesthetic qualities, social, cultural, and psychological considerations, and political attributes. This chapter looks briefly at some of the major theories that influence collection development.

Literary and Aesthetic Theory

Historically the *literary and aesthetic* aspect of collection development has exerted the strongest influence in school and public library collections. This approach has long insisted that only the best literature be made available to children and youth. The literary and aesthetic approach places as much emphasis on genre as on content.

Making choices from a literary or aesthetic point of view is challenging. Each item must be judged according to exacting criteria. If it is a nonprint item, is it well produced in terms of literary and aesthetic appeal? If it is a written work, is it well written and original? Are the writing and dialogue (in the case of filmed materials) subtle and poetic? If it is a film product, do its visuals and framing evoke a response to its originality and inner beauty or truthfulness? How are the characters presented? Do we as readers or viewers really care about them? Is there real depth to their development, or are they merely plastic figures and stereotypes? Is the plot interesting? Does the story line or plot have enough complexity to challenge the reader or viewer? Are literary allusions and symbolic meanings introduced and used with skill? Even if the story is set in the past or in the far distant future, can children and youth of today appreciate the work's underlying purpose or theme in terms of contemporary life?

Donelson and Nilsen's *Literature for Today's Young Adults* is a basic guide to literary criticism. The major elements the authors cover include the *plot* (story line) *theme* (underlying meaning), and *mode* (how the story is written, e.g., comedy, romance, irony/satire, tragedy); *character and character development, point of view of the author, tone* (the author's attitude toward the subject, characters, and readers), *setting* (the context of time and place), and *style* (how the story is written, combining all the major elements of literary construction).[1] Journals for youth that exemplify the literary approach are *Lion and the Unicorn* and *Phaedrus*. Other theoretical approaches used in the study of literature include queer theory/gay and lesbian studies, feminism, cultural studies (including cultural materials), aesthetic theory, gender and sexuality, race and culture, Marxist theory, narratology, phenomenology, reader response theory, and postmodernism. The Internet is an excellent avenue for finding out more about these approaches. For example, Dino F. Felluga, an assistant professor of English at Purdue University, maintains a site titled "Undergraduate Introduction to Critical Theory," which offers definitions for some of these approaches with citations for additional sources and links.[2]

One purpose of good literature is to challenge us and to help us grow in some way. The literary and aesthetic approach to collection development gives much weight to human and social values as well. Within this approach, we expect authors to interpret human values and to comment upon them with enough insight to provoke thought and perhaps even to offer guidance and direction to the reader or viewer. We likewise expect authors to help broaden and expand our understanding of human behavior, and we expect them to contribute to history and literature through their ideas. Collectively we expect a work to reward us through its literary beauty and as a commentary on the human experience.

Moral Theory and Approach

The moral theory or approach to the evaluation of literature centers around the discernment of or instruction in what is good and evil. Taken to extremes, this approach holds that the sole purpose of literature is to teach what is considered to be good behavior within a society and culture and to condemn what is evil. The history of children's literature is filled with examples of this approach. In colonial America, the major purpose of literature written especially for children was to impart religious information and to save children's souls from damnation. By the mid-nineteenth century, the focus had shifted to instilling patriotism, the work ethic, and concern for the less fortunate. This moral approach is still with us and continues to greatly influence how literature for children and youth is perceived by many. Many people still see literary works for the young as an important influence in creating a moral society.

Today we live in a multicultural society where many moral issues are not always clear. For example, many people hold that allowing lesbians and gay men to adopt children or to raise their own children is morally corrupt. Others disagree, claiming that it offers positive diversity in a heterogeneous society.

Selection criteria generally recognize that a moral approach is desirable and that the theme of a work should have well-recognized moral underpinnings. What modern selection criteria warn against is an overly didactic tone or approach in conveying the moral message.

Authors and reviewers of youth literature often find themselves in conflict with those who feel that authors and producers of materials for youth should be allied with them in their quest for moral truths. When faced with such expectations, authors often answer that their role is not to associate themselves with proponents of certain moral answers to social problems, but to craft stories so that moral questions and the dilemmas posed by moral choices are presented to young readers and viewers in all their complexity.

Sociological and Cultural Theories and Approaches

The *sociological approach* also has a long history in terms of selecting materials for school library media centers. Basically, this approach sees literature as a means of expressing and reflecting social and cultural ideas and behaviors. Adherents appreciate the literary and aesthetic aspects of literature, but they expect literature to play an active role in influencing society and culture. Three basic interpretations of the sociological approach to literature have evolved over the years. Simply stated, they are that, (1) literature reflects society, (2) literature controls society, and (3) literature influences society.[3] The first view holds that all literature reflects what is authentic in society. This approach has little interest in using literature to bring about change, seeing it as a diagnostic and descriptive tool.

The "literature controls society" approach is very traditional. It holds that literature is very powerful and that it can control society. Through literature individuals can be controlled in thought, word, and actions. Historically, this view of literature has been used by government, religion, and social organizations to ensure that established norms, beliefs, and behaviors are uniformly adhered to and practiced by individuals.

The "literature influences society" approach holds that literature is a powerful tool in bringing about change in society. Through the collective responses of individuals to literature and the ideas in literature, society can be influenced for the better.

In recent decades the "literature influences society" approach has been most influential in collection development practice. Literature and materials have been seen as important agents in influencing the behaviors and attitudes of individuals in society and, in so doing, in facilitating positive changes in society and culture.

Of course various political and society agendas can use this approach in justifying the selection of items for collections. Generally speaking, following the guidance of such organizations as the Association for Library Services for Children (ALSC), a division of the American Library Association and the International Reading Association, selection criteria influenced by this approach abound in the literature of collection development. This approach calls for the selection of materials that will help bring about a more compassionate understanding of human beings. It is sensitive to how minorities are presented and it expects works to help foster a better appreciation of the aspirations, achievements, and problems of minorities. It is likewise concerned that the role of women in society is positively presented, avoiding stereotyping.

On the other hand, this approach can be used in ways that promote specific agendas. Some might even claim that the sociological approach invites political or even propagandistic approaches to collection development, which can come from either the right or the left. A good example of a leftist pressure group was the Council on Interracial Books for Children (CIBC), which ceased to exist in the early 1980s. Donelson and Nilsen described the group as "worrisome" because of the coercive methods it used to discourage educators from purchasing, stocking, or using books and other items it found unacceptable.[4] Its basic approach was to question all media for youth that did not actively attack social ills such as racism, sexism, materialism, ageism, and so on. CIBC held that authors, publishers, and producers had an obligation not only to attack these ills, but to aggressively work for their eradication from society. The council was particularly concerned that certain messages, although well-meaning, nevertheless often held destructive information regarding minority groups. The only way to avoid such messages was to insist that authors, publishers, and producers actively creative and distribute media that promoted and insisted on the redress of injustices. Through its publications it attacked such well-regarded books as Paula Fox's *The Slave Dancer* and Harper Lee's *To Kill a Mockingbird*.[5] In the view of Donelson and Nilsen, CIBC was "a call for censorship based on social awareness."[6]

Many organizations on the political right also see youth literature as a means of bringing about changes in society. The American Family Association is an example of a rightist organization that holds views that they consider to be traditional and honorable American values based on God, country, and family, which should be reflected in media directed at youth.[7]

This movement also has its intellectual base. In her book *One Nation, Two Cultures*, social historian Gertrude Himmelfarb observes that the counterculture of the 1960s has become the dominant culture of today, while the culture of the 1950s, which represents the ideals upon which the United States was founded, has become a dissident culture. She believes that we now live in a morally decaying society and holds that the previous culture, with its respect for strong family values, a belief in an absolute standard of truth and morality, and respect for religion and authority, was the cornerstone upon which the nation was built. This traditional culture is now being replaced by cultural relativism, unbridled sexuality, and rejection of tradition, personal responsibility, authority, and most institutions.[8]

Psychological Theories and Approaches

Psychology is "the science that deals with mental processes and behavior [and] the emotional and behavioral characteristics of an individual, group, or activity."[9] The *psychological approach* has a long history in the evaluation and criticism of literature. One of the best-known applications of psychology to literary criticism is *psychoanalytic theory*. Influenced by Freudian psychology, this approach seeks to understand how authors use the minds and behaviors of their characters to paint their unique development history and their relationship to other characters and to their social and cultural environments. The electronic journal *Psyart: A Hyperlink Journal for the Psychological Study of the Arts* is an example of the interplay of psychological theory and serious literary analysis.

School library media collections have also benefited from the application of psychological understanding and theory to collection development. Selection criteria used by school library media specialists often reflect *behaviorism* and *social learning theories*. Behaviorism assumes that specific behavior codes and norms presented through literature or other media products can be integrated into the minds of readers or viewers and that individuals' behavior can therefore be modified and changed through reinforcement, modeling, and the manipulation of situational cues. Social learning is closely related in that behavior can be influenced greatly by the modeling and observation of socially desirable behaviors and attitudes.

Ecological systems theory and *sociocultural perspective theories* are related to the above in that they too seek to explain how behaviors are learned and acted out. Ecological systems theory holds that children and youth are part of complex systems of relationships and that they are affected by multiple levels of environments ranging from the immediate family to school and on to broad cultural values, expectations, and programs. These influences help shape their personalities and ways of thinking and contribute to their development. Sociocultural perspective theory maintains that youth are constantly internalizing essential features of the social dialogues that go on around them. From these dialogues they form psychological structures that they use to guide and determine their own behavior. Children learn the expected norms of their communities and cultures through dialogues with more knowledgeable members of the community.

Similarly, *ethnomethodology theory* states that people are continually trying to make sense out of their world and to create their own understandable social structure through their actions and interactions. People in fact create their own realities from what they know about the world around them.

A guide for the selection of materials for school library media center collections may not state explicitly that it is based on any particular psychological theory or group of related theories, but the evidence is not hard to discover. The following questions reflect the influence of the psychological and social theories discussed above:

• Does the story avoid an oversimplified view of life?

• Is prejudicial appeal readily identifiable by the potential reader/viewer?

• Are characters created with individual human qualities or are they stereotypes of any cultural group?

• Does the story give a broader understanding of human behavior without stressing differences of class, race, color, sex, education, religion, or philosophy?

• Is the book or item free from derisive names and epithets that would offend minority groups, children, young adults, women?

Community Psychology Theories

The community psychology approach is reflective of some of the above theories. At a basic level, community psychology states that how community workers interpret the role of their organization influences how that organization can and will influence the behavior of the community it serves. Penland and Williams observe that communities are filled with unique and valuable information that must be identified, selected, and organized in ways that are meaningful to the community and that will affect the lives and behaviors of those who live there.[10] Community psychology is very much involved in analyzing and studying the community, and helping to bring about change in the community through relevant programs and services. Programs, services, and resources made available are not based solely on the judgment of a professional staff, but grow out of what the community needs and how it has expressed those needs. Therefore, community psychology's influence on the selection of library resources has been its insistence that the selection and acquisition of resources be justified by community needs and the involvement of the community in determining those needs. In a school environment this includes students, faculty, staff, and parents. Of course the approach goes well beyond resource selection and involves management as well as program planning and evaluation and the integration of resources into programs and services. Elements of community psychology that are applicable to the selection of resources include the following:

- Promoting continuous study and review of the community.
- Identifying the information and education needs and interests of various publics in the community.
- Identifying community resources that can be used for programming as well as the various programs sponsored by agencies and groups in the community.
- Providing a clearinghouse and publicizing information about needs, interests, resources, and programs.[11]

Although Penland and Williams address their remarks to public librarians, many of their ideas have relevance to school library media specialists as well. In recent years, school communities have become very much concerned with parental needs and interests, and have developed programs designed to encourage parental participation and input.

With the advent of newer forms of information technologies, school librarians are now better equipped to adopt many of the elements of community psychology. For example, many schools have local Web sites that list information about the school and related resources. School librarians are often called on to manage these Web sites or to help evaluate and select resources to be mounted on the school's Web page. The Web site for Wells Branch Elementary School in Round Rock, Texas (a suburban community of Austin), is managed by the school librarian, who has special training in Web site construction and design. She selects resources to be mounted on the Web site, publicizes the availability of the site, and promotes access to it. (Search the site at www.roundrockisd. org/wellsbranch.)

Essentially, community psychology promotes the basic idea that professionals who manage community institutions have a responsibility to develop missions, goals, and programs that will influence the behavior of the community. As school library media specialists make decisions about the kinds of resources they will bring into the center, they often have a vision of the school and its library playing a vital role in the lives of those who live and work in the community. Resources selected for the library then become a necessary linkage in the development of a positive community psychological base for school and the community it serves.

Feminist Theory and Approaches

Feminist theory and approaches to selection of resources have had a great influence on the publishing, production, and selection of materials for school library media collections. Feminist social theory holds that there must be political, economic, and social equality of the sexes and that society must be challenged to recognize and provide for those rights. Rosalind Sydie of the University of Alberta writes this about feminist social theory and its influence across disciplines:

Feminist theory examines women in the social world and addresses issues of concern to women, focussing on these from the perspective, experiences, and viewpoint of women. It cuts across conventional academic disciplines (e.g. feminist history, geography, literature, science) and develops ideas and approaches that are useful in a wide variety of these disciplines. Not only have feminists critiqued conventional methodological approaches, they have developed new methods—placing more emphasis on the experiences of women and new forms of knowledge. . . . [F]eminism is closely engaged with the social world—feminist theorists tend to be women who theorize about their own experiences and interaction, it is concerned with the everyday lives and experiences of women and their social interactions, and it is often connected to women's groups, social reform, and broad social and political movements, organizations, and institutions.[12]

Felluga offers this definition of feminist literary theory:

Feminism is a way of analyzing the position of women in society. It critiques the ways in which representations of gender produce, transform, and transcend social stereotypes about women and men. In this critical approach, one examines why certain cultural behaviors are gendered and how that labeling has been limiting and/or empowering to women and men in society.[13]

An excellent scholarly guide to literary feminist study is *Encyclopedia of Feminist Literary Theory*, edited by Elizabeth Kowalewski-Wallace (New York: Garland, 1997). Kay Vandergrift of Rutgers University has written extensively on children's and young adult literature from a feminist perspective. Her scheme "Model of Female Voices in Youth Literature," which reflects a feminist critique of youth literature, is one of the most complete yet published.[14]

The following criteria, collected from several sources illustrate the influence of feminist ideology and theory on collection development.

- Does it [the item under consideration] present a positive picture of the role of women and avoid stereotyping?
- Does it offer an opportunity to better understand and appreciate the aspirations, achievements, and problems of . . . women?
- Does the story give a broader understanding of human behavior without stressing differences of class, race, color, sex, education, religion, or philosophy in any inimical way?
- Do materials under review reflect equality of [the] sexes?
- Are both males and females portrayed as active, avoiding the passive female stereotype?
- Are both males and females shown as capable of making decisions?
- Both males and females should be engaged in a variety of work tasks and recreations.
- Avoid stereotypical family roles and patterns where father is head of household, final authority, less involved in child rearing tasks.
- Avoid the use of sexist language.
- Avoid presenting both males and females as sexual objects.

Criteria such as these offer guidance in how to look at and evaluate an information item or a work of fiction. They also serve to make the selector sensitive to very complex psychological and social issues. In doing this, they advance feminist theory and social ideology. Ideally such criteria should help librarians and others acquire items that will have a positive social, cultural, and behavioral impact on students and others who use them.

The change in the status of women is based on cultural acceptance, and cultures are generally conservative and slow to change. Beginning in the nineteenth century with the call for the vote for women and the gradual opening of the professions to women, feminist victories have certainly occurred, but many argue that the movement has not yet changed broad-based cultural expectations and institutions. The feminist movement has been revolutionary, but it is an interrupted revolution.[15] Selection criteria based on feminist theory are a small but important aspect of this continuing social revolution.

Cognitive Theory

Cognitive theory includes several families of thought, among them Gestalt theory and Piaget's theory of cognitive development. Generally, cognitive theory holds that information comes to the individual in multiple channels of influence and that the individual has a need and the ability to impose order and logical patterns on this incoming information. The cognitive theories seek to explain how individuals process and order this information. *Gestalt theory* holds that learning is holistic, modular, subjective, naturalistic, and phenomenological. Individuals do not see new information in isolation from previous information they have received. The way information is processed by an individual is very subjective and very natural to his or her need for comfort and survival, and it is based on what has occurred or is occurring in the person's life. In other words, "learning is the active building of knowledge through dynamic interaction with information and experience."[16]

Piaget's *cognitive-development theory* asserts that psychological structures are necessary and predictable for learning and that it is the logical structuring of relationships by the child that determines its understanding of the world. As the child develops he or she actively and logically constructs knowledge.

Cognitive influences in selection criteria are reflected in statements that focus on factors found in media that might help the user structure and experience knowledge. Such criteria be applied both to the technical evaluation of materials and to the social and cultural aspects of information contained in them. The following questions illustrate cognitive considerations:

- Are the concepts presented appropriate to the ability and maturity of the potential reader?
- If the story is fantasy, is it the type that has imaginative appeal and is suitable for children? For young adults?
- Does a story about modern times give a realistic picture of life as it is now?
- Does the story avoid an oversimplified view of life?
- Do characters speak in a language true to the period and section of the country in which they live?
- Is there good plot construction with logical development?

- Are the illustrations realistic in relation to the story?
- Are illustrations located properly for the greatest usefulness?
- Are the page layouts well designed?

These criteria are all concerned with helping the user process information and/or concepts. The assumption is that if an item is well designed, accurate, and logically presented, then the reader/viewer can use his or her cognitive skills to bring order to the information and help develop a positive and accurate view of the world.

Information theory is a type of cognitive theory that is mechanistic and system-based. It proposes that people process information in much the same way that computers do. As with any system, information is received and processed by the individual, resulting in outputs that are behavioral. Although stated in less mechanical terms and with some modification, the current information literacy approach is based on cognitive information theories of how we process information internally. *Information Literacy Standards for Student Learning* defines information literacy, stating and defining standards, providing indicators of achieved behaviors, and establishing levels of acceptable proficiency.[17] School library media specialists who select resources to support literacy programs must be aware of these expectations and make acquisitions decisions in accordance with them.

Information Literacy Standards also gives attention to information content areas within the curriculum. For example, the foreign language standards for grades K–4 state that students will be able to present information about family, school events, and their celebrations via letters on e-mail, or in audio and videotapes.[18] To help students meet this standard, the school library media specialist will need to select from a variety of sources, including print and community resources, the Internet, and technical production guides.

Other Theories and Approaches

Closely aligned with cognitive theories and approaches are theories that seek to explain how people learn, how to teach, and how to understand the social and psychological demands placed on the delivery of curriculum. *Learning theory* has many schools of thought, but modern theories are heavily based on cognitive psychology. These theories take information from cognitive science and apply it directly to instructional strategies. Various schools of learning theories have been influential in the design of strategies for teaching information literacy. *Course design theory* is likewise based on cognitive sciences and instructional theory. Basically, course design theories seek to give practical meaning to the principles of how individuals organize information for learning so that better instructional and learning materials can be produced. With the widespread use of the Internet, design theory has become even more important to school library media specialists, who must now make selection decisions about appropriate information and products provided on the Internet. In addition, they must often create and mount information products.[19]

The following selection criteria have been influenced by both learning and design theories:

- Is the size of the book or item appropriate for the intended age or concept levels?
- Is the typography clear and easy to read?
- Is the type size appropriate for the level intended?
- Are the page layouts well designed? Are there ample margins?
- Are the illustrations appropriate and in good taste?
- Is the art or photographic quality acceptable?
- Are captions readable?
- Are illustrations located properly for the greatest usefulness?
- For audiovisual products: Is the fidelity clear? Are pictures clear? Are sequences related and coherent? Are art or photographic reproductions authentic in terms of detail, color, depth, dimension, size proportions? Is framing appropriate? Is the script appropriate for the type of information presented? Is the information complete?
- For Internet Web site designs, the accuracy and scope of information must be considered as well as the authority behind the information. What is the intended audience? Are the format and design of the item suitable for the information presented and for the intended audience? What is its cost in comparison to its overall use? In addition, the interface and command structure must be evaluated for ease of use and effectiveness. What types of training and/or enrichment materials are provided? What external support services are included?
- For instructional products: Are principles of psychological perception used effectively? For example, is the product based on an understanding of how people organize information for retention and learning through their perceptions of relationships, events, groupings, words, objects, people, past experiences, interests, and needs?

Curriculum theory operates in a similar fashion as the above theory. Although curriculum theory has been greatly influenced by cognitive science and bases much of its insight on those principles, curriculum theory also seeks to explain the nature of curriculum and the role it plays in modern education and society as an instrument of improvement and change.[20] Selection criteria influenced by curriculum theory include the following:

- Are instructional objectives based on sound program and learning principles provided?
- Are the instructional objectives appropriate to the intellectual and social maturity of the audience?
- Are the content and supplementary materials accurate, up-to-date, honest, and complete?
- Do materials show a bias toward any single point of view?
- Do materials lend themselves to decision making when appropriate?
- Is racial, sexual, and other stereotyping avoided?
- Are support and supplementary materials such as teacher's guides provided?
- Are materials organized for easy access?

USING THEORIES AND CONCEPTS

Many of the above theories have overlapping concepts, and taken together they provide guidance for those charged with building school library media center collections for diverse populations. The individual specialist will probably use all these theories at some time in making selection decisions. Based on personal and professional philosophies and approaches to living, each media specialist will feel more comfortable with some theories and approaches than with others. Research in helping professions such as psychology, teaching, and nursing indicates that good helpers use the techniques and theories that suit them best.

Theories are not mutually exclusive. That is, a selection decision may often combine elements from several theories. Good theory leads to good practice, and can also help defend good practice if and when selection decisions come under attack.

BIBLIOGRAPHIC THEORIES AND APPROACHES

Although bibliography and bibliographic theory are used in many professions and academic disciplines, the discussion here will focus on library and information science concepts. In libraries bibliographic control is at the core of bibliographic theory. At the basic level bibliographic control includes all of the processes and tools used to impose order on large quantities of titles and products, including books, periodicals, reports, studies, audiovisual materials, software programs, films, recordings, archival and manuscript items, pictures and images, and digitized information.[21] Major elements of bibliographic control include tools and processes designed to aid in a variety of tasks, including the following:

- location of items in collections through such tools as online catalogs and union catalogs
- bibliographic description of individual items as presented through catalog and other bibliographic records prepared according to standard codes and/or rules
- correct identification of items through descriptions that distinguish one item from another
- verification or ascertaining of bibliographic correctness (i.e., making sure that records prepared for the item reflect the actual item precisely)
- selection of items for collections[22]

Although not all authorities consider selection to be a part of bibliographic control, it is included here because of its important conceptual relationship to bibliographic tools and the bibliographic process.

The building of library collections has always depended upon reliable selection tools prepared by authorities. *Booklist* was among the first major critical selection tools made available to the professional community. Its purpose was to help librarians make wise selection decisions and build useful collections. Although initially aimed at public librarians, *Booklist* has had extensive influence on school library media center collection development.

For the most part, selection aids consist of reviews written by professionals who are competent to make judgments about materials. Although similar to the literary reviews in publications such as the *New York Times Book Review*, they are written especially to provide guidance to librarians. They also include acquisition information (e.g, prices, ISBNs, and so forth) so that the materials under review may be ordered.

Selection aids generally fall into three major categories:

- Aids for building standard collections (e.g., the H. W. Wilson Company's *Standard Catalog* series)
- Aids for selecting new and current materials (e.g., *School Library Journal, Booklist*, [now includes *Subscription Books Bulletin*]
- Aids for selecting special types of materials and/or formats (e.g., *Magazines for School Libraries* by William Katz) and others (R. R. Bowker, 1969–   ).

When evaluating a selection aid for use or purchase, several elements must be considered. First, consider the tool a professional reference aid and evaluate it much as you would a reference item. Pay attention to these factors:

- What is its authority (i.e., publisher, association, editor, compiler, etc.)?
- Who is the publisher, producer, or contributor?
- What is the audience (e.g, school library media specialists or public librarians)?
- What is its overall purpose?
- What is its scope (i.e., what is included, what is not included)?
- How are titles selected for inclusion and/or review?
- How is it arranged and designed?
- What types of special features does it offer (e.g., articles, commentaries, special lists, columns, links to other sources, etc.)?
- What is its publication or issue frequency and/or edition history?
- What kinds of bibliographic or acquisition information does it provide?
- What types of reviews are provided, and by whom are they written? Are the reviews short but informative? Are they long and analytical? Are they written for the lay public or for professionals such as librarians and teachers? Are they written by the editorial staff, literary authorities, or volunteer professionals active in the field?
- What is the cost of the aid? Can you afford it? If you had to make a choice would it be a first purchase choice, basic to your collection development needs; a second purchase choice, fundamental to the maintenance of a well-developed collection; or a third purchase choice, something nice to have, but not essential?

It is always advisable to physically examine a selection tool or to become familiar with it before purchase. The following steps are helpful in evaluating a new tool:

- When examining a review copy, read the introduction and preface. This will often provide information on scope, purpose, uses, and authority. Selection tools that take the form of periodicals seldom have introductions, and it might be necessary to consult a standard guide to periodicals. *Magazines for Libraries* (various editions) provides excellent reviews of such selection aids. If the review is electronic, consider its interface and interactive design features.
- Examine the table of contents or menu and search features.
- Examine the copy for content characteristics, special features, and arrangement.
- Summarize in a few words the major characteristics of the tool.
- State how it can be used in developing and maintaining school library media center collections.

Types of Reviews

In her classic book *Living with Books: The Art of Book Selection* Helen Haines identified three basic types of professional book reviews, publisher's annotations, reader's annotations, and technical or librarian's annotations. Publisher's annotations are basically marketing tools designed to sell a book or to promote items in positive ways. They appear in publishers' catalogs and Web sites and other promotional literature. School library media specialists can use them in making collection development decisions, bearing in mind that they are marketing tools and, as such, their descriptions are not impartial.

The reader's annotation is especially designed to promote the reading or use of an item. It is short and positive, and based on professional judgment about what potential readers or users will find useful and interesting. Reader's annotations find wide use in library reading, viewing, and promotional materials.[23]

Most important to us here are technical or librarian's annotations, which are written for librarians and others who make collection development decisions by experts (librarians and other professionals who are knowledgeable about materials and the review process). These reviews appear in professional publications such as *School Library Journal* and *Booklist* as well as in other professional communications such as Web sites.

Technical annotations are short and include vital selection information. A well-conceived and well-written technical or librarian's review will have these elements:

- Complete bibliographic identification and acquisition information, including price.
- A brief summary of the item's content.
- A statement as to its appropriateness in terms of audience (age, grade, reading, and concept and difficulty levels).
- Its curriculum applications as well as its personal value for individuals.
- An analysis of its strong and weak points.
- Comparisons with similar items (i.e., other works by the same author, other books or items on the same subject, etc.).
- Special aspects of the item of which a selector should be aware.
- Recommendations as to purchase and type of collections for which it might be best suited.

CONCLUSION

Selecting items for a collection is a complex task. It is both an intellectual and an applied process. Some knowledge of the most influential social and cognitive theories is useful for those responsible for making selection decisions. An understanding of theory can also help one justify decisions should they come into question.

Fortunately, a number of bibliographic tools and aids are available to help in the selection process, including tools of bibliographic records such as *Books in Print* (including its electronic versions); guides to recommended items for purchase, such as the *Standard Catalog* series published by the H. W. Wilson Company; and review media such as *School Library Journal* and *Booklist*. Taken together these tools and processes encourage and promote the idea that high quality decisions can be consistently made by school library media specialists as they continually seek to build and improve their collections.

NOTES

1. Kenneth L. Donelson and Alleen Pace Nilsen, *Literature for Today's Young Adults*, 5th ed. (New York: Longman, 1997), pp. 43–73.
2. Dino F. Felluga, "Undergraduate Introduction to Critical Theory," http://omni.cc.purdue.edu/~felluga/theory.html.
3. M. C. Albrecht, "The Relationship of Literature and Society," *American Journal of Sociology* 59 (March 1954): 425–26, 431–32.
4. Donelson and Nilsen, *Literature*, 5th ed. pp. 383–84.
5. Ibid.
6. Kenneth L. Donelson and Alleen Pace Nilsen, *Literature for Today's Young Adults*, 3rd ed. (New York: Scott, Foresman, 1989), p. 434.
7. American Family Association, available at http://www.afa.net/.
8. Gertrude Himmelfarb, *One Nation, Two Cultures* (New York: Alfred A. Knopf, 1999).
9. *The American Heritage Dictionary of the English Language*, 4th ed. (New York: Houghton Mifflin, 2000), available at http://www.bartleby.com/61/57/P0635700.html.
10. Patrick R. Penland and James G. Williams, *Community Psychology and Co-ordination* (New York: Marcel Dekker, 1974), p. viii.
11. Ibid., p. 148.
12. Rosalind Sydie, *Natural Women, Cultured Men: A Feminist Perspective on Sociological Theory* (Toronto: Methuen, 1987). Abstract by Paul Gingrich available at http://uregina.ca/~gingrich/f1500.htm.
13. Felluga, "Critical Theory."
14. Kay Vandergrift, "Journey or Destination: Female Voices in Youth Literature," in *Mosaics of Meaning: Enhancing the Intellectual Life of Young Adults Through Story*, edited by Kay E. Vandergrift (Lanham, MD: Scarecrow Press, 1996), pp. 17–46; Kay Vandergrift, "Female Protagonists and Beyond: Picture Books for Future Feminists," *The Feminist Teacher* 9 (Fall/Winter 1995): 61–69; Kay Vandergrift, "Reconstructing the Study of World War II for Gender Equity," *Knowledge Quest* 28 (May/June 1998): 38–43; Kay Vandergrift, "Model of Female Voices in Youth Literature," available at http://www.scils.rutgers.edu/special/kay/model.html.
15. Robert W. White, *The Enterprise of Living: A View of Personal Growth*, 2d ed. (New York: Holt, Rinehart and Winston, 1976), pp. 356–57.
16. American Association of School Librarians and Association for Educational

Communications and Technology, *Information Literacy Standards for Student Learning*, p. 2.

17. Ibid.

18. Ibid., p. 22.

19. Andrew Bonime and Ken C. Pohlman, *Writing for New Media: The Essential Guide for Writing for Interactive Media, CD-ROMs, and the Web* (New York: John Wiley and Sons, 1998); Lisa Graham, *The Principles of Interactive Design* (Albany, NY: Delmar, 1998); User Interface Engineering, *Web Site Usability: A Designer's Guide* (North Andover, MA: User Interface Engineering, 1999); User Interface Engineering, *Eye for Design* (bimonthly periodical). The User Interface Engineering items are available at 800 Turnpike Street, Suite 101, North Andover, MA, 01845, e-mail, uie@uie.com.

20. Malcolm Skilbeck and Richard Cotter, "Curriculum Design," in *Encyclopedia of Educational Media, Communications, and Technology*, 2d ed., edited by Derick Anwin and Ray McAleese (New York: Greenwood Press, 1988), pp. 131–35.

21. William A. Katz, *Introduction to Reference Work: Basic Information Sources*, 6th ed. (New York: McGraw-Hill, 1992), Vol. 1, pp. 59–62.

22. Robert B. Harmon, *Elements of Bibliography: A Guide to Information Sources and Practical Applications*, 3d ed. (Lanham, MD: Scarecrow Press, 1998), p. 7.

23. Helen Haines, *Living with Books: The Art of Book Selection*, 2d ed. (New York: Columbia University Press, 1950), pp. 125–44.

Collection Development Policy: A Management Approach

4

Policy and how it is created and maintained play a crucial role in all institutions in society today. Developing sound policy and executing it well are at the heart of good and fair management. This is certainly true of the role policy plays in creating and maintaining collections for school libraries. What is policy? *Webster's* provides several definitions, perhaps the most useful for our purposes being "a definite course or method of action selected from among alternatives and in light of given conditions to guide and determine present and future decisions."[1] *Dictionary of Professional Management* defines policy as the official authoritative statement of rules, judgments, decisions and guidelines that is used to (1) define, describe, interpret and prescribe long-range objectives, intentions, functions and procedures; and (2) guide and regulate activities of a group or organization.[2]

Included in these definitions are several important concepts that influence the management of school library media collections. A collection development policy can be expected to provide a theoretical overview that explains the educational, social, and cultural rationale for the development of the collection. It should also state directions, guidelines, controls, and standards for the overall management of the collection. The policy should also outline elements within and external to the school that must be coordinated within the selection and evaluation process.

At the operations level, a good policy statement establishes methods for planning and carrying out day-to-day operation of the collection. Further, it outlines who is responsible for collection development decisions and operations. It addresses how to review challenged materials and the need for fairness and due process.

COLLECTION POLICY IS OFFICIAL AND AUTHORITATIVE

A school library media collection development policy must be official and it must be authoritative. It becomes official after having been reviewed and approved by the governing board of the school system. When it becomes official, it carries legal and professional obligations that cannot be ignored. The official policy is an open statement to the community and to teachers, administrators, staff, students, and parents describing the collection and how it is to be managed. Because it has been approved by an elected or appointed governing board, it becomes authoritative, carrying the weight and authority of social, legal, and political accountability.

POLICY AS THEORY AND CONCEPTUAL GUIDE

Although a policy is not a theoretical or conceptual discussion, it must be based on a thorough understanding of the various theoretical and conceptual elements that influence collection development. These elements must be reflected and articulated well in the policy narrative itself. Theory in application gives direction to what we do and explains why we do it. A detailed, clearly written policy document also serves as a means of educating and informing various client groups about the role collection development plays in the total program of the school and about the role that librarians, teachers, administrators, and others play in the process of developing and maintaining viable collections.

Generally, an explanation of collection development can be based around six concepts:

• Culture and its general expectations
• Society and the requirements for social order
• The role of modern education as a cultural system
• Institutions such as schools and the roles they play in society and culture
• Curriculum analysis and mandates
• Group and individual needs

Culture refers in part to the body of learned behavior of human societies. To have a workable society, individuals must cooperate so that activities carried on within the society satisfy both social and individual needs. Learned activities are handed down from generation to generation within the society and become a part of the social order. Human activities are so numerous and complex that most cultures must rely on systems that are based on ideas as well as structures that include constructs and propositions expressed as symbols. Culture is then transmitted from generation to generation through the ideas and symbols inherited in and understood within the culture. Such systems are necessary to communicate cultural knowledge and to coordinate activities within the culture.[3]

Education in some form is necessary in all cultures for this knowledge to be transferred, and schools and their curricula are fundamental to this process. In recent years, educators have viewed the curriculum as a means of selecting necessary elements from the culture. By using cultural analysis, a meaningful curriculum can be planned to successfully transfer cultural values through the formal educational process.[4]

COLLECTION DEVELOPMENT, CURRICULUM ANALYSIS, AND CULTURE

Although the relationship of culture to curriculum and collection development may appear to be remote and abstract, it is one of the driving forces behind how librarians select resources for their various user groups. Culture sets the broad parameters of values, needs, and expectations; and curriculum analysis identifies those elements in terms of how they need to be integrated into learning and instruction in schools. In its broader sense, curriculum takes the many expectations and needs of culture and forms them into programs of instruction in language, literature, science, health and safety, and other areas.

In a broader sense, curriculum can also mean all instruction that takes place either in school or out of school, both planned and unplanned.[5] Collection development policy is a management plan for building and managing the school collection over time. This policy must be based on a clear understanding of the official curriculum as well as the unofficial curriculum of a school. Collection development policy must also consider other influences on learning and student development and needs. A collection development policy is a formal plan of operation that states in broad terms how the collection is to be managed and developed over a period of time. As such, the policy needs to address a number of considerations:

The goals and objectives of the collection

The perceived weaknesses and strengths of the collection

Methods and means to be used to address weaknesses and to maintain strengths

Limitations to be placed on the collection:

> What will not be collected

> The degree to which an area will be developed (e.g., completely and exhaustively; representatively; or narrowly and selectively)

In complex library environments, the collection development plan can be extensive and exhaustive in detail. The best examples of these are university and special collection development policies, many of which are now being published on individual library or institutional Web sites.

Evans, based on his reading of *Understanding You and Them*, by C. E. Cortes and others (Boulder, CO: Social Science Education Consortium, 1976), suggests a number of reasons for having a formal collection development plan.[6] The policy is a communication instrument that informs everyone about the collection's nature, scope, and priorities. It helps focus thinking on the organization's priorities for the collection, and it helps foster commitment to collection priorities.

The policy can also be used as an assessment instrument in that it can aid in collection evaluation and deselection. A good policy also sets standards for inclusion and exclusion. It can therefore serve as an assessment tool for determining the effectiveness of the collection development plan. It will likewise aid in budget allocations. The policy also helps with personnel matters in that it can help reduce personal, intellectual, and department biases in making choices. It also helps in training and educating staff members, and over time it ensures consistency in judgments. It also is useful in handling complaints, and it can be useful as a public relations and public information device.

FORM AND STRUCTURE OF A COLLECTION DEVELOPMENT PLAN

Over the years, general agreement has been reached about the form and structure that an official collection development policy should have. Evans suggests that all librarians who are charged with developing a policy first consult two fundamental works in this area, the second edition of *Guide for Written Collection Policy Statements* (1996) and *Guide for Writing a Bibliographer's Manual* (1989), both published by the American Library Association. Evans draws heavily on these two sources in preparing guidelines for formulating a collection development policy.[7] He further suggests that policies should have four central elements.

The first element is a brief description of the community to be served. For a school district, this would include an account of the district's main characteristics. For the building-level school, this would include a description of its population. The description, although brief, should present a succinct profile of the school district or the local school in terms of population, missions and objectives, and the curriculum structure it has developed.

The second element is a brief description of the client group to be served. In the case of schools this will include students, staff, teachers, and administrators. Limits placed on services provided to other groups in the community (e.g., parents, volunteers, businesspersons) should be noted.

The third element is a statement concerning the parameters of the collection to be maintained. This should include the subject areas and types of materials to be collected as well as the format of materials and the technological support systems that certain formats will require.

The fourth and final element is a detailed description of the service programs that the collection will support.

In a school library media center this statement will outline the major elements of the curriculum and will explain how the collection contributes to meeting curriculum and learning objectives as established by the school district. In addition, the statement will need to address issues related to recreational and developmental requirements, cultural enrichment and diversity, and the information needs of staff, teachers, administrators, students, and other important groups of persons closely associated in some way with the school.

Evans outlines some basic elements that can be used to support the above requirements. These include an explanation of culture, heritage, and social values as they influence collection development; attention to the experiences of ethnic groups and ethnic relationships; information needs and survival skills required for successful living in a complex society; changes in society and how those changes affect culture; and educational requirements and educational materials required for a diverse society and culture.

In addition, within the last few years, collection development policies have needed to address technology, especially computer developments. Technological developments have impacted collection development policies through their influence on facilities and facility redesign, the need for production facilities, and access to advanced information databases and formats such as various forms of CD-ROM technologies and the Internet.

SCHOOL COLLECTION DEVELOPMENT POLICY

The school library media collection development plan is often referred to as the selection policy. As such, it reflects most of the points made above. A school collection development plan may be designed at the district level, at the school building level, or at both levels.

A school collection development plan intended to serve an entire school district or system should address several basic elements. The following discussion is based on models for school district collection development policies suggested by the American Association of School

Librarians (AASL). Various publications AASL offer the following guidelines for designing a policy.

1. Overall Statement of Policy. This initial statement explains the general policy of the governing board regarding the selection of materials for school libraries within the system. For example, such a statement might read:

The policy of the Board of Education of Union School District is to provide a wide range of learning resources at varying levels of difficulty, with diversity of appeal and the presentation of different points of view to meet the needs of students, teachers, and other interested parties as defined in this policy.

2. Objectives of Selection. This section offers definitions of terms used in the document. Basic terms such as "learning materials" will need to be defined. This section also should provide an overall rationale for the selection of materials to meet learning and teaching objectives. It often presents examples of materials that can be expected to be acquired under these definitions and procedures. Examples can include textbooks, supplementary materials, trade books, reference materials, charts, maps, CD-ROMs, videotapes, computer programs, microfilms, and Web and Internet sources.

3. The Role of the Professional Staff. The policy will state the expected role of the professional staff in making selection decisions. Presented here are details on how the professional staff will perform its duties. For example, the staff's role could be described as follows: Provide materials that will enrich and support the curriculum, taking into consideration the varied interests, abilities, learning styles, and maturity levels of the students served.

4. Responsibility for Selecting Materials. This is an important section because it is here that the governing board delegates the responsibility for the selection of materials to the professional staff employed by the system. The policy must state that all selections by the professional staff are made under the authority delegated by the board. The policy may further state that although many persons, including parents, students, teachers, and community members, may be involved at an advisory level, the overall responsibility for coordinating the selection of materials and making recommendations rests with the professional library media staff.

5. Criteria for Selection of Learning Resources. This section outlines the how and why of selecting materials. One of the most important criteria to be stated here is that all decisions must support and be consistent with the general educational goals and mission of the school district as well as those of individual schools within the district. Likewise, selection must meet the requirements for helping to provide enrichment and support for individual users. The policy may also suggest specific standards and outline problem areas that should not be overlooked in selection, including controversial issues and newly evolving concerns such as the needs of at-risk students.

6. Procedures for Selecting Materials. The evaluation process is presented in more detail in this section. Suggestions are made on the kinds of selection aids to be used in making decisions. In addition, this selection should also reemphasize who is involved in the selection process and the nature of their involvement. Problem areas such as how to evaluate gifts and how to process recommendations for purchases should be discussed here.

7. Challenged Materials. The importance of this section of any collection development policy document cannot be underestimated. Several provisions need to be addressed here:

- **Statement of Policy**. This section should present a clear statement affirming that any citizen has the right to question and challenge materials selected and acquired by the school libraries of the district and that such protests must follow a prescribed form for requesting reconsideration of the item or items in question.
- **Provisions for Handling Complaints**. Complaints may be handled either informally or formally. Both approaches should be described in detail, giving lines of communication and authority. Requests for a formal reconsideration require procedures that generally establish a committee to hear complaints and to make recommendations. Decisions regarding formal complaints may always be reviewed by higher-level hearing bodies or committees until they reach the governing board of authority, where a formal and legal resolution of the conflict is made.

8. Supplements. In school districts with several schools, one official policy must apply to all schools. Nevertheless, because each school is different, the local building-level library may wish to add an official supplement to the policy explaining how the school is different and how selection of materials in that school will address its unique requirements in different ways. For example, if the school serves a large number of students who do not know English well, then the collection policy will need to address the needs of such students more vigorously than a school in the same district with a more homogeneous, English-speaking student body.

POLICY ANALYSIS AND ADJUSTMENT

Culture and society change and evolve over time. Even immediate circumstances change, and a school collection development policy must adjust to those changes. In management theory *policy adjustment* is a term applied to the need for change.[8] Policy adjustment recognizes that no policy can be written in stone and that changes must be made after due consideration. Policy adjustment is a process that allows either temporary or permanent changes to be made in response to requests or needs that may become apparent from several sources, including parents, teachers, administrators, and people in the community. For example, the policy might be altered to state in more specific ways that materials will be acquired to reflect diversity and cultural awareness. An explanation outlining how changes are officially made to the policy must be made a part of the document, so that when changes are made they are official.

In recent years, the literature has advised those responsible for collection development to pay more attention to electronic information sources, digitalization, and information support technology. Likewise, library media specialists need to be aware of changing cultural and social situations that have strong implications for collection development adjustments. For example, the needs of students who are at risk for failure for various reasons fall into this category. A collection development policy statement can be adjusted to respond to such needs and to state how these problems will be addressed in terms of identification and selection of materials.

Closely related to policy adjustment is *policy analysis*. Policy analysis is a management process that is used to objectively measure and evaluate questions, issues, problems, concerns, and information that relate to and are affected by policy.[9] Policy analysis is generally undertaken to improve existing policy or to correct problem areas in policy. It has three major components, all of which are designed to bring about better policy:

• Develop, continue, or improve goals, objectives, and mission priorities.
• Develop necessary guidelines for action.
• Suggest alternative actions for improvement.[10]

Policy analysis uses both qualitative and quantitative measures. *Guide to the Evaluation of Library Collections*, published by the American Library Association, outlines several kinds of measurements. Among these are:

Collection-centered measurements.
> Use standard checklists, catalogs, and bibliographies to measure the existing collection against authoritative recommendations.
> Compile use statistics and make comparisons with other similar libraries or collections.
> Apply published standards and guidelines against the collection.

Use-centered measurements

> Study circulation patterns.
>
> Study shelf availability (what is or is not on the shelves at given times and periods).
>
> Study requests for interlibrary loan.
>
> Conduct user surveys and focus group sessions.
>
> Conduct document citation studies of projects.[11]

Measurement approaches may also employ more qualitative methods, such as conversations with teachers, students, and parents, and your own observations. Systematically recorded anecdotes also offer evidence of collection development needs and adjustments.

PROCEDURES FOR CREATING THE COLLECTION DEVELOPMENT POLICY

There are several ways to initiate a collection development plan. In large school systems, the governing board will usually instruct all units under its charge, including library programs, to develop and present policies and policy plans for approval that explain the operations of their units. In smaller districts the library supervisor or even librarians may have to take the initiative and ask the board to implement a collection development plan. In small single-school districts where there might be only one or two librarians, the initiative for an official policy will likely have to come from the librarians themselves. Such requests will usually go from the librarians to the principals and then up the chain of command to the official governing body.

In some situations an officially approved collection development policy may be difficult to establish. Some board and staff members may see such a policy as fraught with political and social questions that they do not want raised. If so, it becomes imperative to launch an education and information campaign to explain that such a policy is important because it offers protection and fairness for all parties involved in the selection process, including the staff, students, parents, and members of the community.

Once the decision has been made to write a policy, the governing board or some other appropriate official will appoint someone to chair a policy development committee comprised of a variety of individuals representing the many constituencies with an interest in the development of the collection: librarians, teachers, administrators, staff, parents, and, when appropriate, students. The committee is then charged with drafting a basic policy statement for submission to a review board or to an officially appointed individual. After the reviewing board or individual has read the document and made revisions and recommendations, the policy may then be submitted for comment to selected groups within the community, perhaps committees of teachers, parents, and students. Once these groups have commented on the draft, it goes back to the policy development committee for final review and revision. The committee then has the discretion of sending it back to those who have suggested revisions for their comments. After all reviews and revisions have been made, the document is sent to the official governing body for review and final adoption.

It is customary to have a public hearing on the document to inform the community about what the official board is considering. Usually the official board will invite comments and reactions to the policy before it votes, and an informed constituency is important. Another benefit of an open hearing is that it offers an opportunity to gather support for the policy, which can be voiced to the board. It also is a good way to find out if anyone opposes the policy and to determine the nature of the opposition. If opposition is voiced, the policy development committee may need to explain the policy better or perhaps develop a strategy to counter the arguments voiced by those who disagree with the policy.

Once finally approved, the policy then can be printed and distributed widely. All library staff members should be instructed on its use, and others in the school community should be informed of its content. To reach as many interested groups of people as possible, a condensed version might be developed and given out as a public information item.[12]

A number of useful resources have been developed to help in the construction of a policy statement. These include:

- *Collection Development Policies and Procedures*, 3d ed., edited by Elizabeth Futas (Phoenix: Oryx Press, 1995)
- *Collection Development and Collection Evaluation: A Sourcebook*, edited by G. E. Gorman and Ruth H. Miller (Metuchen, NJ: Scarecrow Press, 1995)
- *Acquisitions Management and Collection Development in Libraries*, 2d ed., by Rose Mary Magrill and John Corbin (Chicago: American Library Association, 1989)
- *Collection Development: Past and Future*, edited by Maureen Pastine (New York: Haworth Press, 1996)
- *Library Collection Development Policies: A Reference and Writer's Handbook*, by Richard J. Wood and Frank Hoffmann (Lanham, MD: Scarecrow Press, 1996)
- *Collection Assessment and Management for School Libraries Preparing for Cooperative Collection Development*, by Debra E. Kachel (Westport, CT: Greenwood Press, 1997)
- *The Collection Program in Schools: Concepts, Practices, and Information Sources*, 3d, ed., by Phyllis J. Van Orden and Kay Bishop (Englewood, CO: Libraries Unlimited, 2001).

Individual schools as well as school districts often make their selection policies available through Web sites. For examples, see the following:

- "Alemany High School Library Collection and Collection Development Policy," available at www.geocities.com/Athens/Sparta/7543/collection.htm
- Scecina Memorial High School, "Collection Development Policy," available at www.hinet.palni.edu/~scecina/cdpol.htm)
- Round Rock Independent School District, Round Rock, Texas, "Instructional Materials Selection and Adoption Policy," available at www.tasb.org/policy/pol/private/246909/LPM/EFA(L)-X-246909.html

POLITICAL PROCESSES INVOLVED IN ADOPTION

The official adoption of a collection development policy is a political and social process. In this age of conflicting values over the role of education, opposition to the policy is a strong possibility. This is especially true in areas where there is a history of political conflict over public policy issues. In *The Dynamics of Achievement: A Radical Perspective* Dieter Seibel makes some suggestions for helping guide a proposed policy to adoption.[13] He advises those who plan new programs and operations, including policy changes to follow these summarized steps:

- **Evaluate the overall situation.** Take into account your own skills as well as the skills of your supporters. What resources do you have at hand to promote your agenda? What are the real challenges to having the policy adopted?
- **Set objectives for the policy's adoption.** Establish both long- and short-term goals. Focus on the immediate goals first and make these realistic and obtainable. Rank these objectives in order of priority.
- **Cultivate the drive to be successful.** A personal drive for success is important to success. Consider your reasons for reaching the goals. Place some personal emotions behind reaching your goals. At this point place less emphasis on the intellectual and analytical aspect of the project and more on the emotional. An emotional undertone to your approach communicates sincerity and helps highlight the importance of the policy in terms of professional management. Of course, always remember that this is a professional undertaking and that all of your actions and behaviors must reflect high professional and personal standards.
- **Become assertive, but not aggressive.** Learn to speak up on the issues and to defend the contents and directions taken in the policy. Be able to answer questions put to you in a strong and authoritative manner.
- **Cultivate confidence in yourself and in those around you.** Build this confidence around a self-appraisal of yourself and your supporters.
- **Build your approaches around strengths.** Awareness of your strengths will have come from prior analysis of existing staff and school and community

resources, skills, and attributes. All approaches to justifying the policy should be based on a clear understanding of those skills and resources.

- **Use leverage**. As in any situation, when we face opposition we will sometimes find ourselves and our supporters weak or unprepared. It is at times like this that we must place our efforts where they will be the most effective. We must know where we have leverage that can make a difference. *Force field analysis* is one method that can help us understand just what our true leverages are. (A discussion of force field analysis follows later in this chapter.)

- **Ask questions**. In any situations where opposition or a lack of understanding might occur, it is necessary to ask the right questions at the right time. A skilled leader will know how to ask questions to uncover dangerous assumptions that might be held by some people. Uncovering those assumptions is essential to the successful passing of the collection development policy.

- **Communicate your ideas on the issues effectively**. Communication is vital to the successful adoption of the policy. This includes the written document as well as how it is presented to the board and the community. Effective communication is also important in defending and explaining the policy before the board and before its detractors.

- **Work with others and cultivate group activities**. Getting the policy approved is not a one-person operation. Someone needs to head the effort, but it will take many people to effectively see the policy through to its final reading and adoption by the official board. Personal networking as well as formal group meetings and consultations will be required. The person given the responsibility for presenting or at least getting the policy ready for presentation to the board should be able to work with people individually as well as with groups in a more formal setting.

UNDERSTANDING GROUP WORK

As noted, obtaining official approval requires an understanding of the political and social processes at work. Policy formation and hearing groups are a part of this political and social process. They have lives of their own. This is especially true when groups are composed of elements that hold differing views or values concerning issues.

Realistically, we can expect varying views to be expressed concerning a collection development policy, especially when the policy is presented for open hearings or debates. Before one takes charge of a hearing where the collection development policy is to be presented, it is useful to understand group dynamics. Napier and Gershenfeld identify the following stages of group development as typical:[14]

The Beginning. When a group first comes together there are uncertainties. People have only their experiences with other groups to know what to expect. Self-protection for all involved is important. Some may seek to establish control immediately, while others may wait to see what will happen. It is a time of observing, gathering data and information, and deciding personal roles. Initial moves are often polite, tentative, and superficial.

Movement toward Confrontation. After the initial probing has occurred and boundaries, lines of authority, and roles are established, usually the group will move into confrontation. Confrontation may not mean conflict, but it does mean that differing views and values will be expressed, considered, and debated. The good group leader will note the types of boundaries that are being set and the level of power and in-group leadership that is being established. The leader may find him or herself in an awkward position because often the power base may shift from accepting the official leader to one of suspicion. The official leader may become a source of criticism. General complaints may be voiced about how things are getting done or how decisions are being made and by whom, and other issues of freedom and control will be voiced.

Depending on a variety of things, the group may become more assertive, and some members may become rather aggressive. Power and personal influence become very important. Leadership within the group changes as positions are better understood. Although the group may experience some anger and hostility, there will also be affective behavior and even some humor. This is probably a much more realistic phase than the beginning stage with its superficiality and generalities. If the group reaches a point where decisions are not being reached, then a confrontation of some sort will likely occur in order to get the group back on task.

Compromise and Harmony. At this stage, when conflict comes out into the open, it is addressed in some fashion so that the group can continue with its work and improve its effectiveness in addressing the issues at hand. Usually this period reveals a new openness and a willingness to respect each other's views and boundaries and to avoid signs of hostility. Although issues and problems are raised and everyone is encouraged to speak up and be heard, there is underlying pressure not to raise questions or to engage in behaviors that might break up this newfound harmony. The real problem here is that issues are over-analyzed and no real decisions are made. Compromise and harmony are gained at the expense of efficiency and group integrity. This inefficiency soon leads to disillusionment and increasing tension.

Reassessment: Uniting Emotions and Tasks. This is a critical stage in most groups. The group may feel the need for more structure so that it can meet its objectives and responsibilities. A call for strong and decisive leadership may be heard. This may not succeed because fundamental questions and issues are not being addressed. If the group decides to address the underlying reasons for its ineffectiveness, questions of member roles, decision-making procedures, leadership, and communication patterns will likely be scrutinized as well as the personal behaviors that facilitate or inhibit the group's effectiveness. This is a period of reflection on the group's goals, performance, resources, and final accomplishments. It is a time of emotional reassessment and realignment of tasks.

The Maturing Process: Resolution and Recycling. It is not reasonable to expect that conflict can be avoided in a working group. Groups will always have periods of tension and conflict. As with people, some groups mature and are able to deal with conflicts and tensions and meet their goals and obligations. Other groups may not mature and therefore fail. If the group cannot resolve its issues, an impartial group facilitator or mediator may be called in to help restructure the group and its dynamics. The group process is complex and needs more study than this brief analysis can provide.

The above discussion should not discourage librarians or other educational leaders who have the responsibility for marshaling a collection development policy through to official adoption. Rather, it should alert leaders to an awareness of the power of the group and how essential it is to understand group processes. The success of a campaign for the formulation and adoption of an official collection development policy may hinge on how effectively the various groups have been managed during the policy development stages.

FORCE FIELD ANALYSIS: AN APPROACH TO PROBLEM SOLVING

One helpful theory in facilitating decision making and problem solving in groups is *force field analysis*. Psychologist Kurt Lewin, who developed a force field analysis theory for group dynamics, explained that in groups as well as with decision-making processes in general, when forces are increased for change in a given direction, then counterforces in the other direction often develop, bringing situations back to the status quo. If changes are to happen and decisions are to be made, efforts must be directed at enhancing the forces for change and reducing or keeping constant resistant forces.[15]

The use of force field analysis as a problem-solving technique promotes a diagnostic approach to looking at the factors causing a problem. Force field analysis also encourages one to look beyond the obvious and to consider new ways of responding to problems. In addition, it helps focus attention on the possible repercussions of any decision.

In force field analysis exercises, forces likely to promote the desired change are listed and given numerical values indicating how powerful they are perceived to be in influencing change. Similarly, forces likely to inhibit change are also identified and given numerical weights indicating

Figure 4.1
A Force Field Analysis Diagram

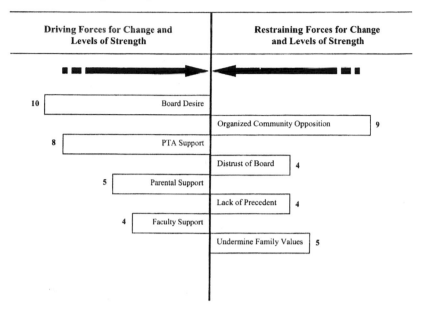

their strength. For example, Figure 4.1 indicates that the following forces have been identified and assigned numerical strengths based on the assumption that they will promote change: expressed desire from the board for a policy document (10); PTA leadership support (8); influential parental support (5); faculty support (4). Likewise, the following forces have been identified as likely to cause resistance: organized opposition from certain community groups (9); distrust of the school board (4); lack of precedent for a policy (4); feelings in some quarters of the community that a policy would undermine family values (5). Once identified, these factors can then be charted, as in Figure 4.1.

Because the support of the school board is so great in this example, the decision might be made to seek ways to increase the power of that factor by one or two points. Perhaps a better public relations and information campaign directed at individual board members might be effective. It might not be possible to influence any of the well-entrenched restraining forces, therefore perhaps the decision might be made to seek ways of increasing the power of the positive forces, such as support from the PTA leadership, parents, and faculty.

Force field analysis is only a tool. As with any other policy change activity, success depends on gathering and assessing facts and data and identifying and outlining plans of action. Careful attention to personal, cultural, social, and political climates will lay a sound foundation for the final adoption of the policy.

PUTTING THE POLICY IN ACTION

In practical terms, a well-developed collection development policy will eliminate many problems before they arise and will help settle arguments even after a policy is in place. As its heart, the policy represents a consensus of how to build a collection of materials. It likewise outlines how First Amendment rights and the right of individuals to have access to information are to be protected.

In management terms, after a policy has been adapted and becomes an official statement of operations, it is then a part of everyday administration and practice. Rules, procedures, and other types of operational decisions can then be made following the principles outlined in the policy. The policy can also act as an administrative guide in that it sets forth the ideals and standards by which the collection is to be measured.

CONCLUSION

Good policy makes good management. A good collection development plan is fundamental to the consistent development of any collection. A good policy document does several things. It states a library's philosophy and ideas about collections, and it lays down ground rules for the development of those ideals. Perhaps one of the most important aspects of good policy development is that it ensures fairness and protects the rights of individuals to a wide variety of information, resources, and ideas. We live in a diversified world, and clear understanding of that world must be reflected in how we set policies and build collections. Good policies ensure the rights of all to information. At the same time, policies can help us celebrate our differences as well as our commonalities.

NOTES

1. *Merriam-Webster's Collegiate Dictionary*, 10th ed.
2. I. S. Banki, *Dictionary of Professional Management: Authoritative, Comprehensive* (Los Angeles: Systems Research, 1997), p. 810.
3. Roy D'Andrade, "Culture," in *The Social Science Encyclopedia*, 2d ed., edited by Adam Kuper and Jessica Kuper (London: Routeledge, 1966), pp. 161–63.
4. Denis Lawton and Peter Gordon, *Dictionary of Education* (Sevenoaks, Kent: Hodder and Stoughton, 1993), p. 66.
5. Ibid.

6. G. Edward Evans, *Developing Library and Information Center Collections*, 4th ed. (Englewood, CO: Libraries Unlimited, 2000), pp. 70–71.

7. American Library Association, *Guide for Written Collection Policy Statements*, 2d ed. (Chicago: American Library Association, 1996); American Library Association, *Guide for Writing a Bibliographer's Manual* (Chicago: American Library Association, 1989), pp. 5–15.

8. Banki, *Dictionary*, p. 810.

9. Ibid.

10. Ibid.

11. American Library Association, *Guide to the Evaluation of Library Collections* (Chicago: American Library Association, 1989), pp. 5–15.

12. Evans, *Developing*, p. 86.

13. Dieter Seibel, *The Dynamics of Achievement: A Radical Perspective* (Indianapolis: Bobbs-Merrill, 1974).

14. Rodney W. Napier and Matti I. Gershenfeld, *Groups: Theory and Experience*, 6th ed. (Boston: Houghton Mifflin, 1999), pp. 429–36.

15. Ibid.

Protecting the Collection from Censorship

5

INTRODUCTION: OBLIGATIONS AND LAW

One of the most important professional responsibilities of librarians is to protect library collections and the information available through libraries from censorship. This must be accomplished with integrity and professionalism within the framework of social, cultural, and legal norms and according to professional ethics.

Chapter 4 discussed the importance of an official collection development policy in seeing that items are carefully and fairly considered if their presence in the collection is challenged. This chapter outlines some of the legal, social, and ethical factors that must be considered within the framework of censorship and what that means in terms of a democratic society. It also outlines some of the major legal and ethical issues now facing American librarians concerning censorship. The discussion will focus on the social and cultural role school library media center specialists play within American democracy. It describes some of the pressures now being placed on school librarians by forces in society that see educators, including school library media center specialists, as playing a role in preventing the erosion of the social order and traditional values.

Public and school libraries are now facing censorship pressures as they attempt to serve the needs of a broad-based population. This chapter will consider significant court rulings that have influenced and continue to influence the role of the American school library media community in terms of First Amendment rights. Recent court rulings concerning Internet accessibility in public libraries for adults as well as children and adolescents also require discussion. The examples given here are American, but the principles of intellectual freedom and how they are being interpreted in the United States have international implications as information and information distribution become more and more global through electronic transmissions.

THE EDUCATIONAL AND THEORETICAL ROLE OF THE SCHOOL LIBRARY MEDIA SPECIALIST

As with most branches of librarianship, school library media specialists have worked for over a century under a very oppressive and unflattering cultural stereotype.[1] It is the stereotype reflected in the mass media of the librarian as rigid, physically unattractive, and socially isolated. Unfortunately, the librarian stereotype is so ingrained in the minds of the population that it has prevented librarians and much of their work from being taken seriously by society.

The professional and theoretical literature of school librarianship demonstrates just how out of touch this stereotype is with reality. The educational role of the school library media center specialist has been well articulated through a series of standards and guidelines dating from the 1920s. This educational role has always reflected progressive educational theory, promoting reading and literature, curriculum development, the social responsibility of citizens in a democracy, information literacy, and lifelong learning.[2] Newer guidelines continue this progressive ideology by drawing upon contemporary learning theory and relating it to the role school media center specialists play in helping students to develop skills in accessing, evaluating, and using information in its many formats and environments.[3] It is apparent that the professional role of the media specialist as an information facilitator is now being questioned by some external sources with different views on the place of information and access to information in students' lives. Many of these views and the means used to see that they become public policy raise serious constitutional questions.

THE U.S. CONSTITUTION

American constitutional law deals primarily with government powers, civil rights, and civil liberties. The U.S. Constitution is a rigid document in that it cannot be changed by ordinary forms of legislation.[4] The American judiciary has enormous power to interpret the meaning of the Constitution. The right of the judiciary to interpret the Constitution was affirmed by the Supreme Court in 1803 in *Marbury v. Madison*.[5] What this means today is that all laws, regulations, ordinances, and orders passed by governments and boards that act in the name of governmental authority in the United States must conform to the principles of constitutional law. Constitutional law also governs many actions of private individuals, corporations, and organizations.

Among these constitutional principles is freedom of speech, guaranteed under the First Amendment to the Constitution. The freedom of speech clause gives people the right to express their thoughts and opinions without governmental restrictions.[6] However, it is not an absolute freedom, and the courts have ruled that the government can restrict speech under certain circumstances. Examples are rulings on child pornography and materials that have been judged by courts to be obscene. Courts have ruled that child pornography and obscene materials have no First Amendment protections.

The problem American courts face today is how to apply constitutional law in a diverse and complex society where many points of view are expressed openly. This is not an easy task, and many court interpretations of First Amendment rights and legal censorship are viewed as inconsistent. In fact, most First Amendment scholars consider the current American approach to regulating indecency in particular as flawed and inconsistent.[7] Such inconsistent court interpretations of what can be legally censored by government and other social entities have placed school library media collections in a vulnerable position.

According to the *Oxford English Dictionary*, the word "censorship" came into the English language in 1591 and was used to indicate a judgment. *Black's Law Dictionary* defines censorship as the act of inspecting publications, films, and the like for objectionable content.

Historically, censorship has a strong connection with governmental actions and degrees. Roman censors were government officials who had great power. They could invade family life and other forms of personal conduct, investigate how political duties were being performed, and decide whether public gatherings were permissible based on moral grounds. They had no superiors, and acted in accordance with their own values and Roman tradition.[8]

According to Martha Boaz, censorship has generally been viewed as "an effort by [a] government, private organization, group, or individual to prevent people from reading, seeing, or hearing what may be considered as dangerous to government or harmful to public morality."[9] Mary Hull defines censorship as "the practice of supervising conduct or morals" and a censor as "someone who examines materials and prohibits what he or she considers morally, politically, or aesthetically objectionable."[10]

A major problem lies with whether censorship is to be considered an official act of government in removing or prohibiting citizen access to information and materials, or whether it is to be seen as an attack from any quarter on any item or source of information including books, curriculum, and Web sites.[11] The American Library Association sees censorship as an overt "attempt to remove books and other items from a school, denying all other children access to the work."[12]

The American Library Association recognizes and supports the rights of parents and other interested parties in a community to question materials acquired for library and curriculum use, and it does not see such challenges as censorship. In fact, over the years, ALA has recognized the following levels of expressions of concerns regarding materials in a library collection:

- **Inquiry.** An information request, usually informal, that seeks to determine the rationale behind the presence or absence of a particular item in a collection.
- **Expression of Concern.** An inquiry that has judgmental overtones. The inquirer has already made a value judgment on the material in question.
- **Complaint.** An oral charge against the presence and/or appropriateness of the material in question.
- **Challenge.** A formal written complaint filed with the library questioning the presence and/or appropriateness of specific material.
- **Attack.** A publicly worded statement questioning the value of the material, presented to the media and/or others outside the library organization in order to gain public support for further action.
- **Censorship.** The removal of material from open access by any governing authority by its representatives (board of education/trustees, principals, library directors, etc.).[13]

In recent years some organized groups such as Focus on the Family that have been involved in questioning materials acquired by school libraries have insisted that they are not involved in censorship when they raise questions about the appropriateness of items in collections. They strongly object to being labeled as censors. Their objections lie largely with what they see as a blanket condemnation of their actions as censorship by librarians and others when they challenge particular books or authors.

THE WHY AND WHEREFORE OF CENSORSHIP

Censorship has been a part of human history since the beginning of recorded time. Almost all societies practice it in one way or another. In the United States and Canada in recent years, complaints about materials acquired for school library media centers have increased greatly. Most complaints stem from conflicts in values.

Challenges come to school library media center specialists because of a desire on the part of adults to protect young people from harmful information and images. These complaints generally center on sex, violence, ideology, political beliefs, social commentary, and religion. For example, the National Coalition to Protect Children and Families (NCPCF) is especially opposed to material that they consider pornographic. They cite research that indicates to them that exposure to pornography leads to increases in rape, child molestation, and general crime.[14] On the other hand, the concerns of Focus on the Family are based more on religious beliefs. This organization was founded by James Dobson, a former clinical professor of pediatrics, in 1977 in response to what he saw as both internal and external forces that were causing the disintegration of the American family. He believed that society had provided no comprehensive, rational, and biblically based approach to combat this erosion. The mission of this organization is to combat what it sees as assaults on the family. It does this by focusing its energies on promoting "reasonable, biblical, and empirical insights so people will be able to discover the founder of homes and the creator of family, Jesus Christ."[15]

VALUE FORMATION

Values, beliefs, and moral reasoning are at the heart of censorship attempts. Values formation, both in society and within the individual, is a complex process that involves the interaction of cultural social, and psychological forces. Numerous philosophical, religious, political, and psychological theories have been formulated in an effort to better understand values and their place in human discourse. In these discussions over the centuries, truths and values have been debated countless times.

Basic to these debates are idealism and empiricism. Idealism holds out the possibility that certain kinds of knowledge or truth exist independent of actual experiences or observational verification. Religious beliefs are examples of such systems. Idealism allows individuals to establish and apply standards of objectivity based on a given system of knowledge that is self-evident to the individual. In so doing truth is imposed on the world. Empiricists believe that all truth must be derived from facts. Knowledge of the world is not imposed by prior truths, but must be acquired by actual experience. According to this philosophy, because experiences are never complete, complete truth can never be obtained.[16]

The philosopher Immanuel Kant gave some attention to how idealism and empiricism might be reconciled. He argued that scientific knowledge or empirically gained information about the world is genuine knowledge. It is spatial and temporal knowledge of the world as it appears to the individual. We come to understand the world by the very act of trying to understand and conceptualize it through experiences. Nevertheless, apart from this experience-based knowledge exists another type of awareness that cannot be experienced or intelligibly ascribed. Insight into this reality can be achieved only by moral actions that are universally understood. Kant maintained that if no such moral standards existed and if moral behaviors were relative, then human communication would be impossible.[17]

Ideologies are collections of values and beliefs that help inform people about correct actions. These values and beliefs offer structure and order and become a part of social arrangements and interactions. Values reinforce beliefs and goals, and they justify actions and the machinery necessary for effective actions. Sociologists and other social scientists tend not to look at values as truth, but as empirical variables in social life that inform behavior. In other words, people think and act upon what they believe to be true based on their own realities.[18] Government, law, politics, education, religion, social and cultural configurations, and economics are just a few examples of the machinery that enables values and beliefs held by individuals and groups to become institutionalized, controlling, and pervasive.

UNDERSTANDING VALUES AND DEFENDING THE LIBRARY COLLECTION

What does all of this have to do with censorship? Censors and others who are concerned with materials in library collections will bring to the table a variety of values and concepts. From a cultural and social perspective, if librarians and school library media specialists are to be socially responsive to their environments, they must understand these views and concerns and respect their theoretical origins.

THE LAW AND CENSORSHIP

As we have seen, censorship is a part of human culture. It is a means of social control, and some form of it has been codified into laws of all nations. Various countries interpret censorship differently, depending on the cultural, social, moral, religious, and political values the nation wishes to uphold or suppress. Depending upon what is important and valued in a culture, offenses against established codes of conduct and expression may be labeled as treason, heresy, or obscenity.

As stated earlier, virtually all First Amendment scholars consider the current American approach to regulating indecency to be flawed and inconsistent.[19] Nevertheless, federal law today requires that for items to be adjudicated obscene, they must be judged on a tier of facts. These

include community adult standards; an item's appeal to prurient interests; the description of sexual conduct in a patently offensive way; sexual
conduct defined as obscene by applicable state law; and whether the
work taken as a whole lacks serious literary, artistic, political, or scientific
value.[20]

The development of this tier has been an ongoing evolutionary legal
and social process. The United States and Canada, as well as other
English-speaking countries, have been greatly influenced by English
common law, and many of these countries' early censorship laws were
directly influenced by both common law and English legislation. Legal
experts contend that modern censorship laws began with the Obscene
Publication Act (Lord Campbell's Act) of 1857 and were further codified
in *The Queen v. Hicklin* (L.R. 3Q.B.360) of 1869, where a high English
court ruled that the test of literary morality was "whether the tendency
of the matter charged as obscenity is to deprave and corrupt." In this
ruling the test of obscenity as applied by the court was whether a father
could read a work aloud in his own home. Based on this ruling, many
literary works were seized, their authors and publishers prosecuted, and
books destroyed. In 1913 in *United States v. Kennerly* (209 F. 119), although sympathetic to the free expression of ideas, an American court
ruled against the defendant because the publication under review fell
within the limits of the Hicklin test. Even in its time in both the United
States and England the Hicklin legal test for obscenity was criticized for
reducing literary standards to what was morally proper for the young
and for forcing authors to avoid or distort social reality. This test of
obscenity remained in British law for a century and in American law
until the 1930s.[21] In 1954 an English legal interpretation set aside the
Hicklin test and established a distinction between "filth for filth's sake
and literature." The judge ruled that literature should not be condemned
because it deals with the "realities of life, love, and sex" and instructed
the jury that sex is not dirty or a sin and that the literary-moral-legal
test ought not to be what is suitable for a fourteen-year-old schoolgirl to
read.[22] In 1954 changes were made in Lord Campbell's Act, and in 1959
a new Obscene Publications Act was passed by the British Parliament
that provided that

a work was to be read and judged as a whole and that testimony of expert
witness[es] could be admitted as evidence in relation to the literary, artistic, scientific, or other merits of the work; that a person should not be convicted if
publication was in the interest of science, literature, art, or learning and that book
publishers and authors could speak in defense of the work even though they
had not been summoned in the case.[23]

In the United States in the 1950s two court decisions narrowed the
legal definition of obscenity and in effect overturned much of the Hicklin

test. These included interpretations involving *Ulysses* by James Joyce (1933) and *Lady Chatterley's Lover* by D. H. Lawrence (1959). Rulings in these two cases noted that the literary aspects of works must play a central role in determining obscenity. In the *Ulysses* case the courts ruled that the work must be judged as a whole, not on the basis of its parts. In 1957 in *Butler v. Michigan* (353 U.S. 380), a challenge was made against a state statute that tested obscenity in terms of how the work might affect children. The court ruled that the Michigan statute reduced adults in Michigan to reading only what was fit for children and declared the Michigan law unconstitutional.[24]

In the 1960s Ralph Ginzburg and Edward Mishkin were found guilty of obscenity, Ginzburg for distributing obscene materials through the mails and Mishkin for publishing *Fanny Hill*. In 1966 the U.S. Supreme Court upheld the obscenity convictions of both Ginzburg and Mishkin based not on literary content, but on the supposedly offensive ways the works in question were promoted and advertised. In the Mishkin case the Court did allow *Fanny Hill* to be distributed in the United States, but only because the Court had not heard evidence of how it was advertised.[25]

In *Ginsberg v. New York* (390 U.S. 692) the Court, in upholding the conviction of a merchant who sold "girlie" magazines to a sixteen-year-old boy, introduced the concept of "variable obscenity," which meant that obscenity was not an absolute and could vary with circumstances. The Court allowed that the protection of children from the harmful effects of obscene materials was such a variable.[26]

The important *Roth v. United States* (345 U.S. 476), heard by the U.S. Supreme Court in 1957, declared that obscenity was not protected by the Constitution and that "obscene materials were without redeeming social importance." Along with the test that obscene materials deal with sex in a manner appealing to prurient interest, the ruling introduced the new test of whether the average person applying contemporary community standards would find the work taken as a whole appealing to prurient interest.[27] *Roth* also rejected what remained of the Hicklin test as unconstitutional. In 1964 in *Jacobellis v. Ohio* (84 S. Ct. 1676) the *Roth* test involving community standards was further refined to mean national standards, not necessarily local standards.[28]

The landmark *Miller v. California* (413 U.S. 15), decided by the Supreme Court in 1973, contained what was meant to be a clear and unambiguous test of obscenity. *Miller v. California* remains the fundamental legal guide and test for obscenity in the United States today. The basic guidelines to come out of this ruling involved whether

the average person, applying contemporary community standards, would find that the work, taken as a whole, appeals to the prurient interest; whether the work depicts or describes in a patently offensive way, sexual conduct specifically defined by the applicable state law; and [whether the] work taken as a whole lacks serious literary, artistic, political or scientific value.[29]

In this ruling Justice Warren Burger stated that community standards meant statewide standards, not just the standards prevailing in the local trial community.[30] This definition of community standards is no small matter. In an obscenity trial in Austin, *Rees v. Texas* (909 S.W. 2d), the jury was instructed to consider community standards to be representative of the average person in Texas and not the average person living in the traditionally more liberal Travis County, where the offense occurred.[31] Although statewide standards can be considered community standards, in *Jenkins v. Georgia* (1974) the Supreme Court noted that "juries do not have unbridled discretion" in determining obscenity.[32]

CHILDREN AND PORNOGRAPHY

In the last decades of the twentieth century court rulings involving child pornography have augmented the above decisions. The U.S. Supreme Court, in ruling that obscenity has no protection under the Constitution, has also ruled specifically that photographic child pornography is especially excluded from First Amendment protection. *The United States Code* (USCS) defines current federal law regarding child pornography (Section 18, paragraphs 2251 [2000] and sections of paragraphs 2252A [2000] and 2256 [2000]). The Child Pornography Prevention Act of 1996 especially criminalizes child pornography as it has appeared and developed on the Internet. However, in December 1999 parts of that act were declared unconstitutional by the Ninth Circuit Court of Appeals (*Free Speech Coalition v. Reno*, 9th Cir, no. 97–16536). The ruling may indeed affect the production and distribution of virtual pornographic images of children by recognizing that such images are products of the imagination and not reality.[33]

This court declared that certain provisions of the law were "so vague that a person of ordinary intelligence cannot understand what is prohibited." The court reasoned that this vagueness further invited arbitrary interpretation of law by the police and ruled that "[t]he First Amendment prohibits Congress from enacting a statute criminalizing the generation of computer images of fictitious children engaged in imaginary but explicit sexual conduct."

Regarding pornographic virtual images of children, the court issued several rulings that are now under appeal to the U.S. Supreme Court by the federal government.[34] In this ruling the court seemed to be saying that a product of the mind (e.g., creative imagination or factual reporting) is currently not criminalized by existing case law, and that laws that might be passed to control evil ideas (e.g., the real or fictionalized depiction of child-child or adult-child sexual relationships not involving photographic images of real children) cannot meet constitutional requirements of the First Amendment.[35]

No librarian wishes to see children exposed to pornography and its harmful effects. The Internet, although educationally powerful in many ways, is a major provider of pornography today. Demands are being made by society and government that librarians take precautions to see that children are not exposed to this type of material. The challenge is to protect free access and First Amendment rights while at the same time exercising good professional and legal judgment about the right to information in a free society.

COURT RULINGS AFFECTING SCHOOL LIBRARIES

The well-known 1982 Island Trees case, *Board of Education v. Pico* (457 U.S. 853) is considered one of the most important cases directly involving school library media centers to reach the U.S. Supreme Court. Nevertheless, two earlier cases have a bearing on censorship in school library media centers as well. In 1969, in *Tinker v. Des Moines Independent School District* 393 U.S. 503), the Supreme Court recognized that while in school students have certain First Amendment rights and that schools may limit those rights of expression only if a student's conduct is materially and substantially disruptive to the work and discipline of the school. But in 1972, in *Presidents Council, District 25 v. Community School Board No. 25* (457 F. 2d 289), the U.S. Court of Appeals, Second Circuit, upheld the right of the school board of the district to remove *Down These Mean Streets* from its school libraries. The court held that the book had dubious literary or educational merit and that the local school board was acting in accordance with the authority given to it by the state to select materials for schools. The court saw no constitutional infringement in the board's actions. This ruling was important because for some years after it was often cited by judges who gave school boards the right to remove books from libraries.[36]

A different view was taken by a federal appeals court in *Minarcini v. Strongsville City School District* (541 F. 2d 577). In this situation the local school board had refused to let a teacher use Joseph Heller's *Catch-22* or Kurt Vonnegut's *God Bless You, Mr. Rosewater* in class and also ordered that Vonnegut's *Cat's Cradle* and the Heller novel be removed from the school library. The board also ordered that students and teachers not discuss the books in class. The court ruled that the board was in error by having the books removed from the library. The ruling recognized that the school library was a storehouse of knowledge and a privilege that has been created by the state for the benefit of students in schools. That privilege could not be taken from students through the removal of books based on a board's displeasure or disapproval.[37]

A year later the U.S. District Court for Massachusetts in *Right to Read Defense Committee of Chelsea v. School Committee of the City of Chelsea* (454 F. Supp. 703) ruled that the board had no constitutional right to remove from the school library the poetry anthology *Male and Female Under Eighteen*, which contained the poem "The City to a Young Girl." The court's reasoning was as follows:

- The School Committee (the school board) had no absolute right to remove the book from the library;
- Compelling public policy speaks against any public authority having unreviewable power of censorship;
- The power of a school committee [to sanitize] the school library of views divergent from its own is alarming. . . . What is at stake in this case is the right to read and be exposed to controversial thoughts and language—a valuable right subject to First Amendment protection.[38]

BOARD OF EDUCATION, ISLAND TREES, NEW YORK V. PICO

On March 2, 1982, the U.S. Supreme Court heard arguments in its first case involving the removal of books from school libraries. The argument brought to the Court involved the Board of Education of the Island Trees School District having removed several books from a high school library in the district. In *Board of Education, Island Trees, New York v. Pico* (457 U.S. 853) the central question presented to the Court was, Can a school board remove books from a school library to promote moral, social, and political values without violating First Amendment rights? Issues raised by this question centered on the motivation of the school board and the students' rights to receive information. In the 5–4 judgment, with no majority opinion, the plurality opinion favored the plaintiffs in affirming that a board of education cannot simply remove books because of the ideas and values expressed in them.

In this ruling the Court defined the right of students to receive ideas and to learn as an "inherent corollary of rights of free speech and press," and it affirmed the right to receive information in a number of contexts. Through this ruling students become beneficiaries of First Amendment rights of access to information in school library media centers and libraries. *Pico* further gives support to students' right to learn from materials already available to them, and it lends approval to such educational goals as encouraging individual autonomy and the appreciation of diverse points of view. As such, the ruling protects against the removal of books based on ideological content.[39]

In this ruling the Court did allow books to be removed by boards of education for sound educational reasons and for legitimate purposes of limiting students' exposure to excessive vulgarity. Nevertheless, the board's reasons for removing books from school library media centers must be based on educational grounds that can be subject to court challenges.

Eight of the nine judges disclaimed any intent to undermine the authority of the school board to control curricula and to establish and apply curricula that transmit community values (including respect for authority and other social, moral, or traditional values). The dissenting judges also agreed that school boards must have broad discretionary powers to promote "civic virtue." In his minority opinion Justice William Rehnquist stated that it is

permissible and appropriate for local boards to make educational decisions based upon their personal, social, political or moral views. In short, action by government as educator do not raise the same First Amendment concerns as action by government as sovereign.[40]

Writing in the *Texas Law Review* in October 1983, Tyll Van Geel outlined some of the other issues and judicial conflicts and interpretations that faced the Court in deciding this case. For example, both the Supreme Court justices and those in the lower courts had to face three basic points in this dispute: (1) the students' rights regarding freedom of belief; (2) the rationale for the government's desire to indoctrinate students; and (3) the role of the judiciary in protecting First Amendment rights within the context of public education. In an earlier ruling the Supreme Court had recognized and protected students' rights to free speech and had insisted that schools remain a marketplace of ideas rather than becoming institutions to foster a homogeneous nation. The Court had also insisted that public school officials cannot impose a "pall of orthodoxy" on the classroom.[41]

On the other hand, both Supreme Court and lower court rulings had likewise recognized the proper function of public schools to inculcate students. Such indications from the courts gave and continue to give support to those who wish to have the rights of school authorities enforced and protected in overseeing policies and procedures such as the selection of materials for classrooms and school library media centers.[42]

Although involving First Amendment rights, challenges to government officials' decisions to remove materials from a school library could not be easily approached by the Court in *Pico* using the traditional means of resolving First Amendment conflicts. The central test became whether an order by the governing board to remove books is based on reasonableness and legitimate pedagogical concerns. The *Pico* decision also underscored the Court's view that students have a right not only to receive information but also to learn and to be taught.

Although the Court was clear in saying that this ruling concerned only the removal of books from a school library by a board, the case did present other constitutional issues. The role of government in restraining free speech of individuals is not clear or obvious when the government refuses to purchase a book for a library. With *Pico* and other rulings the Court indicated that governmental boards may not prescribe certain orthodoxies to be adhered to within a school by withdrawing unacceptable books from a school library. The removal of books from libraries may be challenged on this basis as well as on grounds that such removal is a violation of the right to receive information.

Based on this principle, the selection and acquisition of materials may also be challenged if the refusal to purchase certain items is a clear and persistent practice that in effect prevents certain ideas from being made available to students. The Court has recognized that a school cannot buy all books or materials relating to a topic or idea, and that officials must make decisions about what will be acquired, but *Pico* implied that constitutional rights have been violated if it can be shown that a persistent pattern of refusal to purchase certain types of materials is present. Records of selection decisions and official selection policies might be used by courts in deciding whether such unconstitutional practices have been systematically followed.[43]

In line with rulings in *Pico*, Van Geel argued that to test whether government has impinged upon First Amendment rights of free speech, courts must consider the motives of a board that refused to allow the purchase of materials and whether those motives present governmental restraint on the right of free speech of private individuals.[44] A federal court has also ruled that if a book has been removed from a library and as a result of this removal students cannot gain access to the book through other means, then in effect students have been denied access to this material and their constitutional rights may have been violated.[45] *Pico* is now the legal standard set by the Supreme Court that all lower courts follow in determining whether the First Amendment rights of students have been violated in issues involving school library media center collections.

Slowly the influence of *Pico* has begun to appear in court rulings and legal reviews relating to school library media centers and other information access issues. In 1995 a federal district court found that the school board of Unified School District No. 233 in Kansas had violated the First Amendment rights of its students by ordering the removal of *Annie on My Mind* from a school library in the district (*Case v. Unified School Dis-*

trict No. 233, 908 F. Supp. 864, 1995). The court ruled, based on *Pico*, that books may be removed if they are "pervasively vulgar" or lacking in "educational suitability," but that it is unconstitutional to do so if such removal will deny students access to ideas with which school officials disagree. School board members claimed that the book was removed by board vote because it was "educationally unsound," but testimony in the four-day trial convinced the court that students' First Amendment rights had been violated because of considerable evidence of "viewpoint discrimination" on the part of the board. The court reasoned that the board had interpreted "educational unsoundness" to mean anything different from their own agreements. The book in question had received much literary recognition, including being selected by the American Library Association as one of the "Best of the Best" books for young adults.[46]

Pico has been effective in that it has been cited numerous times in legal reviews and arguments in the defense of First Amendment rights of students and in limiting school boards' authority to interfere with students' rights to information and ideas.[47] The judgment in *Case v. Unified School District* cost the school district more than $85,000 in court costs and fees. *Pico* has not proven to be an isolated ruling affecting only school media center collections. A search in law review journals and court rulings indexed through the LEXIS/NEXIS database (Academic Universe) indicates that *Pico* has been cited widely in journals and case reports. Most of these citations appeared in discussions concerned with free speech of students and access to information within libraries, and in arguments concerned with the constitutional limits placed on school boards' authority to interfere with students' rights to information.

CENSORSHIP AND THE INTERNET

In recent rulings, the Supreme Court has extended to the Internet the highest level of First Amendment protection, and in doing so has recognized its enormous reach and public forum appeal. At this writing it is unclear whether this concept will remain, as the Court may be asked to consider other aspects of Internet information delivery.

In ruling that much of the Communications Decency Act of 1996 was unconstitutional, the Court recognized that Internet speech is to be afforded "strict scrutiny standards" for free speech (47 U.S.C. 230, 560–61, declared unconstitutional in *Reno v. ACLU* [521 U.S. 844, 1997]).

Strict scrutiny standards are the highest that courts can consider in determining constitutional issues. The Court in its ruling recognized that the government did have a legitimate interest in protecting children from harmful content found on the Internet, but it felt that some sections of the law as written were too broad to achieve that goal and that these sections would suppress a far greater spectrum of speech than was constitutionally permissible.[48]

The debate over how to protect children from harmful and obscene materials found on the Internet is ongoing. In October 1998 the Child Online Protection Act (47 U.S.C.A. 231 [Supp. 1999]) was signed into law by President Bill Clinton. It was an attempt by Congress and the president to address some of the issues raised by the Supreme Court in *Reno v. ACLU*. The American Civil Liberties Union (ACLU) also opposed this law, claiming that it is still too broad and is a serious threat to freedom of speech. The law was struck down by the U.S. District Court for the Eastern District of Pennsylvania on February 1, 1999, with the ruling upheld in June 2000 by the Third Circuit Court of Appeals.[49] In early 2001, the U.S. Department of Justice asked the Supreme Court to review the Third Circuit Court's decision. This request by the government was supported by the National Law Center for Children and Families. In May 2001, the Court agreed to review the case (*Ashcroft v. American Civil Liberties Union, et al.*)[50]

At this writing federal courts are facing new issues raised in the Children's Internet Protection Act (CIPA) and the Neighborhood [Children's] Internet Protection Act (NCIPA) (Public Law 106–554), signed by President Clinton on December 21, 2000. According to the ALA, the acts placed restrictions on the use of funding available through the Library Services and Technology Act, Title III of the Elementary and Secondary Education Act, and on the Universal Service discount program known as the E-rate: "These restrictions take the form of requirements for Internet safety policies and technology which blocks or filters certain material from being accessed through the Internet."[51] The law, which was to become effective on April 20, 2001, was challenged in court by the American Library Association and other groups based on claims that it was unconstitutional.[52] Under law, appeals to this ruling will go directly to the Supreme Court.

The Loudoun County Library in Virginia presented the courts with one of the first Internet situations involving First Amendment rights violations involving public libraries. The library board had adopted a policy of filtering the Internet for the intended purpose of blocking out pornography. In its policy statement the board stated that "library pornography can create a sexually hostile environment for patrons or staff," and it noted that filtering was needed to protect children from "harmful" materials. Shortly after the filtering program was added to library computers, People for the American Way (PFAW) and the American Civil Liberties Union filed a complaint against Loudoun County and its officials—the library board and its library director—claiming that they were in violation of the Civil Rights Act of 1964 by denying library patrons access to protected speech.[53] In its ruling, *Mainstream Loudoun v. Board of*

Trustees of the Loudoun County Library (24 F. Supp. 2d 552, E.D. Va. 1998), the court found that the library and its officials were in violation of the act. The court wrote that the library's policy was unconstitutional because it was not based on "strict scrutiny" principles in that it was not narrowly tailored to show a compelling government interest, and that the library had restricted the access of adults to materials based on whether they were suitable for children. The court also found that the library's policy of deciding which sites to block was not sufficiently explained. The court noted that procedures for contesting specific blocked sites by patrons lacked sufficient explanations.[54] In fact, the court felt that the procedure established for requesting that a site be unblocked had a "chilling" effect on free access to speech.[55]

The court reasoned that the library had acquired Internet publications and had made them immediately available through the Internet, but at the same time had a policy that effectively removed them based on content, which in effect became a "content-driven policy." The court felt that this content-driven policy of regulating access to speech on the Internet was subject to unqualified First Amendment scrutiny—the strict scrutiny the Supreme Court applied to Internet regulations in *Reno*.[56] In an analysis of this case, legal scholar and author Matthew Kline argued that the library's policy was an internal management decision that had the effect of controlling adult behavior and of restricting adult access to public discourse.[57]

As the Supreme Court had reasoned in *Pico*, this court also saw the public library as an open forum for discussion and ideas, while the school library was subject to the mission and objectives of the school, operating under the informed oversight of its governing board. It must not be forgotten that in *Pico* the Supreme Court also established a "right to receive" rationale for students using school library media centers. This rational also guided the court in its *Mainstream Loudoun* decision.

ALA's Core Values Task Force has stated that one of the association's important values is "assurance of open access to intellectual resources." The association has also gone on record as opposing the use of Internet filters in libraries. The association claims that the use of filters can lead to First Amendment rights violations and that filtering systems are not effective in weeding out undesirable materials.[58]

Another problem public libraries now face is how to protect children from undesirable Internet materials. Historically, the ALA has claimed that libraries cannot and should not act *in loco parentis* and has insisted that parents have the primary responsibility for supervising their own children in the use of materials and services offered through the public library. In recent years this policy has come under attack by groups such as the American Family Association who assert that because the public

library is a social institution within American culture it has a responsibility to supervise and protect children who use its services and materials, just as do schools and other membership groups. The problem is
intensified by issues such as how to protect children from harmful materials in constitutional and professionally sound ways while at the same
time affording adults access to legally protected information.

The Internet and Our Children: A Community Partnership, published by
the Illinois Library Association,[59] is a useful document in understanding
the theoretical and culture role that the American public library community has defined for itself in recent years. It addresses such issues as
hallmark library policy positions concerning the Internet; policy development at the local level; the limited usefulness of filters; assertion of
the library's role in information navigation; denial of the government's
right to limit access; and individuals' information needs and the right to
know and have information available.[60]

School library media centers also have a role to play in this broad
debate. Although the role of the school is different than that of a public
library, societal experiences of public librarians often influence decisions
made by school library media specialists on Internet access. Society and
courts to a large extent have recognized the strong parental role that the
school plays in guiding and educating children. Society recognizes that
school library media specialists, along with other school officials, have
an obligation to make sound educational decisions in the selection and
use of materials. This obligation certainly extends to materials and information found on the Internet. Material selection policies can address
these issues in legally defensible ways by establishing criteria and explaining how electronic information is evaluated and acquired for the
collection. In line with court rulings, clearly stated selection policies provide media specialists, teachers, administrators, and parents with specific
information regarding the kinds and types of electronic information
available and how they are accessed through the library media collection
and its electronic information services. Modern educational theory and
cognitive psychology allow media specialists as information mediators
to directly supervise the use of the Internet by students in the library
media center. As suggested by Van Geel, they cannot carry this selection
of sites and supervision and guidance to the point of making judgments
about political, social, and cultural orthodoxy.[61] The Supreme Court,
through *Pico* stated that officials who manage school library media collections have this right as long as the selection of materials is carried out
in ways that do not promote a given orthodoxy or conformity to a certain
belief system and do not curtail students' First Amendments rights to
receive information.[62]

CONCLUSION

As we move into the twenty-first century, most institutions are in the midst of reevaluating and refining their roles, missions, and goals. This is certainly true of school library media centers. One of the dominant challenges media centers and libraries face in democratic societies is defining their core values. It is clear that in the United States, media specialists and librarians face a new era of legislation and litigation over both existing laws and case law regarding intellectual freedom.[63]

School library media specialists and other librarians will be called upon to play a decisive role in this debate by defining the role media centers and libraries play in American democracy and explaining how they will protect intellectual freedom and access to information and materials. Paul Burden, a reference librarian at a public library, observed in *American Libraries* that "anyone who is denied access to needed information cannot truly pursue the happiness that is everyone's inalienable right."[64] How this right is to be protected underscores a debate that will certainly help define American democracy and society in the future.

NOTES

1. Pauline Wilson, *Stereotype and Status: Librarians in the United States* (Westport, CT: Greenwood Press, 1982).

2. W. Bernard Lukenbill, "Learning Resources and Interactive Learning Principles," *Drexel Library Quarterly* 19 (spring, 1983): 91–116.

3. American Association of School Librarians and Association for Educational Communications and Technology, *Information Literacy Standards*, pp. 2–3.

4. *Black's Law Dictionary*, 7th ed. (St. Paul: West Group, 1999), p. 307.

5. *Marbury v. Madison*, 1 Cranch 137, 5 U.S. 137 (1803), available at http://caselaw.lp.findlaw.com/scripts/getcase.pl?court=US&vol=5&invol=137.

6. *Black's Law Dictionary*, p. 675.

7. J. H. Samoriski and others, "Indecency, the Federal Communications Commission, the Post-Siker Era: A Framework for Regulations," *Journal of Broadcasting and Electronic Media* 39 (Winter 1995): 51–57.

8. Martha Boaz, "Censorship," in *Encyclopedia of Library and Information Science*, edited by Allen Kent and Harold Lancour (New York: Marcel Dekker, 1970), Vol. 4, pp. 328–38.

9. Ibid., 328.

10. Mary Hull, *Censorship in America: A Reference Handbook* (Santa Barbara, CA: ABC-CLIO, 1999), p. 1.

11. Ibid., p. 2.

12. Ibid., pp. 5–6.

13. Texas Library Association, *Intellectual Freedom Handbook*, 5th ed. (Austin: Texas Library Association, 1996), pp. 23–24, available at http://www.txla.org/doc/iflhbk.html.

14. Hull, *Censorship*, p. 6.

15. Focus on the Family, available at http://www.family.org/welcome.

16. Eric Carlton, *Values and the Social Sciences: An Introduction* (London: Gerald Duckworth, 1995), pp. 3–6.

17. Ibid., p. 14.

18. Ibid., pp. 16–17.

19. Samoriski and others, "Indecency," pp. 51–57.

20. *Black's Law Dictionary*, p. 1076.

21. Alleen Pace Nilsen and Kenneth L. Donelson, *Literature for Today's Young Adults*, 6th ed. (New York: Longman, 2001), pp. 412–13.

22. Boaz, "Censorship," p. 331.

23. Ibid.

24. Nilsen and Donelson, *Literature*, 6th ed., p. 413.

25. Boaz, "Censorship," p. 333.

26. Nilsen and Donelson, *Literature*, 6th ed., p. 414.

27. Ibid., pp. 413–14.

28. Ibid., p. 414.

29. Ibid., pp. 414–15.

30. Ibid., p. 415.

31. W. Bernard Lukenbill, "Erotized, AIDS-HIV Information on Public-Access Television: A Study in Obscenity, State Censorship and Cultural Resistance," *AIDS Education and Prevention* 10 (June 1998): 241.

32. *Jenkins v. Georgia*, 418 U.S. 153 (1997), available at http://www.law.umkc.edu/faculty/projects/ftrials/conlaw/jenkins.html.

33. "Virtual Child Pornography Law Struck Down by 9th Circuit on First Amendment Grounds," *Legal Intelligencer*, December 22, 1999, National Child section, p. 4.

34. Jay Lyman, "U.S. Supreme Court to Examine Virtual Child Porn Law," *NewsFactor Network*, January 24, 2001, available at http://www.newsfactor.com/perl/story/6940.html.

35. "Virtual Child Pornography Law," p. 4.

36. Nilsen and Donelson, *Literature*, 6th ed., p. 418.

37. Ibid.

38. Ibid., pp. 418–19.

39. Tyll Van Geel, "The Search for Constitutional Limits on Government Authority to Inculcate Youth," *Texas Law Review* 62 (October 1983): 197–297.

40. Matthew Hilton, "Options for Local School Districts Reviewing Local Governance and Moral Issues Raised by the Equal Access Act: The Gay-Straight Student Alliance in Utah," *Brigham Young University Education and Law Journal* 1 (Spring 1996), available at Lexis-Nexis Academic Universe, Legal Search, http://web.lexis-nexis.com/universe, http://firstsearch.oclc.org/. Rehnquist's remarks available at http://www.tourolaw.edu/patch/Pico.

41. Van Geel, "Search."

42. Ibid.

43. Martin D. Munic, "Education or Indoctrination—Removal of Books from Public School Libraries: *Board of Education, Island Trees Union Free School District No. 26 v. Pico,*" *Minnesota Law Review* 68 (October 1983): 213–53.

44. Van Geel, "Search."

45. Munic, "Education."

46. "Recent Cases, Briefly Noted: Removal of Book from Library," *Entertainment Law Reporter* 18 (August 1996), available at Lexis-Nexis Academic Universe, Legal Search, http://web.lexis-nexis.com/universe.

47. Lexis-Nexis Academic Universe, Legal Research, searched April 20, 2000, using keyword "Pico," available at Lexis-Nexis Academic Universe, Legal Search, http://web.lexis-nexis.com/universe.

48. Joel Sanders, "The Regulation of Indecent Material Accessible to Children on the Internet: Is It Really Alright to Yell Fire in a Crowded Chat Room?," *Catholic Lawyer* 39 (Summer-Fall 1999), available at Lexis-Nexis Academic Universe, Legal Search, http://web.lexis-nexis.com/universe.

49. *American Civil Liberties Union et al. v. Janet Reno*, Memorandum, 3rd District Court for Eastern District of Pennsylvania, February 1, 1999, Civil Action, no. 98–5591, available at http://www.aclu.org/court/acluvrenoII_pi_order.html; "*ACLU v. Reno* II Victory," *American Civil Liberties Union Freedom Network News*, June 22, 2000, available at http://www.aclu.org/news/2000/n062200b.html.

50. "Supreme Court Will Review Child Online Protection Act," *Computer & Online Industry Litigation Reporter*, June 5, 2001, p. 3, available at http://web. lexis-nexis.com/universe.

51. American Library Association, "CIPA & NCIPA Legislation," available at http://www.ala.org/cipa/legislation.html.

52. *Freedom to Read Foundation News* 25, no. 4–26, no. 1 (April 2001): 1, available at http://www.ala.org/cipa/ftrfnewsarticle.html.

53. Sarah E. Warren, "Filtering Sexual Material on the Internet," *Florida Bar Journal* 73 (October 1999), available at LegalTrac, http://web5.infotrac. galegroup.com; http://web2.infotrac.galegroup.com.

54. Matthew Thomas Kline, "*Mainstream Loudoun v. Board of Trustees of the Loudoun County Library* (Public Library's Blocking of Certain Internet Information.) (Annual Review of Law and Technology)," *Berkeley Technology Law Journal* 14 (Winter 1999), available at LegalTrac, http://web5.infotrac.galegroup.com.

55. Ibid.

56. Ibid.

57. Ibid.

58. American Library Association, *Libraries and the Internet Toolkit* (Chicago: American Library Association, 2000), available at http://www.ala.org/ internettoolkit.

59. Illinois Library Association, *The Internet and Our Children: A Community Partnership* (Chicago: Illinois Library Association, 2000).

60. Illinois Library Association, available at http://www.ila.org/pdf/ internet.pdf.

61. Van Geel, "Search."

62. Ibid.

63. C. James Schmidt, "Sex-and-Violence Ratings for Libraries," *American Libraries* 31 (April 2000): 44.

64. Paul R. Burden, "The Key to Intellectual Freedom Is Universal Access to Information," *American Libraries* 31 (September 2000): 48.

Technology, Education, and Information

6

INTRODUCTION: TECHNOLOGY AND CULTURE

Technology has always been a part of human evolution and culture. Unlike other species, humans have a capacity to think systematically, and early in the evolutionary process, humankind learned to create tools and techniques that helped solve problems and modify living environments. In so doing, we became toolmakers, artists, and technologists. Today technology and tools are hallmarks of society, culture, and education.

The history of the twentieth century was one of technological and scientific development, the rise of strong national states, and competition for natural resources. These national and economic forces have influenced and promoted the development of all kinds of technologies. The term "technology" comes from the Greek *techne*, "art, craft," and *logos*, "word, speech." In ancient Greece it meant a communication or discourse about the arts, both fine and applied. It first appeared in English in the seventeenth century, where it was restricted to references to the applied arts. Gradually these applied arts were called technologies. By the early twentieth century, the term embraced many processes and ideas in addition to tools and machines. Educational, instructional, and information technologies later came to be included among this array. By the mid-twentieth century, technology was seen as "the means or activity by which man seeks to change or manipulate his environment." Today many feel that it is now difficult to distinguish between scientific inquiry and technological activity.[1]

EDUCATIONAL AND INFORMATION TECHNOLOGY

Educational technology is the scientific and systematic application of both technical tools and understandings of psychological, biological, and social factors that in positive combinations can foster better student learning. Instructional technology, although often used together with educational technology, is somewhat more specific in that it means the application of tools and processes for the teaching of specific types of information and/or subjects.[2] The term "information technology" embraces technologies that help produce, manipulate, store, communicate, or disseminate information.[3]

DEVELOPMENT OF MODERN EDUCATIONAL TECHNOLOGY

Textbooks have been used in some form as instructional media for centuries. Hornbooks first appeared in the 1440s. These were not books at all, but little wooden paddles on which were fastened lesson sheets written on vellum or parchment. The lessons were covered with transparent horn and bound along the edges with brass. The battledore, another early educational technology invented by a helper of the famous printer John Newbery, was used from 1746 to 1770. Battledores were made of three folding cardboard leaves and consisted of alphabets, easy reading, numerals, and woodcut illustrations. In 1657 Moravian bishop and educator John Amos Comenius produced what is now considered the first picture book for children, *Orbus Pictus*, another hallmark in instructional technology. In an effort to interest children in learning, the bishop included materials that would attract their attention, interest them, and promote learning "by sport, and a merry pastime."[4] Although often referred to as a picture book, his *Orbus Pictus* was actually a teaching device whereby much of the information was presented visually.[5]

In the early part of the nineteenth century textbooks soon replaced hornbooks and battledores as standard fare for instruction. Textbooks became the instructional technology norm with the spread of universal schooling because they helped to maintain uniformity in instruction, reinforced national values, and assisted poorly prepared teachers. Textbooks remain an important part of elementary and secondary education and continue to reflect cultural values and expectations.[6] In the United States the *McGuffey Readers* and Noah Webster's *Blue-Backed Speller* became the standard textbooks for instruction and influenced the learning of many generations of chlidren.[7] Although the progressive education movement had encouraged new ways of teaching, rote learning and recitation and the use of the blackboard dominated educational practice and instructional technology for decades. Boardwork, including use of the blackboard or chalkboard, as it is now called, has some technological advantages. Among other attributes, boardwork in general encourages personal human verbalization and promotes "group memory" and structure.[8]

Military Training

Military conflict have always been important in the development of technology. From these conflicts come not only military technologies, but also scientific and applied science information that have broad implications for society. Military conflicts also require that personnel be educated and trained. World Wars I and II were particularly demanding in this regard. During these wars the American military in particular devoted considerable resources to training personnel. This included basic education as well as health and war technology training. For example, during World War I the U.S. Army used film to both inform the public about its efforts and needs and to train personnel in warfare. During both wars the armed forces faced the problem of having to train and educate huge numbers of people. Educational films were first introduced in 1910 and made some progress during the 1920s and 1930s, but it was during World War II that the usefulness of the training film was tested and accepted. Films could be used widely, reached large numbers of people, and ensured uniform instruction. The U.S. military devoted considerable time and expense to the perfection of training films, and much research was done on the psychology of learning and how learning principles could be transferred to the training needs of the military. These early efforts helped lay the foundation for modern educational and instructional technology.[9]

Higher Education

Generally higher education did not follow the military model in terms of investing significantly in new educational technology. For the most part, the textbook and lecture methods dominated higher education well past the mid-twentieth century. Although a 1946 ALA report recognized the importance of college and university libraries in furthering both research and instruction, as late as the 1970s American library standards and guidelines for college and university libraries continued to emphasize the importance of collecting print media over other formats.[10] In 1972 the Carnegie Commission in its report *The Fourth Revolution* attempted to modify that practice and recommended that nonprint information be maintained as part of the unified information instructional resources in colleges and universities.[11]

Among elements of higher education, the community college movement was the first to adopt newer forms of educational technology vigorously. We see strong evidence of this in the 1960s and 1970s. The mission of the community college was instruction and learning rather than research. The community college was seen as both a standard academic institution and as a source for technical skills training. Because it had to address the needs of a wide array of students, it was also expected to provide remedial training. Many community colleges employed educational technology staffs that were trained in learning theory as well as the application of media to learning and teaching problems. Faculties were often encouraged through consultation services and reward systems to incorporate newer educational technologies in their classes.[12,13]

Although not as abundant, examples of educational technology in colleges and universities other than community colleges can also be found. For example, Evergreen State College in Olympia, Washington, developed an extensive educational technology and collaborative learning model for instruction early on and continues to use it today.[14,15]

Nevertheless, not until the widespread introduction of computers and digital technology were some aspects of the newer educational technology model fully accepted by colleges and universities. Because computers and informational technology are now so pervasive and clearly impact both the transfer of information and learning, one of the important questions in higher education today is how to standardize and integrate educational and information technologies into the instructional process. Principles and techniques of educational and instructional technology acquired over the last several decades together with new research into information architecture (IA) and the psychology of learning are adding new energy and importance to this movement.

Secondary and Elementary Education

Modern-day educational technology was first introduced into elementary and secondary schools through the use of film and audio products such as radio, the 35mm filmstrip, the 16mm educational film and the 35mm slide. (In earlier years, the lantern slide was used.) The early school museum movement in major cities likewise influenced the development of educational technology. In their educational programs for students museums used interactive learning principles supported by the use of exhibits, machines, objects, drawings, models, and field visits. These approaches and tools offered students firsthand learning experiences and reinforced many of the learning principles upon which educational technology is based.[16]

Educational film production began early in the twentieth century. Before World War II companies such as ERPI Classroom Film, Eastman Classroom Film, and Films Incorporated had established markets. By the 1950s and 1960s educational film production was well established. Companies such as Coronet Instructional Films, McGraw-Hill Films, National Geographic Society, and Encyclopedia Britannica Educational Films had joined the educational market. Educational film libraries such as those at Indiana University and Iowa State University and at land-grant colleges and universities, museums, and government agencies increased in number, leading to the establishment of the U.S.-based Film Library Information Council.[17] As films and other formats became more accessible teachers were increasingly encouraged to make use of them to augment their instruction.

Other forms of educational technology were quickly introduced during the 1950s and 1960s. Provisions for educational television channels were adopted by the Federal Communications Commission (FCC) in 1952. During the 1960s and early 1970s programmed learning models were also introduced and encouraged.[18] Individualized instruction was initiated in the 1960s, but by the 1970s its use had waned. Computer assisted instruction, also introduced in the 1960s, proved a disappointment, and by the late 1960s it too had begun to fade from the educational scene.[19] Both of these technologies resurfaced later with the advent of the desktop computer.[20]

In the 1990s demand for educational improvement and accountability grew. As a part of this movement, in 1992 President George Bush established an office to access the state of American education, and the president and vice president encouraged federal officials to seek ways to better use modern technology in the nation's schools. The Office of Science and Technology Policy took a lead role in establishing a research base for this initiative; and in 1994 the Goals 2000: Educate America Act required the secretary of the U.S. Department of Education (now the Office of Education) to construct a "national long-range technology plan for actions promoting higher student achievement through the use of technology in education."[21]

A 1995 report from the Clearinghouse on Information and Technology noted a number of important trends in the area of educational technology in elementary and secondary schools:

- Computers [were] pervasive in schools and higher education institutions. Virtually every student in a formal education setting [had] access to a computer.
- Networking [was] one of the fastest growing applications of technology in education.
- Access to television resources in the school [was] almost universal.

- Advocacy for the use of educational technology . . . [had and was increasing] among policy groups.
- Educational technology [was] increasingly available in homes and community settings, including public libraries.
- A new insistence [had developed] that teachers . . . become technologically literate.
- Educational technology [was] perceived as a major vehicle in the movement toward education reform.[22]

A 1995 report by the RAND Corporation agreed with many of these findings, but voiced the need for planners and policy makers to learn more about the effectiveness of computer and network-based technology in elementary and secondary education. The RAND data also indicated that the use of computer technology was not evenly distributed. While some schools were heavily involved in computer technology, in others its use appeared to be marginal. Computer technology was limited to small groups of teachers who appreciated its potential for providing students with access to new resources. The report identified the following major issues as needing further attention: determining effectiveness of computer technology based on research; equity of availability of the technology, especially to minority, poor, and special-needs populations; costs and the restructuring of school budgets to accommodate the need for computer technology; retraining and equipping teachers to effectively use computers; ensuring that both pre- and in-service education provides for significant training in computer technology; and assuring that a plentiful supply of high quality content software is available. The report noted that software presented particular problems. It stated that software content must be specific to school and state standards and expectations, but that the educational market offered limited incentives for its development. Even if a high number of schools require software, sales are small in comparison to the business community.[23]

Information Architecture

Although relatively new to the scene, information architecture is fast taking its place within the broad structure of educational and instructional technologies. Information architecture is based on an understanding of information and focuses on the design of Web sites, which it considers to be the containers of information. IA has been called a three-way marriage among the information technology corporations, graphic designers, and researchers and librarians with the ability to focus on making what is complex very clear.[24] Stated another way, it is "the foundation for great Web design. It is the blueprint of the site upon which all other aspects are built—form, function, metaphor, navigation and interface, interaction, and visual design. Initiating the IA process is the first thing [one] should do when designing a site."[25]

CURRENT ISSUES IN EDUCATION

School library media specialists and their programs will be greatly affected by how educational problems are identified and solutions presented. Papers given at the Secretary's Conference on Technology 2000, sponsored by the U.S. Office of Education, as well as position papers developed by the North Central Regional Educational Laboratory address some of these issues.[26,27,28] Among them are how to

- use educational technology to increase student achievement;
- support the development of standards for education technology in learning and accountability;
- ensure the equitable use of education technology and address the problems of access to information technology often determined by race, economics, and location (e.g., "the Digital Divide");
- restructure the educational community so that new educational technology can be better integrated into teaching and learning. This includes the virtual classroom concept;
- use technology to enhance the learning of special populations and at-risk students;
- promote the concepts of learner-centered education where the learner is actively involved in constructing knowledge;
- develop knowledge-centered learning where the learner acquires the ability to think, reflect, and solve problems because of access to ideas and concepts of others configured in different ways;
- create a learning community where there is a shared interest in a topic, task, or problem and where there is a respect for a diversity of perspectives, abilities, and skills;
- encourage the development of a learning community that promotes teamwork, provides tools for sharing perspectives, and encourages knowledge production as a shared goal and outcome;
- prepare teachers to adjust their relationship in terms of new technology, teaching, learning, and students;
- create better understanding of the psychology and biology of the learner-centered process.

This is not an exhaustive list by any means, but it does help bring focus to the important role technology and the delivery of technology through the school library media center can and will play in the new technology-based educational paradigm of the future.

TECHNOLOGY IN THE SCHOOL LIBRARY MEDIA CENTER

Beginning with the first national standards issued in 1920[29] and continuing to the present, technology has generally been reflected in school library media standards. The theories and practices of educational, instructional, and information technologies have played even more significant roles in recent decades in shaping the standards issued jointly by the American Association of School Librarians and the Association for Educational Communications and Technology. (See Chapter 1 for a discussion of these standards.) It was through these later standards that the idea of the school library media center or instructional materials center was conceptualized by these two influential professional groups. Although instructional technology has always been a part of the school library media center concept, the dominant emphasis was on print media. The later standards helped school library media centers move toward a holistic vision of educational and instructional technology.

Acceptance of newer forms of technology was likewise helped by the management needs of the school library media center. Management technology that helped support cataloging and circulation was first introduced, followed by public access catalogs (PACs) and networking. Today this activity continues, especially in the area of large area resource sharing. The Texas Library Connection is a good example of large area networking. This service includes the "TLC Union Database," a union catalog holding the records of participating libraries in the state. This database permits students and faculty to access a variety of resources. Participating school library media specialists can send electronic requests and retrieve records for well over 27 million book and software items held by participating libraries. Specialists can use the database to download catalog records for their own systems and to aid in developing their local collections.[30]

NEW ROLES FOR SCHOOL LIBRARY MEDIA CENTERS

We cannot consider the new role of the school library media center without first discussing some of the major issues facing all libraries. For some libraries, the captive audience they have always enjoyed may not be there for long. This is the case particularly for academic libraries. Students and faculty have discovered that many of the resources they consulted in the library are readily available online. Major suppliers of books such as Amazon.com now deliver products virtually anywhere.

This in turn has increased user expectations of what service providers such as libraries should have available. Publishers and other information vendors have discovered direct markets for their products in an online environment, possibly forcing librarians into an unfamiliar competitive environment.

This scenario assumes, first, that information on the Internet is acceptable, reliable, and dependable, and that users can make that determination. Second, it seems to assume that users are willing to pay for information. Economist and computer scientist Charles Jonscher asserts that consumers will pay for information only if it will help in meeting tangible, basic goals. Most consumers now are willing to spend only a small part of their income on information products and services such as books, educational materials, and programs.[31]

Partly for economic reasons, libraries will continue to play their traditional role of providing free or inexpensive access to information, while other roles will emerge. The following concepts help define both the current and new agenda for library professionals. The librarian or school library media specialist will play the following roles:

• Acquisitor (e.g., manager of acquisitions)
• Evaluator
• Producer and designer
• Distributor
• Educator
• Counselor and advisor

Librarians and information specialists will still act as gatekeepers, acquiring, selecting, evaluating, and organizing information within their various environments. This role has been under expansion for some decades now, and these developments define the librarian as holding a vertical staff position, acting as an educator, consultant, information architect, community liaison officer, and manager.

In the future, as more information is available and conveniently arranged on the Internet, patrons will not always need to be in the library to access that information. However, the library's role as an educational and community resource will not decrease. Human evolution has not prepared us to remain isolated from community.

To add another dimension to this discussion, in the spring of 2001 the National Commission on Libraries and Information Science held hearings on the topic "School Librarians: Knowledge Navigators Through Troubled Times." The five major questions posed by the commission were:

- What is the role of the school librarian in student performance?
- What is the role of the school librarian in curriculum?
- What is the role of the school librarian in promoting and sustaining literacy?
- What is the role of the school librarian in promoting and sustaining information literacy?
- What is the role of the federal government in supporting school librarians?[32]

The role of the school library media specialist is an evolving one. The school library media specialist has always been an educator, advisor, and consultant, and we can expect these roles to continue to evolve and expand in a dynamic profession.

IMPORTANT CHALLENGES AND ISSUES

Evaluation and Selection

Selecting and evaluating materials and equipment is of primary concern to school library media specialists. It is necessary to place the selection and evaluation process within the context of educational and instructional technology. Robert Heinich and his colleagues offer a number of suggestions on the selection and evaluation of various kinds of media and equipment,[33] including the following:

- Does the material product match the curriculum?
- Are the materials accurate and current?
- Do materials offer motivation and promote interests?
- Do materials provide for learner participation?
- Are materials' technical qualities sound?
- Has the effectiveness of the product been determined through field testing?
- Are materials free from biases and advertising?
- Do materials give grade levels? How is this documented?
- Do materials assist learning with cognitive aids (e.g., overviews, cues, summaries)?
- For computer programs, are clear directions provided? Does the computer program promote creativity?
- For programmed learning, do programs follow standard principles of programming? Are frames parallel to objectives? Do feedback mechanisms provide for remediation and or/branching?
- For equipment, are sound and picture quality high? Is the equipment easy to operate? Is it affordable and reasonably priced? Is it durable and easy to maintain? Can it be easily repaired?

School Library Journal, Booklist, The Electronic Library, and *Science Books and Films* are just a few examples of professional publications that offer review and guidance in the selection of software.

SELECTING ELECTRONIC MEDIA

G. Edward Evans and Margaret R. Zarnosky, university librarians, note that the selection of electronic media raises many issues for libraries. These involve ownership, access, user and institutional needs, fees, and user selection of information versus the traditional gatekeeper role of the library.[34] Vicki L. Gregory, a university library resource specialist who echoes many of these same concerns, gives concrete and practical guidance by providing checklists and worksheets.[35] Evans and Zarnosky suggest that knowledge of local needs and the "local mix" will be required to address many issues involved with electronic media.[36]

Without question, collection development policies must take electronic formats into consideration. Criteria for selection and evaluation must be applied consistently across formats. Paul Metz suggests the following guiding principles:

- Establish a rational for the acquisition of each resource (both print and electronic).
- Meet faculty and student information needs.
- Provide access to electronic resources and integrate them into library programs.
- Maintain balance among disciplines and instructional needs (for both print and electronic resources).
- In terms of electronic resources, give priority to:
  - Integrity of the resource
  - Economic benefits in terms of the greater number of users
  - Currency and availability
  - Content
  - Functionality
  - Access by remote users
  - Resource sharing capabilities
  - Archiving and replacement of content

Cost and the budgetary requirements for electronic media must also be considered. The American Association of School Librarians (AASL) and the Association for Educational Communications and Technology (AECT) make a strong case for budget support:

Creating an information literate society is an expensive task. The school library media program requires a level of funding that will give all students adequate opportunities. . . . The school library media program requires a budget that supports the continuous collection of information in all formats and that provides the instructional infrastructure that will help students learn to use that information in creative, meaningful ways.[37]

For small software packages and CD-ROMs prices are generally set, but the pricing of large electronic databases will vary on an individual basis, often determined by the modules and options acquired.[38] Funds for the purchase of electronic media can come from the school library media center budget, but in most cases the budget must be supplemented. This can be done through special allocations. In the Austin Independent School District in Austin, Texas, bonds approved by voters allowed the system to both upgrade its print collections and purchase computer equipment and software for all schools in the district. In many cases, grants and entitlement programs from governments as well as funding from foundations and businesses offer support.

It is clear that the standard school library media center budget cannot absorb the total requirements for electronic materials. As with audiovisual materials, special allocations above the general budget will need to be obtained. Generally this means that a center will need a start-up budget aside from the general center budget. It is difficult to say what proportion of the budget should be devoted to electronic media. Again, local needs and expectations should determine that. Balance and needs should always be the guiding force here. As a matter of course building-level school library media centers can often afford to buy CD-ROMs and software much as they purchase reference materials or periodical subscriptions. Because of the expense, acquiring large bibliographic data and reference collection files such as those produced by the H. W. Wilson Company and the Gale Research Group generally requires cooperative purchasing arrangements within school districts or between larger jurisdictions.

The question often arises about how to justify the continuation of the print collection with so much information and material now being made available electronically. Recreational and critical literary reading has not shifted to electronic media, and some users will always require retrospective materials and data. This need is particularly prevalent in the humanities and social sciences. Another important point is that electronic media are not necessarily the most complete or comprehensive.[39] Libraries, especially academic and special libraries, have been somewhat accommodating in accepting and often substituting electronic bibliographic and reference materials for print versions. But it is clear now that both print and electronic media are needed because each meets different needs. Likewise, there is little indication that teachers at the elementary and secondary levels are demanding reduction of print collections. In fact, research has shown that teachers for the most part are conservative in their use of computers and electronic media.[40] There is little evidence that teachers prefer electronic resources over print media in the preparation and citing of resources used in written work and projects. It seems clear that instruction in literacy skills, including critical thinking skills and information skills, still requires a balanced approach using both print and electronic media.[41]

Copyright and Licensing Considerations

As materials are selected and produced, copyright laws and fair use considerations must be understood and followed.[42] The law and the interpretations of copyright protections are subject to frequent changes. The Copyright Office of the Library of Congress offers access to these changes and new interpretations.[43] Copyright requirements and licensing requirements for both building-level and jurisdiction- or consortium-level purchases must be adhered to rigorously when acquiring and using electronic media. Even small, inexpensive software programs such as word processing programs are governed by licensing agreements spelled out in the documentation that comes with the software. Institutional and jurisdiction-level licensing agreements generally include such directives as permission to load, what constitutes a legal copy, reproduction and/or copying rights, access levels, and requirements for protection against unauthorized use. The licensing agreement of the H. W. Wilson Company is a good example of what a producer will require.[44] A review of copyright laws as well as licensing expectations is suggested when dealing with electronic data. Knowledge of copyright laws is especially needed in the content design of Web sites.[45]

Web Site Evaluation

As noted, Web sites and the Internet are valuable information resources. Nonetheless, thorough evaluation and a high degree of scrutiny are required before Web sites can be recommended for students. Books and other sources are available to meet the demand for assistance in Web site evaluation. These include *How to Evaluate and Create Information Quality on the Web*, by Janet E. Alexander and Marsha Ann Tate (Lawrence Erlbaum Associates, 1999), and by the various educational institutions.[46] (Chapter 7 gives more information on Web site evaluation.)

Metz reminds us that electronic resources have not reduced the need for traditional collection development values and goals, but they have increased the need to be more aware of such issues as ownership, long-term availability of resources, educational and instructional expectations, user needs, legal requirements, and consortial issues.[47]

THE INTERNET AND WEB INFORMATION DELIVERY SYSTEMS

Although the Internet was originally conceived by the United States government as a means of sharing scientific and technical research among scientists, with the development of HTML (hypertext markup language) and the World Wide Web, it quickly grew to encompass many other uses, many of them commercial. Some of these commercial ventures are research and bibliographic resource-based, such as services offered by the Gale Group and the H. W. Wilson Company. Others, such as INET, are instruction-based.[48]

INET claims to be the world's largest educational resource on the Internet, offering links to over 200,000 sites that have been professionally reviewed for appropriate content. These resources include daily newspapers, books, demographic resources, encyclopedias, lesson plans for teachers, museums and photo galleries, and a host of other resources.

NetSchools Constellation is a "one-on-one commercial, Internet-based approach to educational technology." It is built around the concept of offering a laptop computer and Internet access to every student. An infrared wireless network allows the laptop to travel with the students, offering them word processing, math, e-mail, and Internet access. Teachers have notebook personal computers (PCs) that allow them to monitor and control students' laptops (including e-mails and Internet access). The system provides the Academic Information System (AIS), which contains a curriculum browser that is correlated with national, state, and local curriculum standards; local school resources; lesson planning and achievement assessment; and test preparation and reporting. The system likewise provides an extensive library of high-interest content in a variety of areas. This site includes tutorials, homework help, databases, and research and media resources. All of these resources are selected by the NetSchools editorial team of education professionals. The company claims that its vision is to offer the most powerful new technologies available to its clients. To further this vision its Internet-based approach to learning is school-centered and delivers high-quality educational applications that, it claims, will enhance student achievement.[49] Literature provided by the company says little or nothing about the direct role of the local school library media center, its resources, or its personnel in this configuration. It might be assumed by potential consumers that the AIS software allows for linkage to the local school library media center.

Other Web-based systems which for the most part are not commercial include the Library of Congress sites America's Library and American

Memory; European Schoolnet; Virtual LRC; the international Virtu@l School sites; KidsClick: Web Search for Kids by Librarians and Yahooligans: The Web Guide for Kids. These sites are very inclusive. For example, the Virtual LRC offers access to curriculum, reference, and bibliographic support systems such as Big Hub, Bibliomania, BUBL Information Service, Study Web, Michigan Electronic Library, Smithsonian, Suite 101, InfoPlease.com, the LibrarySpot, and the Awesome Library.[50]

In addition, the Web is offering an increasing number of links to university library Internet subject guides, museums, zoos, biological gardens, and art galleries. Sites developed for or by children and older students are also available. Other educational services can be found on the Web as well. For example, VHS (Virtual High School), a project of the Hudson (Massachusetts) Public Schools and the Concord Consortium, supported by a U.S. Office of Education grant program, offers Web-based high school appropriate courses.[51] A useful guide to Web-based sources is *Internet Resource Directory for K–12 Teachers and Librarians*, 2000/2001 ed., edited by Elizabeth B. Miller (Libraries Unlimited, 2000/2001).

FILTERING AND GOVERNMENT CONTROL OF THE WEB

The Internet and the Web cannot be discussed without reference to government control and social expectations. Filtering programs are now being promoted as one way of ensuring that only appropriate materials come to libraries and schools. An early problem faced by these filtering devices was their reliance on selected keywords to eliminate inappropriate sites. Some keywords, such as "breast," succeeded in eliminating useful sites such as those on breast cancer because somewhere in their contents they contained the designated word. Another problem with early filter programs was that they often blocked all sites on servers that were known to carry pornographic materials. Vendors claim that later versions of these programs have succeeded in limiting some of these problems.

The role the government should play in protecting children and youth from pornographic materials has been a burning issue for years. The federal government and many state governments have enacted laws designed to protect children from inappropriate Web sites they might encounter in school and public library environments. Most of these laws have raised constitutional issues of free speech, and most have been challenged in the courts or modified through legislation based on court rulings.

Generally the library community, through various library associations and groups, has opposed filtering, asserting that it is an unconstitutional infringement on freedom of speech and freedom of information. The American Association of School Librarians has collected and or developed a number of documents that should be useful to school library media specialists as they create policies and procedures for dealing with Web site issues.[52,53]

In 2000 the U.S. Congress commissioned the National Research Council (NRC) to examine ways of protecting children under age eighteen from pornography and other inappropriate materials found on the Internet. This included exposure to sexually explicit material, online sexual harassment and solicitation, and the ability to download sexually explicit materials. The National Research Council is a private, nonprofit organization that provides independent advice to the government on matters of science, medicine, and technology. It is also a part of the National Academies, which include the National Academy of Sciences, the National Academy of Engineering, and the Institute of Medicine. The study originated in a congressional mandate to the attorney general under Public Law 105–314 (Protection of Children from Sexual Predators Act of 1998), Title IX, Section 901. Under this directive, in the spring of 2001 the NRC held hearings across the country to gather opinions and advice from parents, teachers, librarians, and other interested parties.[54] Chapter 5 discusses the legal implications of filtering in more detail.

OTHER ISSUES OF IMPORTANCE

Media Equipment

Heinich and his colleagues suggest *Directory of Video, Multimedia, and Audio-Visual Products* (Fairfax, VA: International Communication Industries Association (ICIA), annual; text and CD-ROM) as a useful guide to media equipment. The *Librarian's Yellow Pages*, available in print and online editions, is another directory that is useful for locating equipment suppliers.[55] School library media specialists should not overlook the guidance in equipment and software selection and review provided by the ALA bimonthly publication *Library Technology Reports*[56] and by ALA TechSource, the ALA division that publishes *Library Technology Reports*. TechSource, through its Web site and other avenues, provides information on new technological developments of concern to school library media specialists.[57]

Conservation of Materials

Conservation of materials is another issue that is receiving more and more attention. This is especially true regarding all forms of media, paper, film, and digitized information. As school library media specialists move more into the digitized environments and begin to share their resources through networking and Web environments, methods, policies, and conservation practices will need to be seriously considered.

Information Architecture and Design

The subject of information architecture and design, although addressed previously, needs special attention here. It is clear that school library media specialists are now producers of information. Understanding learning psychology, behaviors, and theories as well as how to select and configure information for traditional and electronic environments is vital to creating an effective educational environment based on technology.[58]

The Virtual Classroom

The school library media specialist's role in the virtual classroom is still being defined. Evidence from commercial undertakings as Net-Schools Constellation as well as more traditional classroom settings suggests that school library media specialists must be assertive in defining what they can do and how they can do it within the virtual classroom. As the virtual classroom evolves, school library media specialists must make sure that their skills and education are put to use by those who are influencing the development of the virtual classroom, the evolution of the traditional classroom, and the electronic information environment. In this regard, the school library media specialist will need an understanding of how psychological principles are being applied to technologies. Research is greatly needed in all of these situations in terms of how the school library media specialist is or can be involved in helping to develop both theory and practice.

Distance Education

The role of school library media specialists in distance education must likewise be considered. Distance education can be defined as learning where the learner and the teacher are physically separated. Distance education has existed for many years using traditional technologies. For example, customarily many colleges and universities have offered correspondence courses that rely on the mail and print technologies. Newer programs use more advanced technical and multidirectional communication. Distance education programs can use a variety of technological configurations, including radio, telephone, television, and computers.[59]

The needs created by small schools' involvement in distance education warrant serious consideration. The TI-IN network, located in Texas, is a satellite system that serves high school students across the United States. It is designed to reach small schools or schools that need specialized courses. The question that arises is who is responsible for providing resources at such sites? Some high schools in remote areas in Texas and Alaska offer their students advanced high school as well as college courses through distance education technologies. Resource management problems arise and must be addressed. For example, a high school in the remote regions of the Big Bend country of West Texas may have a total of twenty-five students, with four taking a distance education course in microbiology from a regional community college. Perhaps students there are likewise allowed to take a Web-based course in microbiology prepared by a high school provider in the eastern United States or Canada. Such a school is not likely to have either a library media center or a school library media specialist. Who, then, has responsibility for providing the needed resources? Who must advocate for adequate materials to serve the needs of students at such distant sites, the local school authority or the provider of the instruction?

Information Literacy and Critical Thinking Skills

Low information literacy skill levels are common among both teachers and students. Improving information literacy and critical thinking skills has been a driving force of school library media center philosophy for decades. Among the forceful voices for this are the AASL and the AECT. Their contributions to information literacy are discussed in more detail in Chapter 1.

Some librarians complain that in their attempts to introduce students to the Internet teachers construct poor assignments that result in students searching in a helter-skelter fashion. Many school library media specialists have learned that they must work very carefully with teachers and their instructional needs to make sure that appropriate Web sites are identified and cataloged or listed, making them readily accessible to students when needed. Some teachers do not realize the limits of their research skills and do not ask for assistance from the school library media specialist. As one specialist said, "We just pick up the pieces [from the teacher's instruction] and do the best we can from there." Parents, staff, and administrators also need to develop better information literacy skills. Organizations offering guidance and support in information literacy and critical thinking skills include the AASL and the National Forum on Information Literacy, whose membership includes a wide array of educational and communication organizations, all of which share an interest in information literacy and critical thinking skills.[60]

Aside from the important standards and guidelines developed jointly by the American Association of School Librarians and the Association for Educational Communications and Technology, which emphasize both information and critical thinking skills, some useful works in information literary recommended by the forum include

- *Information Literacy: Educating Children for the 21st Century*, 2d ed., by J. A. Senn and Patricia Senn Breivik (NEA, 1998)
- *Student Learning in the Information Age* by Patricia Senn Breivik (Oryx Press, 1998)
- *How School Librarians Help Kids Achieve Standards: The Second Colorado Study* by Keith Curry Lance, Christine Hamilton-Pennell, and Marcia J. Rodney (Hi Willow Research and Publishing, 2000, distributed by LMC)

LMC, located in San Jose, California, offers a number of practical guides to help the school library media specialist understand and deliver information literacy instruction, including the following:

- *Information Literacy: A Review of the Research* by David V. Loertscher and Blanche Woolls (Hi Willow Research and Publishing, 1999)
- *Helping with Homework: A Parent's Guide to Information Problem-Solving* by Michael B. Eisenberg and Robert E. Berkowitz (ERIC Clearinghouse on Information and Technology, 1996)
- *From Library Skills to Information Literacy: A Handbook for the 21st Century*, 2d ed., by the California School Library Association (Hi Willow Research and Publishing, 1997)[61]

Libraries Unlimited also carries a number of useful guides on information literacy, such as Nancy Pickering Thomas's *Information Literacy and Information Skills Instruction: Applying Research to Practice in the School Library Media Center*, edited by Paula Kay Montgomery (1999).[62] Greenwood Press has a number of subject-oriented guides to using the Internet resources to promote critical thinking skills. Among others, these include *Using Internet Primary Sources to Teach Critical Thinking Skills in History* by Kathleen W. Craver (Greenwood Press, 2000) and *Using Internet Primary Sources to Teach Critical Thinking Skills in World Languages* by Grete Pasch and Kent Norsworthy (Greenwood Press, 2001).

EQUAL ACCESS TO INFORMATION TECHNOLOGY

Equal access to the Internet is also a major concern today. One of the initiatives of the Institute of Museum and Library Services (IMLS), a federal office, is to help address this problem. The Institute feels that "librarians are information navigators who help people find information they need and want" and that "museums provide an incredible variety of dynamic education experiences to support a lifetime of learning."[63] The institute has identified four essential tools for bridging the "digital divide": *literacy*, the foundation for all information use; *access* to free public information; *training* to empower individuals to find and use information effectively; and *content*, the rich source material that is needed to make the Internet a truly powerful information resource. These tools involve technology innovation, access to information, physical access, intellectual access (linking), and training in access skills. This view is reflective of the idea of universal information service in society, as suggested by Jorge Schement and further articulated in his planned book, *The Wired Castle*, which discusses information in the context of families and homes of the future.

Physical Environments and Management

When new technology is acquired, the environment in which it will be placed may need to be structured. Reconfiguration to accommodate new technologies is inevitable. In the future technological and social changes will place demands on the school library media center to provide access to information on a year-round basis, twenty-four hours a day, seven days a week. School library media centers will increasingly offer facilities that will accommodate audio and televised conferencing and distance learning as well as other forms of interactive learning. Adaptive devices will become more abundant in centers to meet the needs of special populations.[64] Administrative technologies and technical staffs to manage this new array of equipment and services will be critical to success. Administrative technologists and staff will increasingly assume responsibilities for maintaining hardware and installing software on school network servers, freeing school library media specialists for educative, administrative, and service roles.[65]

Among useful guides to the administration of the school library media center, including the management of technology and facilities, are

- *Managing Media Services: Theory and Practice* by William D. Schmidt and Donald A. Rieck (Libraries Unlimited, 2000)

- *Managing InfoTech in School Library Media Centers* by Laurel A. Clyde (Libraries Unlimited, 1999)

- *Facility Planning for School Library Media and Technology* (Linworth, 1999), *Technology Planning* (Linworth, 1997), and *Technology Planning for Effective Teaching and Learning* (Linworth, 2001), all by Steven M. Baule

Designing a School Library Media Center for the Future (American Library Association, 2001) by Rolf Erikson and Carolyn Markuson likewise offers many practical suggestions for the planning and design of new quarters.

ADVANCES IN TECHNOLOGIES

Jonscher predicts that we may indeed be nearing a point where every home, office, and school will have all the processing power it can reasonably need. Digitization has allowed accessibility to information not previously available in electronic formats, and the Internet is the most important avenue for telecommunication of digitized information through its standardized protocols.[66]

Early versions of the Internet have been around since the 1960s and 1970s, but it was not until the mid-1990s that it began to have a serious public impact on policies, behaviors, and life in general. Vinton Cerf, a senior vice president at MCI WorldCom, writes that within twenty years the Internet will become ubiquitous, with most access being through high-speed, low-power radio links. Most of the technologies we rely on in daily life will be Internet enabled. Most handheld and fixed household appliances will be connected to the Internet, and they will be able to communicate with one another. For example, if a refrigerator malfunctions, its internal computer will be able to ask for help independently from a control computer at a distant site, and once the help information is received, the appliance will be able to repair itself. An electronic wallet or belt may soon be available that will allow for multifunction operations. From a purse or wallet a person will be able to control appliances, pay bills, offer identification information, send e-mails, page others, search for information, and use a digital camera. New programming and fiber-optic delivery techniques will allow more and more information to be accessible instantly from anywhere in the world.[67] This includes information available in libraries and archives as well as personal health information and geographic information provided by global positioning systems.

Government and social policies will play a significant role in defining the new Internet. Questions of cost, equal accessibility, privacy, and technological developments must be answered. The Internet of the future must be robust enough to withstand all the demands that will be placed on it. If engineers are not able to develop such a system, Cerf predicts that the information and communication future will be fragile.[68]

Today social and technical planners are concerned that silicon-based computer technology may not meet demands past 2020. A logical estimate is that by 2050 computers will be calculating at well beyond 500 trillion bytes per second. Nevertheless, if we need faster computers, what will replace the current technology? Michio Kaku, physics professor at City College of New York, outlines some options. These theoretical possibilities include the optical computer, whereby information is carried on photons, not electrons; the DNA computer, which would transmit information based on the double-stranded DNA model; the molecular/DOT computer, in which molecules or electrons would act as logic gates and switches; and, finally, the quantum computer, which would rely on the direction of the axis on which individual atoms spin to encode information.[69]

As mentioned earlier, libraries as we know them will continue to exist with collections and spaces for users and staff. The immediate goal is to better define the current and emerging role of the library, including the school library media center, and to make changes as needed based on research, professional observations, and developments in society.

CONCLUSION

Technology implies change and new direction; but technology has always been a part of human society and culture. The rapid pace of technological development affects every aspect of our modern world. School library media specialists are now at a technological crossroad. Ahead lie challenges, opportunities, and great rewards as well as uncertainty and the need to retool and restructure. Fortunately, the history of the school library media center and its predecessor, the school library, has always been one based on progressive and enlightened education and social ideas. That history, experience, and cultural background will serve the school library media specialist well in the future.

NOTES

1. "Technology," available at http://www.Britannica_com.htm.

2. Donald P. Ely, *The Field of Educational Technology: A Dozen Frequently Asked Questions*, ERIC Digest EDO-IR-2000–01, ERIC no. 413889 (Syracuse, NY: ERIC Clearinghouse on Information and Technology, March 2000).

3. University of California at Davis, "Information and Technology Glossary," available at http://it.ucdavis.edu/glossary/#I.

4. Paul Saettler, *The Evolution of American Educational Technology* (Englewood, CO: Libraries Unlimited, 1990), pp. 31–32.

5. Ibid., p. 32.

6. A. Woodward, "Textbooks," in *The International Encyclopedia of Education*, 2d. ed., edited by Torsen Husen and T. Neville Postlethwaite (London: Pergamon Press, 1994), vol. 11, p. 6367.

7. Jennifer Monaghan, *A Common Heritage: Noah Webster's Blue-Back Speller* (Hamden, CT: Archon Books, 1983).

8. J. H. Tyo, "Boardwork," in *The International Encyclopedia of Educational Technology*, edited by Michael Eraut (Oxford: Pergamon Press, 1989), p. 245.

9. Saettler, *Evolution*, pp. 184–94.

10. Lukenbill, "Learning Resources," p. 105.

11. Ibid., p. 103.

12. George A. Baker III, Judy Dudziak, and Peggy Tyler, eds., *A Handbook on the Community College in America: Its History, Mission, and Management* (Westport, CT: Greenwood Press, 1994).

13. Rosanne Kalick, ed., *Community College Libraries: Centers for Lifelong Learners* (Metuchen, NJ: Scarecrow Press, 1992).

14. Evergreen College Home Page, available at http://www.evergreen.edu/user/homef.htm.

15. Joe Tougas, "Draft Memo on Instructional Technology at Evergreen State College," available at http://www.192.211.16.13/individuals/tougasj/ITmemo2.htm.

16. Saettler, *Evolution*, pp. 124–34.

17. J. A. Davis, "Film Libraries," in *The International Encyclopedia of Educational Technology*, edited by Michael Eraut (Oxford: Pergamon Press, 1989), pp. 557–59.

18. Saettler, *Evolution*, pp. 293–304, 362.

19. Ibid., pp. 304–7.

20. Robert Heinich, Michael Molenda, James D. Russell, and Sharon E. Smaldino, *Instructional Media and Technologies for Learning*, 6th ed. (Upper Saddle River, NJ: Merrill, 1999), pp. 227–49, 301–14.

21. Thomas K. Glennan and Arthur Melmed, *Fostering the Use of Educational Technology: Elements of National Strategy*, RAND MR-682-OSTP (Santa Monica, CA: RAND, 1996).

22. Eric Plotnick, *Trends in Educational Technology 1995*, ERIC Digest, ERIC no. 398861 (Syracuse, NY: ERIC Clearinghouse on Information and Technology, 1996).

23. Glennan and Melmed, *Fostering*.

24. "Richard Saul Wurman's Understanding," available at http://www.understandingusa.com/intro.html.

25. John Shiple, "Information Architecture. Lesson 1," available at http://www.hotwired.lycos.com/webmonkey/98/28/index0a.html.

26. North Central Regional Laboratory, "Technology," available at http://www.ncrel.org/sdrs/areas/te0cont.htm.

27. Barbara L. McCombs, "Assessing the Role of Educational Technology in the Teaching and Learning Process: A Learner-Centered Perspective," in *The Secretary's Conference on Educational Technology 2000*, available at http://www.ed.gov/Technology/techconf/2000/mccombs_paper.html.

28. Margaret Riel, "White Paper: New Designs for Connected Teaching and Learning," available at http://www.gse.uci.edu/mriel/whitepaper.

29. National Education Association and North Central Association of Colleges and Secondary Schools, Committee on Library Organizations and Equipment, *Standard Library Organization and Equipment*.

30. "Texas Library Connection," available at http://www.tlcic.esc20.net.

31. Charles Jonscher, *The Evolution of Wired Life* (New York: John Wiley and Sons, 1999), p. 227.

32. U.S. Commission on Libraries and Information Science (NCLIS), "Hearing on School Librarians: Knowledge Navigators Through Troubled Times," April 26, 2001, Cincinnati, Ohio, *Federal Register*, March 14, 2001.

33. Heinich and others, *Instructional Media*, pp. 101, 105, 115, 151, 171, 191, 219, 246, 327, 373, 385.

34. G. Edwards Evans and Margaret R. Zarnosky, *Developing*, p. 211.

35. Vicki L. Gregory, *Selecting and Managing Electronic Resources: A How-to-Do-It Manual* (New York: Neal-Schuman, 2000).

36. Evans and Zarnosky, *Developing*, p. 208.

37. American Association of School Librarians and Association for Educational Communications and Technology, *Information Power*, pp. 109–10.

38. Paul Metz, "Principles of Selecting for Electronic Resources," *Library Trends* 48 (Spring 2000): 711–28.

39. Evans and Zarnosky, *Developing*, p. 215.

40. Glennan and Melmed, *Fostering*.

41. Frank Ferro, *How to Use the Library: A Reference and Assignment Guide for Students* (Westport, CT: Greenwood Press, 1998).

42. Heinich and others, *Instructional Media*, pp. 387–92.

43. Library of Congress, Copyright Office, available at http://www.loc.gov/copyright.

44. H. W. Wilson Company, "Database and Software License Agreement," available at http://www.hwwilson.com/abouthw/weblic.htm.

45. Erica Peto, "Copyright and Licensing for Educators," available at http://www.kent.wednet.edu/staff/epeto/copyright.html; American Association of Law Libraries and others, "Principles for Licensing Electronic Resources," Final Draft, July 15, 1997, available at http://www.arl.org/scomm/licensing/principles.html.

46. Germantown Academy, "Evaluating Web Sites for Curriculum Use—A Guide for Teachers," available at http://www.germantownacademy.org/technology/internet/evaluation/EvalSites.htm.

47. Metz, "Principles," p. 28.

48. INET, available at http://www.inetlibrary.com.

49. NetSchoolsConstellation, available at http://www.netschools.com.

50. Virtual LRC, available at http://www.virtuallrc.com.

51. Hudson Public Schools, "Virtual High School," available at http://www.hudson.k12.ma.us/district_init/home.htm.

52. American Association of School Librarians, "Statements on Filtering," available at http://www.ala.org/alaorg/oif/filtersandfiltering.html.

53. American Association of School Librarians, AASL Technology, available at http://www.ala.org/aasl/tech_menu.html.

54. National Research Council, "Tools and Strategies for Protecting Kids from Pornography and Their Applicability to Other Inappropriate Internet Content," available at http://www4.nas.edu/cpsma/cstb/itas.nsf/.

55. Librarian's Yellow Pages, available at http://www.librariansyellowpages.com/.

56. *Library Technology Reports* (bimonthly); descriptions available at http://www.ala.org/library/alaperiodicals.html.

57. ALA TechSource, available at http://www.techsource.ala.org.

58. Heinich and others, *Instructional Media*, pp. 15–21.

59. Ibid., pp. 275–99.

60. "National Forum on Information Literacy," available at http://www. infolit.org.

61. LMC Web site, available at http://www.lmcsource.com.

62. Libraries Unlimited catalog, available at http://www.lu.com.

63. Institute of Museum and Library Services and the University of Missouri-Columbia, "Web-Wise 2001—The Digital Divide: A Conference on Libraries and Museums in the Digital World," Washington, D.C., February 12–14, 2001.

64. Heinich and others, *Instructional Media*, pp. 353–54.

65. Sharyn Van Epps, "Vision to Reality: Transforming the School Library into the Information Technology Hub of the School," *MultiMedia Schools*, March/April 1999, available at http://infotoday.com/MMSchools/MMStocs/mar99toc.htm.

66. Jonscher, *Evolution*, p. 213.

67. Vinton Cerf, "What Will Replace the Internet?," *Time*, June 19, 2000, pp. 102–3.

68. Ibid.

69. Michio Kaku, "What Will Replace Silicon?," *Time*, June 19, 2000, pp. 98–99.

7

Tools and Aids for Selection

PART I. FOUNDATIONS

Previous chapters have considered many aspects of selection, including theories that influence how materials are selected; the management of the selection process; selection policies; and legal implications of selection decisions. This chapter looks specifically at tools and aids that have evolved over time to help librarians and teachers make sound selection choices.

JUDGMENT AND DECISION MAKING

Decision making in any environment involves a series of events. In *Judgment in Managerial Decision Making*, Max Bazerman gives some useful descriptions of general decision-making processes used by managers. He defines four basic elements of decision making: *diagnosis* (identifying problems and possible solutions); *actions* (appropriate decisions we make on how to correct or improve the situation); *selection* (choosing from various options); and *implementation* (putting the plan into action).

This type of logical approach to decision making is generally referred to as "prescriptive theory." This management approach is widely taught in schools of library and information science and education and is the approach generally advocated for the selection of school library media materials. In general it prescribes what has to be done and how to do it. It addresses the tasks to be completed and tackles problems in a logical way. It likewise suggests resources necessary for good decision making.

Guidelines for material selection policies in schools reflect this prescriptive approach by emphasizing policies; identifying issues (i.e., meeting a school's mission, goals, and objectives for curriculum and general development needs of the school community); and establishing selection criteria and the logical steps to take in reviewing, selecting, deselecting, and removing materials.

Institutions generally recognize the usefulness of this approach, but we realize that this norm is not always reached. Behavioral science has attempted to understand how far afield decision makers can move from the prescribed norm, and it studies ways of helping them reach the objectives set by the prescriptive norm.

Another school of thought sees decision making as a naturalistic process. This school views decision making as a messy process and less analytical than that presented and desired by the prescriptive, normative approach, and contends that in reality decision making may be biased on a number of grounds, including personal, institutional, national, cultural, social, sexual, and gender-based factors. It is apparent that all these factors can influence how materials are traditionally selected for school library media centers.

Naturalistic theory suggests that decision making is influenced by the "framing of information." This means that information can be packaged, presented, or remembered in certain ways that will influence the outcome of decisions. Personal factors also influence decision making and can lead to a nonrational escalation of commitment to a poor decision.[1]

A number of research studies over the years have illustrated that naturalistic decision making is very much a part of how materials have been and or are now being selected for school library media centers. For example, in his study Charles Busha found that librarians often violated the principles of the "Library Bill of Rights" when faced with selection decisions, and in 1999 a discussion published in *Library Talk* focused on censorship by librarians and media specialists and the conflicts that arise between professional obligations and theoretical values.[2,3]

ORGANIZATIONAL CULTURE, GROUP INFLUENCE, AND SELECTION DECISIONS

The organizational culture of the school community can influence decision making. For example, some school communities may encourage innovation and new ideas and expect faculty to engage in new ways of thinking and teaching—in other words, to "move out of the box." Other school communities may have more conservative expectations. The essence of organizational culture is that it sets norms for expected behaviors within an organization and develops ways and means of enforcing those norms and of imparting them to new members of the organization.[4] A natural extension of organizational culture is the culture of the surrounding community. Community culture and its expectations generally influence a school's organizational culture. The organizational culture of both the community and the school influence and can even drive the selection process of materials for local school library media centers. As we have noted, sometimes these organizational and community cultural factors are in conflict with professional, legal, and ethical expectations of school media center librarians.

Groups, regardless of size, play a large role in determining the climate in which selection decisions are made. These groups can consist of teachers, librarians, administrators, parents, students, individuals from the community, and community organizations. Through organized efforts and other means of wielding power, they can both help and hinder logical, well-considered decision making in the selection of materials. School media center librarians must recognize this reality and learn to work with groups, both to educate them about the selection process and to reinforce their professional responsibilities to make good material selection decisions.

Over the last century, school librarians have recognized that these and other issues make the selection of materials for school library media centers a complex process, and they have come to rely on selection tools and aids and developed by professional authorities to help with these important selection decisions.

SELECTING GOOD MATERIALS

The selection of materials and literature for youth has traditionally followed a prescriptive approach. Historically, books and other literature produced for children and young adults were intended to have a positive effect on their moral, spiritual, and cultural development. Early in the nineteenth century in the United States and Britain, there was a growing recognition that literature for children should meet high literary standards and that it could be a source of enjoyment as well as moral and spiritual training. By the 1860s in both the United States and Britain literature for children had entered a "golden age."[5] High literary and artistic standards were established for children's literature and some of the great classics of the genre were firmly established.[6]

In the United States perhaps the most notable example of the drive for better-quality children's materials was *St. Nicholas Magazine*, founded in 1873 and edited for many years by Mary Mapes Dodge. Under Dodge's leadership, the magazine devoted serious attention to reviewing and critiquing children's literature. In time, it came to represent the "very kernel of American books for children" and greatly influenced the rise of children's literature as an important part of literary artistry.[7]

Thus influenced, by 1880 children's literature and its criticism had reached a new high in terms of public acceptance. From 1880 to just after World War I, literature for children was enjoyed by young and old, and the genre was seen as worthy of serious study and criticism. During this period a standard of literary criticism began to take hold. This canon reflected a romantic and idealized notion about children and viewed children's literature as a means of bringing "life and beauty to childhood."[8] This standard soon developed prescriptive notions about what elements exemplified excellence in literature for children.

At this same time forces were at work that challenged this canon of excellence. The new rotary press printing technology made the mass production of cheap and affordable books possible, and that in turn opened up new markets for book publishers and helped introduce books to a wider audience. Fiction became especially popular, and the dime novel is often seen as an icon representing the new popularity of reading. Nevertheless, cheap publications, sensational fiction, penny novels in England, and the dime novel in America soon challenged and encroached upon the idea that literature for children must be pure and exemplary.[9] Educators, librarians, and others began to speak out against these socalled inferior reading products.

The public library movement and the development of elementary and secondary education for expanding groups of students were contemporaneous with these developments in children's literature. Both the development of public education and public library development were grounded on larger progressive social movements of the period that held that mass education was at the heart of improving society and culture. Libraries reflected much of this ideology in the creation and management of their book collections. Librarians saw children's literature as a means not only of helping to improve education, but also of raising the general level of culture and society,[10] and this was reflected in library collections.

Evidence of this willingness to encourage reading and to bring books to children is well documented through the early outreach programs offered by public libraries throughout the country. Not only were these programs designed to encourage reading, but they had an important underlying goal of encouraging the reading of better literature, thus improving the general cultural base of the community and the nation.[11,12]

However, leaders in the American public library movement did not always speak with a clear, united voice, and criticisms and controversies abounded. To some, the library was a place for study and scholarship, not for trivial pursuits such as the recreational reading of novels. In fact, during those formative years, much debate was directed at the perceived harmful effects that novels might have on the minds of the young and at the public library as a possible center for distributing such materials. While recognizing that larger libraries might well collect such popular materials as cultural research documents, a government report of 1876 suggested that smaller libraries that could not aim for completeness should exercise reasonable censorship of books and not try to satisfy only short-term and undiscriminating demands.[13] The report goes on to quote a statement made in a government report by a senator identified only as Yeager that condemned much of the popular reading materials available to citizens: "The volumes of trash poured forth daily, weekly, and monthly are appalling. Many fine minds, which if confined to a few volumes, would become valuable thinkers, are lost in the wilderness of brilliant and fragrant weeds."[14] This view was commonly held by librarians of the time. An 1899 article in *Library Journal* declared that "the voracious devouring of fiction commonly indulged in by patrons of the public library, especially the young, is extremely pernicious and mentally unwholesome."[15] Another author declared that if the public library existed simply for pleasure and for a low order of entertainment, it failed to fulfill its true mission as an educational institution.[16]

Even during the heyday of this debate some librarians argued that books must be bought to meet needs of their users,[17] and over time most librarians came to realize that popular fiction had its value. Nevertheless, librarians serving youth clearly felt they had an obligation to promote better literature, including fiction, and to discourage the reading of poorer quality materials. A good example of this attitude was the universal condemnation of the Edward Stratemeyer Literary Syndicate (publisher of the famous Nancy Drew series as well as others) by both teachers and librarians. In 1901 librarian Caroline M. Hewins complained that the Stratemeyer books used "the phraseology of a country newspaper," calling a supper "an elegant affair" and a girl a "fashionable miss."[18]

The outcome of all this concern was the development of a highly prescriptive view of how books should be selected and acquired for children and young adults for both school and public libraries. This prescriptive voice greatly influenced today's prevailing paradigm, which over the years has been rather consistently presented in articles, textbooks, and the curricula of schools of education and library schools.[19] In fact, this model of selectivity based on high literary standards became so ingrained as the professional paradigm of good practice that only in recent decades has it been subject to serious review and revision.[20] One of the hallmarks that this prescriptive model encouraged was the development of professional reviews, bibliographies, and reading guides to help librarians make good selection choices.

DEVELOPMENT OF REVIEW SOURCES AND SELECTION AIDS

Selection aids include professional resources such as reviews, lists, catalogs, bibliographies, and other forms of recommendations for materials. The practice of librarians relying on these reviews and recommendations for purchase decisions has a long history.[21] Throughout the years, commercial publishers as well as professional organizations and individuals have influenced, promoted, and encouraged the development of selection aids and review sources.

Librarians in the early American public library movement realized that help was needed to bring standardization to many of the management processes involved in librarianship. We see this reflected in the drive to develop better classification systems and to produce uniformity and standardization in catalog records and subject headings. That same drive for management efficiency also created a desire for aids that could help librarians make logical selection decisions. This need was made more evident by the growing number of public libraries that were being established across the country and the general lack of significant formal library education on the part of many of those who were employed to staff these libraries. Generally the professional leadership felt that if the American public library was to be regarded by the population as worthwhile, then it must be managed well and its collections must be well selected and maintained. School libraries, especially at the secondary level, were beginning to develop, and concern was also voiced there about the quality of materials to be acquired.[22]

The American Library Association recognized its responsibility and in 1905 established the *Booklist* (www.ala.org/booklist) as a tool to help public librarians make good book selection choices. *Booklist* has considered the needs of youth to be part of its mission and has historically devoted considerable space to reviewing materials for children and young adults.

Library Journal (www.libraryjournal.com), established in 1876, also assumed a role in reviewing books for libraries. Like *Booklist*, it was devoted largely to public library interests, but over time its editors began to give more coverage to children's and youth materials through a special review section which eventually was called "Junior Libraries" (1954–1961). In 1961 *School Library Journal* was launched as a separate publication. Today both *Library Journal* and *School Library Journal* (www.slj.com) offer electronic editions that are readily available on the Internet.

The Horn Book Magazine (www.hbook.com) was established in 1924 by Bertha E. Mahony partly in an effort to record the book-centered activities of the Bookshop for Boys and Girls in Boston. An editorial statement by Bertha Field in the first issue declared that the purpose of *The Horn*

Book was "to blow the horn for fine books for boys and girls." This idea helps explain the longtime use of Randolph Caldecott's three jovial huntsmen blowing their horns as the magazine's logo. The magazine soon became noted for including as writers and contributors many of the notable figures in the literary and publishing world of the day, among them May Massee of Viking, Alice Jordan, head of Children's Services of the Boston Public Library, and Anne Carroll Moore, supervisor of work with children at the New York Public Library, as well as her successor, Frances Clark Sayers.

The magazine claims that it has always kept pace with society's changing times. Nevertheless, its hallmark has always been to promote excellence in literature for children. A study by Joan Olson suggested that from its founding in 1924 to 1973 (the end of her study) the magazine consistently placed emphasis on the aesthetic pleasures and the beauty of literature. Olson claims that the magazine often criticized prevailing professional theories that placed emphasis on psychological processes rather than reading and literature as artistic expressions.[23] Although begun as a magazine devoted to the broad dissemination of information about children's literature to the general public, *The Horn Book* today has become one of the standard institutional review sources serving school and library needs.

COMMERCIAL COMPANIES AND PROFESSIONAL ORGANIZATIONS

The first company devoted completely to library bibliographic and reference needs was established by H. W. Wilson in 1885 (www.hwwilson. com). Wilson owned a college bookstore in Minneapolis, Minnesota, and had firsthand experience in the difficulties involved in knowing what books were in print and how to acquire them. To bring the bibliographic confusion in the book industry under control, in 1898 he published *Cumulative Book Index (CBI)*.[24] CBI became an independent journal in 1933 and was published until 1999. *CBI* and *The United States Catalog* were among the first bibliographic tools that attempted to gather information about all books issued by the American book trade and to prepare bibliographic records concerning their description and pricing.

Book Review Digest, first published by the H. W. Wilson Company in 1905, was designed to provide bibliographic citations and digests of reviews of books as they appeared in the professional and literary press. In addition to bibliographic and acquisition information, it also aided librarians in making good selection decisions. It now is available in an electronic format with links to reviews it cites.

In 1908 the company published *Fiction Catalog*, the first in its *Standard*

Library Catalog series, as a guide to the selection of adult fiction for public libraries. The series has expanded over the years to embrace the needs of librarians serving school libraries as well. The first edition of the *Standard Catalog for Public Libraries*, published in 1919, presented a list of nonfiction titles recommended for public library collections. Although the *Standard Catalog for Public Libraries* also focused on the adult library reader, school librarians over the years have found that many of the recommended titles are useful for their own collections. Editors of these publications have recognized this as a value-added service and have made special efforts to highlight such useful book recommendations.

In 1909 the H. W. Wilson Company began to publish a number of titles in its *Standard Catalog Series* directed at the needs of both school and public libraries serving youth. These included *Children's Catalog* (1909), *Standard Catalog for High School Libraries* (1928), which also covered works suitable for junior high school, *Junior High School Library Catalog* (1965), and, most recently, *Middle and Junior High School Library Catalog* (1995). Like other titles in the *Standard Library Catalog* series, these were created to present a "standard" collection of titles based on expert recommendations for elementary, middle, junior high, and senior high school library media centers. *Children's Catalog*, from its inception, was always directed at the collection development needs of both public and school libraries.

In keeping with the company's philosophy of service, all recommendations made by this series are based on professional, expert opinion. A committee of librarians representing both school and public libraries reviews titles for appropriateness and makes the final decisions on what will be included. Yearly supplements are published for each title in the series listing new materials as well as newer editions of older works. Since 1999 *Children's Catalog* has been published in electronic format with links to reviews of recommended books. In 2000 all titles in the company's *Standard Library Catalog* series became available in electronic format.

The *Standard Library Catalog* series has never included recommendations for nonprint items. To help fill that void, in 1965 *The Elementary School Library Collection* was published by the Brodart Company (www.brodart.com). Similar in format to the Wilson publications, it includes audiovisual materials such as computer software as well as books. It is currently available in both print and CD-ROM formats.

The R. R. Bowker Company (www.bowker.com) was established in 1872 with a mission of serving the needs of the book trade. In 1873 it published the first volume of *Publishers' Trade List Annual (PTLA)*. Originally *PTLA* was a collection of publishers' catalogs bound up in one, two, three, or more large volumes per year. In 1948 Bowker issued *Books in Print*, followed by *Subject Guide to Books in Print* (1957). *Children's Books in Print* (1969) and *Subject Guide to Children's Books in Print* (1970) soon followed. Although none of these sources are considered selection aids, over the years they have provided school media center librarians with convenient access to information on the availability of books within the book trade market. In recent years these tools have begun to offer abstracts of reviews of selected items, and the electronic versions of these now offer links to reviews of many of the listings.

PART II. TOOLS AND PROCESSES

METHODS, APPROACHES, AND TOOLS FOR SELECTION

Librarians use various means to make selections for their collections, including publishers' catalogs, visits to bookstores, conference exhibits, talking to publishers' representatives, and reviews and book guides.[25] Lillian N. Gerhardt, editor-at-large of *School Library Journal*, states that selection aids play an important and unique role in building school library media center collections, noting that "book selection demands time, thought, interaction with customers, and knowledge of books intellectually applied." She also says that a fine tradition has evolved and should be respected, by which school media center specialists rely on published reviews, expert subject bibliographies, and lists of titles recommended by national organizations, including both library and professional groups outside of librarianship.[26]

The general consensus is that reviews written for professionals should include the following elements:

• Description of content
• Definition of audience
• Information on scope, tone, style, and point of view of the work
• Comparisons with author's other works and with similar works
• Reviewers' personal opinions
• Appropriateness of art to the text
• Use of the work
• Strengths and weaknesses of the work
• Brevity
• Judgment of literary qualities
• Currency of the review
• Judgment regarding reader appeal
• Information on the attractiveness of the cover and jacket design
• Comments relating to controversies surrounding the subject of the book[27]

Research into fiction reviews published in major aids used to select materials for youth has identified several major elements to consider when evaluating such sources:

- Knowledge of review policies of the journals
- Attention to format characteristics
- Attitudes of the reviewers toward the book (e.g., negative, positive)
- How much coverage and nature of the coverage reviews devote to descriptive, analytical, and sociological elements
- Bibliographic and ordering information[28]

PERSONAL BIASES IN REVIEWS

Most if not all librarians are much concerned that personal biases not influence reviewers and that biases are not reflected in the reviews. Some sources will not accept reviews if obvious biases are detected. That does not mean that opinions cannot be voiced or that complete balance needs to be reflected in a review, only that fairness be maintained.[29]

THE INSTITUTIONALIZATION OF REVIEW SOURCES

Over the years a review system has arisen that is largely directed at the needs of institutions. A core list of review titles used extensively by school library media centers and public libraries would include the following:

School Library Journal
Booklist
Horn Book Magazine
Bulletin of the Center for Children's Books
Horn Book Guide
Kirkus Reviews
Publishers Weekly[30,31]

Other useful tools include *The Book Report Magazine* (http://www.linworth.com/bookreport.html), *Library Journal*, (http://www.libraryjournal.com/about/subscribe.asp), and *Multicultural Review* (http://www.mcreview.com/mainpage.htm).

SELECTION AIDS: FORMS AND FORMATS

Throughout the years, many types of selection aid formats have been used by school media center specialists in the selection process. In *Guides to Collection Development for Children and Young Adults* (Scarecrow Press, 1998) John T. Gillespie and Ralph J. Folcarelli describe over 800 of these in detail. Following the lead of Gillespie and Folcarelli, the descriptions that follow offer examples of the major types of selection aids and formats school media center librarians find useful.

Guides for Building a Standard Collection

As mentioned previously, standard guides are designed to suggest the best materials for establishing a collection. Selections in standard guides represent what is considered best by editors, compilers, or committees. The H. W. Wilson Company's *Children's Catalog, Junior and Middle School Library Catalog, Senior High School Catalog, Public Library Catalog*, and *Fiction Catalog* are excellent examples of a standard list approach to book collection. Another example of a standard list approach is *The Elementary School Library Collection*, (Brodart Foundation, 1977–) which includes nonprint items as well as books in its recommendations.

Guides to Current Materials

Because so many books and nonprint items are published or produced each year, it is necessary to keep abreast of this output. Review journals have been developed over the years to meet this need. For example, *Booklist, School Library Journal*, and *The Horn Book Magazine* fall into this category, as they are published on a frequent and regular schedule and review current materials. Following are brief descriptions of important and major review journals.

- *Booklist* (www.ala.org/booklist) presents reviews of recommended books, nonprint items, and computer programs for use in school media center libraries and public libraries. Essays and reviews cover special topics such as easy reading and foreign language materials. Through its *Booklist* Publications imprint, *Booklist* issues bibliographies, lists, and special monographs designed to help with the selection of materials.

- *The Horn Book Magazine: About Books for Children and Young Adults* (www.hbook.com) is a fine literary review and discussion journal devoted to promoting reading and culture through the reviews and critical analysis of books for children and young adults. Various sections or departments include reviews of newly published books, recommended paperbacks, new editions and reissues, and science books. Special columns are devoted to discussing young adult books, re-reviewing older books, and reviewing Canadian books. *The Horn Book* publishes acceptance speeches by recipients of major children's and young adult book awards, lists new professional publications as they are announced, and includes information on events in the library, publishing, and education areas. It also publishes *The Horn Book Guide*, which is a rather complete listing with annotations and brief reviews of children's and young adult books published in the United States. (See description below.)

- *School Library Journal. For Children's, Young Adult and School Librarians* (http://slj.reviewsnews.com) contains review sections on computer software, audiovisual media, and books. Reviews are written by professionals. Periodicals for school libraries are also reviewed on an occasional basis.

- *Bulletin for the Center for Children's Books* (www.alexia.lis.uiuc.edu/puboff/bccb) offers reviews of children's books and books for adolescents. Reviews are brief, but a rating scale offers a recommendation (e.g., R for recommended, NR for not recommended) and a scale that suggests audience and use (e.g., SpC indicates that subject matter or treatment will tend to limit the book to specialized collections). Reading levels for each book are also provided. Listings of recent award books are also given.

- *The Horn Book Guide to Children's and Young Adult Books* (www.hbook.com/guide) attempts to list and comment on all children's and young adult books published in the United States. Although comments are brief, the guide provides a rating scale indicating the quality of the book and includes a guide to genre and subject area.

- *Kirkus Reviews* (http://www.bpicomm.com/internet/box/print/music_kirkus.html) offers long and detailed reviews of both fiction and nonfiction books for adults, adolescents, and children. Reviews are intended for booksellers and librarians and appear before the books are published, allowing libraries and bookstores to stock in anticipation of demand. The children's section, which must be subscribed to apart from the basic subscription, offers special lists, such as holiday books.

- *Publishers Weekly: The Book Industry Journal* (http://publishersweekly.reviewsnews.com) is a trade journal that offers broad coverage of happenings in the book trade, including children's and young adult publications. Reviews are offered for current books just released by various publishers.

Although research has indeed shown that the review sources listed above are considered the first tier of selection aid choices among many school media center librarians, other equally valuable selection aids are available. The following list is a brief sampling of these:

- *ALAN Review* (www.english.byu.edu/resources/alan) is published three times a year and offers reviews of fiction and nonfiction books of interest to young adults. It is published through the auspices of the National Council of Teachers of English with the interests of English and literature teachers and their students in mind.

- *Appraisal: Science Books for Young People* (www.appraisal.neu.edu) is a quarterly devoted to the review of science and technology books for children and young adults. Each issue covers about seventy science books, which are reviewed twice—once by a school media center librarian and again by a science specialist.

- **The Book Report** (www.linworth.com/bookreport.html) is a review source for print and multimedia material, including online resources, software, and hardware. It considers the needs of curriculum development and highlights social themes and issues that have curriculum and information appeal. In addition to reviews it offers advice about how to integrate books into the curriculum. Overall its offers guidance in allocation of resources, teaching information skills, public relations, technology applications, and school library management.

- **Kliatt**: (www.hometown.aol.com/kliatt) publishes reviews of paperback books, young adult hardcover fiction, audiobooks, and educational software appropriate for young adults in classrooms and libraries. Reviews include most fields of interest—fiction, literature and language arts, biography and personal narrative, education and guidance, social studies, history and geography, science, the arts, and recreation. Newsletter supplements are provided.

- **Parents' Choice** (www.parent-choice.org) is an online review and discussion journal intended for parents. It provides written reviews in all areas of children's media including books, television, home video, recordings, toys, music, games, and computer software.

- **Science Books and Films** (www.aaas.org/~sbf) is published by the American Association for the Advancement of Science and reviews print, film, and software materials in all areas of the sciences for all ages. Its reviews are directed at all types of librarians and educators.

- **The Teacher Librarian** (www.teacherlibrarian.com) is an independent library journal that addresses the needs of professionals who work with children and young adults. In addition to reviews of books and nonprint media, it features articles on current issues and trends. Special sections highlight professional materials in education and librarianship, management, and information technologies. Reviews cover children and young adult books, new nonfiction, best-sellers, video materials, computer software, and Internet resources. It also profiles authors and illustrators as well as leaders in the field. *Teacher Librarian* is a continuation of *Emergency Librarian*, published from 1973 to 1998.

- **Voice of Youth Advocates (VOYA)** (www.voya.com) is a hard-hitting review and discussion journal intended to help librarians who work with adolescents. It reviews films, video games, and fiction of all kinds, including adventure, occult, science fiction, and general fiction. Generous space is given to the reviewing of nonfiction. Pamphlets, professional reading, reference books, and reprints are also reviewed. For books intended for the young adult, a rating system denotes books according to literary quality as well as their likely popularity.

As indicated in most of the above descriptions, Web sites are generally available for these publications. Some sites offer full-text editions of their reviews.

Best Book Lists

Professional and social organizations have an interest in promoting the reading of good literature, and toward that end many organizations have established "best book" lists intended to include what they consider to be the best books within their areas of interest and concern. Standards for inclusion on these lists are high, reflective of the interests and expectations of the various professional groups. Because of the rigors involved in the preparation of these lists, they generally make excellent selection aids. Many of these lists are compiled by committees comprised of professionals and/or experts who devote their time willingly to this work. Some, such as the lists published by *Booklist* and *School Library Journal*, are compiled by editorial staffs who draw upon reviews previously published in their own publications. Following are examples of these lists:

- **American Library Association** (www.ala.org) through its divisions—the Young Adult Library Services Association (YALSA) (www.ala.org/yalsa) and the Association for Library Services for Children (ALSC) (www.ala.org.alsc)—publishes several outstanding best book lists. Each year YALSA publishes its "Best Books for Young Adults" list. Books on this list are published the preceding year and are selected by a committee of librarians. Selections include both fiction and nonfiction and are based on the appeal of the book to young adult readers as well as literary and sociological qualities. YALSA also publishes "Best Films and Videos for Young Adults," basing selection on similar criteria. Following a similar pattern, ALSC publishes "Notable Books for Children" and "Notable Films and Videos for Children." The American Association of School Librarians (AASL) (www.ala.org.aasl) promotes these lists and has links to them through its Web site.

  Booklist division of ALA (discussed earlier) also publishes bibliographies of best books. It draws its selections from reviews of the more outstanding titles that have appeared in the journal during a selected period of time. The Reference and User Services Association (a division of ALA) maintains links to these various lists at its Web site, http://www.ala.org/rusa/.

- **Children's Book Council** (www.cbcbooks.org) over the years, in cooperation with subject area organizations such as the International Reading Association (IRA), (www.reading.org), the National Science Teachers Association (NSTA), (http://www.nsta.org), and the National Council of Social Studies (NCSS), (http://www.ncss.org) has produced outstanding lists of books for children and young adults. Some of their special lists include "Outstanding Science Trade Books for Children" (science books for K through middle school) and "Notable Social Studies Trade Books for Young People" (social science books useful for children in grades K–8). These lists are published once a year in the organizations' respective journals and on their Web sites, and may be purchased from the organizations' headquarters.

- **International Reading Association** (www.reading.org) publishes several lists of best books chosen by children and young adults. Each year the *Journal of*

Reading, a publication of the association, publishes a list of best books based on the votes of children and young adults. *Reading Teacher*, yet another IRA journal, publishes a similar readers-choice list. *Reading Teacher* likewise publishes annually a list of books voted best by teachers of reading and school library media center specialists who field test these books for their usefulness in the curriculum.

Book Publishers, Professional Associations, Independent Compilers, and Editors

Commercial publishers and professional associations find that their customers need and want booklists, bibliographies, and other selection aids for highly recommended titles. To meet this demand they invite authorities to compile, edit, and publish bibliographies and guides. Almost all library science trade publishers and many professional organizations and commercial book publishers publish such bibliographic and selection guides. Many, if not most, make their catalogs available through the Internet. Consulting these online catalogs along with reviews of selection aids in the professional press is an excellent way to keep abreast of important aids as they are published.

Book and Nonprint Awards

Book awards are excellent sources for selecting school library media center materials. Many organizations offer awards as a means of promoting reading or exposing their users to better quality print and nonprint materials as well as computer software items. Literary awards are offered by professional organizations, newspapers, publishers, and special interests groups. Especially useful reference sources to consult for more information about awards include *Children's Literature Awards and Winners*, 3d ed. (Gale Research Group, 1983–) and many Internet sources, such as the Children's Literature Web Guide (www.ucalgary. ca-dkbrown/), Bank Street College of Education Library homepage (www.streetcat.bnkst.edu/), and Amazon.com (www.amazon.com). A brief listing of some of the better known and often consulted print and nonprint awards follows.

National and International Book Awards

• **Aesop Prize and Accolade List** (www.afsnet.org/sections/children/aesop. htm). This prize is awarded by the Children's Folklore Section of the American Folklore Society to the most outstanding book or books incorporating folklore and published in English for children or young adults. The awards committee also compiles the Aesop Accolade List, which includes exceptional books among all the Aesop Prize nominees.

- **American Booksellers Book of the Year Children's Prize** (www.bookweb.org). This award is made each year by the American Booksellers Association. Members of the association vote for the book they most enjoyed recommending. The children's prize was established in 1993.
- **The American Library Association** (www.ala.org):
  - **Alex Awards** (bookawarwww.ala.org/yalsa/awards/divds.html) have been given annually since 1998 to ten adult books that will be enjoyed by young adults ages twelve through eighteen. Books selected for the award must be published in the previous calendar year and marketed primarily to adults. Selections can come from genres that have special appeal to young adults or have strong potential for teen appeal. They must be well written and highly readable. Books selected can be either fiction or fact.
  - **The Randolph Caldecott Medal and Honor Books** (www.ala.org.alsc/cmedal.html). Awarded each year since 1937 by the American Library Association to honor the most distinguished American children's picture book published during the previous year. Honor books are also announced. The medal winner and honor books are announced in January, and the list is published in the early spring in major review journals such as *Booklist, School Library Journal*, and *The Horn Book*. Medal winners and honor books are also listed on American Library Association Web sites. For more detailed information consult Bette Peltola, *The Newbery and Caldecott Awards: A Guide to the Medal and Honor Books* (American Library Association, 1999).
  - **Coretta Scott King Award and Honor Books** (www.ala.org/srrt/csking/cskaw00.html). This award is presented each year by the Coretta Scott King Task Force of the American Library Association's Social Responsibilities Round Table. The award is given to authors and illustrators of African descent whose distinguished books promote an understanding and appreciation of the "American Dream." Awards are selected by a seven-member national jury.
  - **Laura Ingalls Wilder Medal** (www.ala.org/alsc/wilder). This award is given by the ALSC to an author or illustrator of literature for children published in the United States. The award is given every three years in recognition of a body of work that over a long period of time has made a substantial and lasting contribution to literature for children.
  - **Margaret A. Edwards Awards for Outstanding Literature for Young Adults** (www.ala.org.yalsa/edwards). Presented by the Young Adult Library Services Association of ALA to an author in recognition of his or her lifetime achievement in writing for teenagers. It is given to an author whose work helps teenagers to better understand themselves and their world.
  - **Michael L. Printz Award** (www.ala.org/yalsa/printz/aboutaward.html). Presented to the author of a book that exemplifies literary excellence in young adult literature. The award is given to books suitable for ages twelve through eighteen published the preceding year, and fiction, nonfiction, poetry, and anthologies are considered. Selected annually by an awards committee of the YALSA.

- **The Mildred L. Batchelder Award and Honor Books** (www.ala.org/alsc. batch.html). This award, first given in 1966, is presented to an American publisher for the most outstanding children's book first published in a foreign language in a foreign country, and subsequently published in English translation in the United States the preceding year. The award is made to encourage American publishers to seek out outstanding foreign-language books published abroad that will promote communication among peoples of the world. Honor books have been recognized since 1994. The award is administered by the ALSC.

- **Newbery Medal and Honor Books** (www.ala.org/alsc/newbery.html). The medal is awarded annually by the LSC. It is made to an author for the most distinguished contribution to American literature for children for the preceding year. The medal is awarded based on literary quality and quality of presentation for children. Didactic intent and popularity are not criteria. Honor books are also selected. Winners are announced in January. The Newbery Medal and the Caldecott Award are considered the most prestigious awards in children's literature. For additional information refer to Bette Peltola, *The Newbery and Caldecott Awards: A Guide to the Medal and Honor Books* (American Library Association, 1999).

- **Pura Belpré Award and Honor Books** (www.ala.org.alsc/belpre). This award is made every two years by ALSC and the National Association to Promote Library Services to the Spanish Speaking (REFORMA), a division of ALA. It honors Latino writers whose works best present, celebrate, and affirm Latino culture experiences in youth literature.

- **Robert F. Sibert Information Book Award** (www.ala.org). This new award administered by the ALSC, is to be presented annually to the author of the most distinguished informational book for children published during the preceding year. The first award was presented in 2001.

- **Américas Award for Children's and Young Adult Literature** (http://www. uwm.edu/Dept/CLACS/outreach_americas.html). Sponsored by the Consortium of Latin American Studies Programs, the award is given in "recognition of U.S. works of fiction, poetry, folklore, or selected nonfiction (from picture books to works for young adults)." Books must be published in the preceding year either in English or Spanish and must deal with Latin America, the Caribbean, or Latinos in the United States.

- **Boston Globe Horn Book Awards** (www.hbook.com/bghb.shtml). This award, begun in 1967, is given for excellence by the *Boston Globe* and *The Horn Book Magazine* in three categories: fiction or poetry, nonfiction, and picture books. Honor books in each category are also selected. Awards are announced in the fall of each year. A jury of three judges representing the *Globe* and *The Horn Book Magazine* make the final selections, and award winners are listed annually in *The Horn Book Magazine*.

- **Bram Stoker Awards for Horror** (www.horror.org/stokers.htm). Given annually by the Horror Writers of America for high achievement in horror publishing. Several categories are honored, including the "Best Work for Young People."

- **Canadian Library Association** (www.cla.ca):
  - **Book of the Year for Children Award** (www.cla.ca/awards/boyc.htm). Awarded by the association to a book published in Canada by a Canadian citizen or a permanent resident of Canada. The award may be for fiction, poetry, or the retelling of traditional literature published in any format (i.e., anthologies and collections).
  - **Amelia Frances Howard-Gibbon Illustrator's Award** (www.cla.ca/awards/afhg.htm). Given by the Canadian Association of Children's Librarians (a division of CLA) to the outstanding illustrator of a children's book published in Canada during the preceding year. Recipient must be a Canadian citizen or a permanent resident of Canada. Text must be worthy of the illustrations.
  - **Young Adult Canadian Book Award** (www.cla.ca/awards/yac.htm). This award recognizes an author of an outstanding English-language Canadian book that appeals to young adults between the ages of thirteen and eighteen. The award is given to works of fiction (i.e., novel or collection of short stories in either hardcover or paperback). The author must be a Canadian citizen or a landed immigrant. The award was established in 1980 by the Young Adult Caucus of the Saskatchewan Library Association and is administered by the Young Adult Services Interest Group of the Canadian Library Association.
- **Christopher Awards—Books for Young People** (www.christophers.org/awards.html). This award is presented each February by the Christophers, a non-profit Christian organization, to books that display "the highest values of the human spirit." The award was first presented in 1949, with the Books for Young People Award added in 1970.
- **Edgar Allan Poe Juvenile Awards** (www.mysterywriters.org/awards). The Mystery Writers of America make two awards each year for the best juvenile novels. The award for "Best Juvenile Novel" was established in 1962, and that for "Best Young Adult Novel" was created in 1989.
- **Giverny Book Award** (www.15degreelab.com/award.html). This is an annual award established in 1998 and given by the selection committee of the 15 Degree Laboratory, currently located at Louisiana State University. The committee consists of biology educators and plant scientists. The award is given to a children's science picture book written in English and published within five years of the award date. The book must teach young readers at least one important scientific principle or encourage the reader toward specific science-related pursuits or inquiry. Artwork, photographs, or graphics must be in harmony with the text and contribute to the story. Works on plants and/or plant science are given preference.
- **Golden Kite Award and Honor Books** (www.scbwi.org/goldkite.htm). Established in 1974, this award is given by the Society of Children's Book Writers and Illustrators to members in recognition of the most outstanding children's books published during the year. Awards are given for fiction, nonfiction, picture book text, and picture illustration. This is the only children's book award given by fellow authors and artists.

- **Governor General's Awards for Children's Literature** (Canada) (http://www.acs.ucalgary.ca/~dkbrown/gg_award.html). These awards, administered by the Canada Council, are the most prestigious literary awards in Canada. They are given for both English and French-language children's books and represent the best books by Canadians, regardless of where they were published.

- **Hans Christian Andersen Medal** (www.ibby.org/Seiten/04_andersen.thm). Presented since 1956 by the International Board on Books for Young People (Switzerland), this is the highest international award given to an author and an illustrator of children's books. It is given in recognition of the excellence of the recipient's entire literary and artistic contribution to youth literature. The award is presented every other year, and selections are made by an international jury of experts in the field of youth literature.

- **The Hugo Award (Science Fiction Achievement Award)** (www.worldcon.org/hugos.html). Named for Hugo Gernsback, this award is given by the World Science Fiction Society. The award is determined by popular vote of the membership. Although no special category for children or young adults is available, the awards do signify what is considered outstanding by science fiction writers, and young adults often find these authors appealing.[32] Other awards given by the society include the John W. Campbell Memorial Award for the Best New Writer, and a Special Award.

- **International Reading Association** (www.reading.org):

  - **International Reading Association Children's Book Awards** (www.reading.org/awards/children/html.) Four awards are given annually for authors' first or second published book in the areas of fiction and nonfiction (in two age categories: younger readers, ages four to ten and older readers, ages ten to seventeen. Books may come from any country and be written in any language, and must be copyrighted during the preceding year.

  - **Lee Bennett Hopkins Promising Poet Award** (www.reading.org/awards/lee.html). This award is given every three years to a promising new poet (writing for children up to grade twelve) who has published no more than two books of children's poetry. The award is given for published works only.

  - **Paul A. Witty Short Story Award** (www.reading.org/awards/witty.html). This award, first given in 1986, is intended to recognize an author of an original short story published for the first time in a periodical for children. The story should exemplify literary standards that encourage young people to read periodicals.

- **The Irma S. and James H. Black Award for Excellence in Children's Literature** (www.streetcat.bnkst.edu/html/isb.html). Established in 1973 in honor of Irma Simonton Black, one of the founders of the Bank Street Writers Laboratory, this award is presented each year for a book that is "outstanding for young children—a book in which text and illustrations are inseparable, each enhancing and enlarging on the other." Selection is made by children based on reading, discussion, and classroom use. Honor books are also announced. The award is presented by the Bank Street College of Education.

- **Jane Addams Book Award and Honor Books** (www.education.wisc.edu/ ccbc/public/jaddams.htm). This award was established in 1953 by the Women's International League for Peace and Freedom and the Jane Addams Peace Association and is presented annually to the children's book that most effectively promotes the cause of peace, social justice, and world community. A picture book category was added in 1993. The award is announced in September of each year.
- **Library Association** (of Great Britain) (www.la-hg.org.uk):
  - **The Carnegie Medal** (www.la-hq.org.uk/directory/medals_awards/shadow/ intro/medals.htm). This award was established in 1937 and is given annually by the Library Association to an outstanding book published in the United Kingdom or written in English and published first or concurrently in the United Kingdom. The award is presented in the summer. Consult Keith Barker's *Outstanding Books for Children and Young People: The LA Guide to Carnegie/Greenaway Winners, 1937–1997* (The Library Association, 1998).
  - **Kate Greenaway Medal** (www.la-hq.org.uk/directory/medals/shadow/ intro/medals/htm). This award was established in 1956 and is presented annually in honor of the most distinguished work in the illustration of children's books published in the United Kingdom. It is presented under the auspices of the Youth Librarians Group of the Library Association. (The Barker work cited above provides more information on this award.)
- **National Book Award for Young People's Literature** (www.publishers weekly.com/NBF/docs/awards.html). This is an award given each year by the National Book Foundation in November to authors in recognition of outstanding literary contributions to children's literature. The awards committee considers books of all genres written for children and young adults by U.S. authors.
- **National Council of Teachers of English (NCTE)** (www.ncte.org):
  - **ALAN Award** (www.ncte.org). An award presented annually by the Assembly on Literature for Adolescents (ALAN), a section of the NCTE, in recognition of authors, publishers, and teacher-scholars who have made significant contributions to adolescent literature.
  - **Award for Excellence in Poetry for Children** (www.ncte.org/elem/poetry). Established in 1977 by the NCTE, it is currently awarded every three years, with announcement of the award being made at the council's spring conference. Past winners have included John Ciardi, Eve Merriam, and Eloise Greenfield.
  - **Orbis Pictus Award for Outstanding Nonfiction for Children and Honor Books** (www.ncte.org/elem/pictus). Presented by the NCTE to promote and recognize excellence in nonfiction writing for children. The award was established in 1990 and is made in honor of Johann Comenius, who published the first information book for children in 1657. Jean Fritz, *The Great Little Madison* won the first Orbis Pictus Award.
- **Nebula Awards** (www.sfwa.org/awards). Presented since 1965 by the Science Fiction and Fantasy Writers of America based on votes by active members of

the association. Several categories are honored: best novel, novella, novelette, short story, and script for audio, radio, television, motion picture, multimedia, or theatrical professional production. Winning short stories and some runners-up are published in an annual anthology. Although no specific categories are given for children's and young adult works, Ursula K. Le Guin, an author who writes for this audience, has won the prize. The novella award often goes to an author of young adult fiction.[33] Other awards given by the organization include the Author Emeritus, Bradbury, and Grand Master Awards.

- **PEN American Center Literary Awards** (www.pen.org/awards/Klein.html). These awards are presented in odd-numbered years in recognition of lifetime achievement for work in a variety of literary genres. One award, the PEN/Norma Klein Award for Children's Fiction, is given to an author who is seen as an "emerging voice of literary merit among American writers of children's fiction." Children's fiction includes young adult fiction.

- **Scott O'Dell Historical Fiction Award** (www.writerswrite.com/books/awards/odell.htm) Author Scott O'Dell established this award in 1981 to recognize the best work of historical fiction brought out by a U.S. publisher and set in the New World.

Reader Advisement and Booktalk Guides as Selection Aids

Reader advisement and booktalk guides also have a role to play in developing and maintaining useful book collections. Reader's adviser guides arose from the need for librarians to serve as advisers to readers who wished to improve and deepen their individual reading activities and backgrounds. Because reading interests, especially among adults, were so diverse, it soon became apparent that guides were necessary to help librarians fulfill this role. To meet this need the R. R. Bowker Company published *Reader's Adviser and Bookman's Manual* in 1921. Over the years this has become a standard aid in collection development. The latest edition at this writing is the fourteenth edition, which was published in 1994 in six volumes. In keeping with its traditional goal of offering guidance on the best literature available, this edition includes expanded references and bibliographic citations to standard and exemplary works in many fields, including the sciences, biography, history, social science, and the humanities. Each subject section provides information on standard reference sources such as dictionaries and encyclopedias, biographies, histories of the field, and definitive works that help define and direct the discipline. Of particular interest to school media center librarians is the new chapter on children's literature. The fourteenth edition also has expanded coverage to include more updated critical and biographical profiles and more material on women writers and culturally diverse topics from around the world.

Building on the success of *Reader's Adviser*, in 1992 Bowker published the first edition of *Young Adult Reader's Adviser*. In describing the work, the publisher noted that "this expertly compiled two-volume resource recommends an extensive list of the finest books for teens. It includes 17,000 bibliographic entries & more than 850 biographical profiles." Both *Reader's Adviser* and *Young Adult Reader's Adviser* are published under the Bowker-Greenwood imprint.

Always on the alert to meet new information and reference needs, in 1995 the Gale Research Group published *Beacham's Guide to Literature for Young Adults*. The goal of this guide is to help librarians and teachers interest young adults of middle and high school age in good literature. The guide is designed to direct teachers and librarians to a core selection of materials that the young will accept and understand. It is designed to help in the study and teaching of literature by offering students guidance in literary research and by helping teachers select novels and books of interest to incorporate into the literary curriculum. Each entry provides title; genre (i.e., biography, novel, short story); publication date; author name; a list of major books for young adults by the author; author's life and contributions; overview; setting; themes and characters; literary qualities; social sensitivity; topics for discussion; ideas for reports and papers; related titles; and further references. Coverage includes both classics and contemporary works. The set, ongoing since 1990, has analyzed 650 titles of interest to young adults, including autobiographies, biographies, historical novels, nonfiction, short stories, adventure, fantasy, Gothic titles, mysteries, mythology, science fiction, and contemporary titles. Volume 9 contains a cumulative index for all volumes and an appendix to titles organized by major themes. Published reviews of this set have generally been good and purchase has been recommended by *Booklist* (July 1990, p. 2113) and *Choice* (July/August 1990, p. 1801).

In 1995 the Gale Research Group released *Beacham's Desktop Guide to Literature for Intermediate Students*. It was favorably reviewed in *Booklist* (February 1, 1996, p. 950), with the reviewer noting that it offered suggestions for lesson plans, learning activities, themes, and the promotion of higher-level thinking skills. Its coverage also references related critical literature such as that found in *The Horn Book Magazine* and *Children's Literature Review*. A similar tool for young adult literature is *Masterplot II: Juvenile and Young Adult Fiction Series* (Salem Press, 1991). In keeping with the tradition of the *Masterplot* series, the strength of this tool lies in its plot summaries. More information can be found in *Choice* (October 1991, p. 254).

The American Library Association through Booklist Publications has also published a reader's guide to short stories, *Short Story Readers' Advisory: A Guide to the Best* (2000), by Brad Hooper. This is a comprehensive reference guide to the critical literature of the short story as well as interview techniques to use in helping users find the short stories they need.

Since 1990 the Gale Research Group has published *What Do I Read Next?* This work appears yearly and is designed to help readers "independently choose titles of interest." Each entry describes a separate book, listing everything readers need to know to make selections. The focus is on similarities between books, for example, similar books by the author or by other authors. *What Do Young Adults Read Next?* (Gale Group, 1994) follows the *What Do I Read Next?* series and provides 1,300 entries that have been selected to meet the interests of young adults in grades 6 through 12. Other recent titles in this multivolume series include *What Do Children and Young Adults Read Next?* Genre/subgenre indexes are included to facilitate research and use. The index is arranged by author within six genres. The guide is available electronically through GaleNet (Consult the Gale Group's online catalog for more details at www.gale.com and *Library Journal*, August 1997, p. 80). *Teen Genreflecting* by Diana Tixier Herald (Libraries Unlimited, 1997) is similar to *What Do Young Adults Read Next?* with more titles but less description by genre. Although limited to books published between 1988 and 1992, it will serve well as a collection development guide and self-education tool for those who have responsibilities for serving young adults. Taken together these sets can be used to build strong, in-depth collections for middle and high school libraries. They offer expert, professional advice on the best literature available.

Booktalk guides are intended to help librarians and teachers "talk" a book to a class or audience. They have been used successfully for years as programming devices by school and public librarians as well as classroom teachers. Their main purpose is to promote a book and encourage the audience to read it. As such, a booktalk is not a review or an extensive analysis. It is really more of a dramatic promotion of the book to an audience.

Typically a booktalk guide will provide a summary of the book, give suggestions for how the booktalk might be presented and on which sections of the book are suitable for reading out loud, and provide a list of related titles or follow-up books the audience will probably enjoy reading as well. These guides can serve as excellent selection aids, especially in the area of fiction. All titles listed have been carefully evaluated for interest and appeal, and they generally have been field-tested with audiences.

Although individual booktalk guides eventually go out of print, they tend to be widely purchased by libraries, where they can be found after the publishers no longer carry them. This is especially true of public libraries that have strong booktalk traditions and programs.

The H. W. Wilson Company has published an excellent series of booktalk guides, as has the R. R. Bowker Company (now published by Bowker-Greenwood). Other well-known library science publishers that have also published booktalk guides include Linworth Publishing, Libraries Unlimited, and Pieces of Learning. For current listings of their in-print booktalk guides, consult each publisher's Web site.

Guides to NonPrint and Electronic Media

Guides to nonprint and electronic media have expanded in the last few decades with the growth of new technologies. The following listing provides a sample of the types of selection tools school media librarians can use in making collection development choices.

Nonprint Bibliographical Enumeration Tools

Bibliographic tools are aids that enumerate and offer a bibliographic record of what has been produced. They generally do not offer critical reviews or guidance on individual titles for purchase.

The National Information Center for Educational Media (NICEM) was founded in 1958 at the University of Southern California (USC) as an experiment to research methods for storing electronic data for the preparation of printed film catalogs. Subsequently, a large master file was compiled from the materials collected by the project. This file consisted of reports of new materials and the cataloging of data sheets from the Library of Congress. In 1967 NICEM contracted with McGraw-Hill to publish print versions of its indexes, and in 1977 NICEM offered its products online through DIALOG, a commercial information retrieval service. Later, after its purchase by a private firm, the NICEM database was produced on CD-ROM. Its computer-retrievable version, now known as *A-V Online*, can be purchased from commercial electronic information vendors. Print versions are no longer published.

Although entries in the *NICEM Audiovisual Database* cannot be considered recommendations, they do serve a useful bibliographic function. This is a comprehensive database of educational audiovisual materials, including videotapes, films, audiocassettes, filmstrips, and other nonprint educational media. Some of its records date from 1900. Over 454,000 indexed items are available, including media in Spanish, French, German, and 130 other languages. Bibliographic records are indexed using the 4,300 education-focused terms found in the NICEM thesaurus.

The R. R. Bowker Company has been most active in the development of guides to media software. For a short time Bowker published *Bowker's Directory of Audiocassettes for Children* (1998), listing audiocassettes produced for listeners from preschool through eighth grade. Other Bowker guides include *Software Encyclopedia 2000: A Guide for Personal, Professional and Business Years* (1999), which is a directory of application software on CD-ROM, and *Microcomputer Software Guide Online,* an electronic service that makes the entire software encyclopedia database available. *Bowker's Complete Video Directory* (2000) and the Gale Research Group's *The Video Source Book* (25th ed., 2000), used together or separately, offer access to a wide variety of videos for children and young adults.

Guides to Periodicals and Reference Materials

Although books, videos, and films are important and provide vital information, in fields such as science and technology, their shelf life is often short. As a result collections require periodicals to provide up-to-date information to users. When developing a school library media collection of periodicals, a basic approach is to consult the major periodical indexes such as *Reader's Guide to Periodical Literature* and *General Science Index,* which are found in many school library media centers, and to make appropriate selections from those periodicals indexed.

Magazines for Libraries, 10th ed. (Bowker, 2000), edited by William Katz and Linda Sternbert Katz, is useful for a critical review of individual periodical titles. The 2000 edition contains the opinions of some 174 subject experts who have reviewed 8,000 selected magazines and journals. These reviews range from popular magazines to academic journals and give attention to periodicals that will appeal to children and young adults.

A Bowker-Greenwood publication that will prove useful in selecting periodicals for elementary and middle school collections is *Children's Magazine Guide: Subject Index to Children's Magazines and Websites* (1948 to the present) (formerly *Subject Guide to Children's Magazines*). The guide indexes fifty-three popular children's magazines and Web sites. For each subject indexed and found in a magazine a carefully selected matching Web site is given. The guide is published nine times yearly.

American Reference Books Annual (ARBA) (Libraries Unlimited, 1970 to the present) is an excellent means of keeping abreast of recently published reference books. Each year major reference books published during the preceding year in many subject areas are reviewed by experts. Another important guide to reference books is the legendary *Guide to Reference Books,* 11th ed. (American Library Association, 1996), edited by Robert Balay. This work has a long history, starting with its modest beginning in 1902 under the editorship of Alice Berta Kroeger. Although academic and scholarly in its approach, this is a fundamental descriptive resource guide to over 16,000 reference titles published worldwide. William Katz's widely used textbook, *Introduction to Reference Work,* 7th ed. (McGraw-Hill, 1997), is also useful as a basic guide to reference materials. Others are

- *"Booklist*'s Editor's Choice Reference Books," published annually in *Booklist*
- *Outstanding Reference Sources for Small and Medium-Sized Libraries*, 6th ed. (American Library Association, 1998), issued under the sponsorship of the Reference and Users Service Association (RUSA)
- *Recommended Reference Books in Paperback*, 3d ed., by Jovian Lang and Jack O'Gorman (Libraries Unlimited, 1999)
- *Guide to Reference Materials for School Library Media Centers*, 5th ed., by Barbara R. Safford (Libraries Unlimited, 1998)
- *Madam Audrey's Guide to Mostly Cheap but Good Reference Books for Small and Rural Libraries* by Audrey Lewis (American Library Association, 1998)
- *Recommended Reference Books for Small and Medium-Sized Libraries and Media Centers*, edited by Bohdan S. Wynar (Libraries Unlimited, 2000).

Leading review journals such as *Library Journal, School Library Journal*, and *Booklist* also publish yearly lists of what their editors consider to be the best reference books published during the preceding year.

Sources for electronic resources include *Purchasing an Encyclopedia: Twelve Points to Consider*, 5th ed., edited by Sandy Whiteley (Booklist Publications, 1996). This gives advice and provides reviews for CD-ROM, online, and print encyclopedias.

Since 1999 MARS (Machine Assisted Reference Section) of RUSA has published annually a guide to outstanding reference sites on the World Wide Web. Consult their Web site (http://www.ala.org/rusa/mars) for information on these selections. Issues associated with the selection and evaluation of electronic media are discussed furthered in Chapter 6.

Other Types of Guides

Numerous other types of selection guides are available for use. These aids include bibliographies and lists; guides for parents and teachers; special bibliographies prepared for students and/or young readers; indexes to media reviews and sources for literary criticism; guides to author information; indexes to works in collections (analytical indexes); guides to nonprint media (including nonprint bibliographical enumeration tools); sources for state, regional, and local materials; and guides to periodicals and reference materials.

COMMERCIAL COLLECTION DEVELOPMENT SERVICES AND DIRECT SALES

For a number of years, vendors or jobbers such as Blackwell (www.blackwell.com), Yankee Book Peddler (www.ybp.com), and Baker and Taylor (www.btol.com) have offered their customers in academic, special, and public libraries collection development services. These services have taken various forms, including approval plans.

For the most part, school media center librarians have not participated in approval plans. Nevertheless, some book vendors or jobbers that market strongly to schools do offer acquisition services to school library media center specialists. Basically, these services operate on a subscription or open enrollment system whereby librarians make selections from a list of titles created by the vendor and then order directly from the company, often through electronic submissions. Companies offering these services that encourage schools to participate include Baker and Taylor, Follett Library Resources (www.flr.follett.com), and Brodart (www. brodart.com). Although somewhat different in approach, Baker and Taylor's service, called the Collection Connection, offers 60,000 children's and young adult books as well as "top rated" audiovisual materials. According to the company, this inventory has been selected by its "expert collection development staff to represent the best in education books and A/V materials."

Follett's service, called TITLEWAVE Internet Edition, is similar. A free online service that offers 85,000 book and CD titles, it permits the librarian to create collection development lists, search for specific titles, and obtain printed results in order to request prices. It also allows librarians to submit orders directly to Follett electronically.

Brodart likewise offers a wide variety of services designed to expedite collection development. Its Collection Builder allows the librarian to customize purchase lists drawn from a database of professionally recommended titles. The McNaughton Children's and Young Adult Subscription Plan allows librarians to select titles from a list of noteworthy new and forthcoming titles with one yearly purchase order. The company's electronic ordering service, ROSE, allows librarians to place orders directly with Brodart. The system is updated daily and reflects current availability. Collection development services are also offered through its "new school openings" program. In this program, lists have been prepared by the Brodart staff and selected from reputable selection aids that reflect the needs of an "opening day collection."

Amazon.com (www.amazon.com) and Barnes and Noble (www. barnesandnoble.com) can also be considered viable vendors for school library media centers through their various custom-focused services designed to sell books. Amazon.com is one of the largest vendors on the Internet, offering books, popular and classical music, videos, and other items to the general public as well as to institutions. The site carries a number of useful links to materials of interest to children and young adults. It offers a great deal of information about many of the books in its inventory, including synopses, published reviews, comments from readers, and lists of similar books bought by other customers. Like other vendors, Amazon.com offers discounts to customers.

Direct sales to libraries are not unusual, and they have a long history often reflective of the nineteenth-century book peddler. The most common approaches today are telephone sales, visits by book sales persons, and marketing techniques designed to sell a product through incentives. All of these can be useful, but the school media center specialist needs to know the product and not be taken in by a "good deal" that may result in acquiring an inferior product for which one has little use. As Lillian Gerhardt reminds us, librarians should show a healthy skepticism toward information provided by the book market. Gerhardt was responding to what she saw as attempts by some library book supply companies to discourage the tradition of relying on book reviews written by professionals and to depend on information developed and supplied by book supply companies. To paraphrase Gerhardt, librarians should rely little on the book evaluations, suggestions, and guidance of people who directly profit from the sale of books.[34]

CONCERNS AND TRENDS

From this survey it is apparent that many well-developed selection aids are available to help school media center librarians make decisions about what to acquire for their libraries. Nevertheless, these aids are expensive, and most building-level school media center specialists cannot afford to purchase many of them. The individual school library media center needs to have at least one selection aid that will allow the library to keep abreast of new materials as they are published and/or produced and one guide that lists what experts consider standard titles needed for a school library media center collection. Many selection guides now appear on the Internet and can be consulted easily.

A major trend is the growth of collection development services available through commercial firms. The advantages to using these services are evident. They save time in the selection, acquisition, cataloging, and physical preparation of items. In addition, some services offer online financial record keeping. The down side is that, with some exceptions, these services often force school media center librarians to order from a preexisting list of titles selected by the vendor.

The greatly increasing availability of electronic information technology is now quickly becoming allied with traditional print-based selection sources in this challenging undertaking. The wise school media center librarian must find ways to use both kinds of sources effectively.

The school and library market continues to dominate children's and young adult book sales. This in turn has affected the nature of book and nonprint reviewing. Many, if not most, reviews of children's and young adult materials are written by professionals for the professional market.

Critic Marc Aronson claims that this review process has not helped the artistic development of writing for children as a serious field of literary expression. In fact, this narrowly focused review process has marginalized institutional reviews and lessened their impact on literary standards for youth literature. He also claims that this institutional focus has not helped parents become better informed about children's literature and media. He calls for the return of the kind of reviewing that predominated in the latter part of the nineteenth century, when children's literature was held in high esteem and when it was reviewed in some of the great literary journals of the time.[35]

CONCLUSION

Collection development is a complex but rewarding task requiring a wide range of knowledge and skills. Fortunately, the library community has long recognized the importance of good library collections and has continually struggled to provided a wide array of aids and support services to help all librarians, including school media center librarians, to make good collection development decisions.

NOTES

1. Max Bazerman, *Judgment in Managerial Decision Making*, 4th ed. (New York: John Wiley and Sons, 1998).

2. Charles H. Busha, *Freedom versus Suppression and Censorship; With a Study of Attitudes of Midwestern Public Librarians and a Bibliography of Censorship* (Littleton, CO: Libraries Unlimited, 1972), chaps. 5 through 8.

3. Robert Hauptman, and others, "Pragmatic Capitulation: Why the Information Specialist Censors," *Library Talk* 12 (May-June 1999): 20–21.

4. Isaac, "Organization Culture," pp. 91–100.

5. John Rowe Townsend, *Written for Children: An Outline of English-Language Children's Literature*, 6th American ed. (Lanham, MD: Scarecrow Press, 1966), pp. 114–15.

6. Peter Hunt, *An Introduction to Children's Literature* (Oxford: Oxford University Press, 1994), pp. 59–61.

7. Humphrey Carpenter and Mari Prichard, *The Oxford Companion to Children's Literature* (New York: Oxford University Press, 1987), pp. 466–67.

8. Anne H. Lundin, "Victorian Horizons: The Reception of Children's Books in England and America, 1880–1900," *Library Quarterly* 64 (January 1994): 31–54.

9. Ibid., p. 52.

10. Miriam Braverman, *Youth, Society, and the Public Library* (Chicago: American Library Association, 1979), p. 15.

11. Joseph Nelson Larned, "The Mission and Missionaries of the Book," *Regent's Bulletin* (University of the State of New York), no. 36. (September 1896): 20. Reprinted in *The Library Without Walls: Reprints of Papers and Addresses*, se-

lected and annotated by Laura M. Janzow (New York: H. W. Wilson, 1927), pp. 283–98.

12. Lowell A. Martin, *Enrichment: A History of the Public Library in the United States in the Twentieth Century* (Lanham, MD: Scarecrow Press, 1998), pp. 57–64.

13. Josiah Phillips Quincy, "Free Libraries," in *United States Education Bureau, Report, 1876*, pt. 1, p. 389. Reprinted in Janzow, in *Library Without Walls*, p. 20.

14. Yeaman, quoted in Quincy, "Free Libraries," p. 21.

15. "Monthly Report from Public Librarians upon the Reading of Minors: A Suggestion," *Library Journal* 24 (August 1899): 479, quoted in Donelson and Nilsen, *Literature*, 5th ed., p. 421.

16. W. M. Stevenson, "Weeding Out Fiction in the Carnegie Free Library of Allegheny, Pa.," *Library Journal* 22 (March 1897): 135, quoted in Donelson and Nilsen, *Literature*, 5th ed., p. 420.

17. Charles Cutter, "Should Libraries Buy Only the Best Books or the Best Books that People Will Read?," *Library Journal* 26 (February 1901): 70–72.

18. Caroline M. Hewins, "Book Reviews, Booklists, and Articles on Children's Reading: Are They of Practical Value to the Children's Librarian?," *Library Journal* 26 (1901): 58, quoted in Donelson and Nilsen, *Literature*, 5th ed., p. 428.

19. Lukenbill, "Learning Resources," pp. 101–3; Caroline Burnite, "The Standard of Selection of Children's Books," *Library Journal* 36 (1911): 161–66.

20. Lillian N. Gerhardt, "Follow the Yellow Brick Road," *SLJ Online*: Opinion, available at www.schoollibraryjournal.com/articles/opinion/20001001_9061.asp.

21. Lillian N. Gerhardt, "Consider the Source: When a Vending Machine Speaks," *SLJ Online*: Opinion, available at http://www.schoollibraryjournal.com/articles.

22. Mary E. Hall, "The Possibility of the High School Library," *ALA Bulletin* 6 (July 1912): 261–63; Martha Wilson, *School Library Management* (New York: H.W. Wilson, 1919).

23. Olson, "Interpretive History of the *Horn Book Magazine*."

24. *CBI* cumulations were released as supplements to H. W. Wilson's *United States Catalog*, first published in 1898.

25. Clare England and Adele M. Fasick, *ChildView: Evaluating and Reviewing Materials for Children* (Littleton, CO: Libraries Unlimited, 1987), p. 3, quoted in Margo Wilson and Kay Bishop, "Criteria for Reviewing Children's Books Applied to Four Professional Journals," *Library Resources and Technical Services* 43 (January 1999): 3–13.

26. Lillian N. Gerhardt, "Consider the Source: When a Vending Machine Speaks. Book Wholesaler's Catalog Versus Reviews," *School Library Journal* 43 (June 1997): 5. Also available at www.schoollibraryjournal.com/articles.

27. Margo Wilson and Kay Bishop, "Criteria."

28. Kay Bishop and Phyllis J. Van Orden, "Reviewing Children's Books: A Content Analysis of Book Reviews in Six Major Journals," *Library Quarterly* 68 (April 1998): 145–82.

29. James A. Baldwin, "Putting Your Trust in Reviews: The Ethics of Book Reviewing," *Library Collection Acquisition and Technical Services* 23 (Summer 1999): 202–3.

30. Bishop and Van Orden, "Reviewing Children's Books," p. 173.

31. Phyllis Kay Kennemer, "An Analysis of Reviews of Books of Fiction for Children and Adolescents Published in Major Selection Aids in the United States in 1979," dissertation, University of Colorado at Boulder, 1980, *Dissertation Abstracts International*-A, 42 (July 1981): 81.

32. Arthea J. S. Reed, *Reaching Adolescents: The Young Adult Book and the School* (New York: Merrill, 1994), p. 422.

33. Ibid.

34. Gerhardt, "When a Vending Machine Speaks."

35. Marc Aronson, "Not a Necessary Purchase: The Journals Judged. Reviewing Children's Literature in General Interest Publications," *Horn Book Magazine* 73 (August 1997): 430.

Creating Information: Cultural Transmission and Critical Thinking

8

INTRODUCTION

Preceding chapters have considered collection development largely from a managerial perspective, paying attention to social and cultural factors that influence the process. This chapter looks at the creative process and how it influences the development of information products. Some of the major problems and issues in modern society and culture that have historically encouraged or impeded the creative process and thus influence the nature of and availability of information products are also discussed.

CREATIVITY AND INFORMATION

The creation of information brings into existence new products, designs, and other elements of communication that promote or enhance the acquiring of knowledge, insight, and wisdom. Books, journal articles, films, videos, and Web sites are not created in a social vacuum. They are cultural artifacts, produced through human creativity, that influence and are influenced by society.

The creative processes have been analyzed and debated since ancient times. Social critics generally agree that some societies, cultures, and historical periods have been more creative and productive than others.

DATA, INFORMATION, WISDOM, AND THE CREATIVE PROCESS

Data, information, knowledge, and wisdom are symbiotic in the creation of informational products. *Data* comprise factual information such as measurements, bytes, or statistics. *Information* is the communication of knowledge or intelligence and requires the organizing of data into a coherent pattern. Information has been defined as taking data and making sense out of them through interpretation and by adding insight and perspective. *Knowledge* relates to the circumstances or conditions that allow information to be understood and communicated. *Wisdom* is the ability to discern inner qualities and relationships, to provide insight, good sense, and judgment.[1]

UNDERSTANDING THE CREATIVE PROCESS

Those who select information products should have a fundamental understanding of how they are created. This understanding adds a further dimension to the evaluative process and helps place products in a logical societal and pedagogical context.

The Greeks are generally seen as probably the most creative people in the ancient world. Their civilization has certainly had the most profound influence on Western art, literature, democratic thought, and history. Scholar Moses Hadas suggests that the Greeks were so creative because they were free from many of the "cognitive restraints" that affected other major societies of the time, such as oppressive religious beliefs. The ancient Greek gods were many and distant, cared little about the lives of humans, and were pleasure loving. Although the Greeks did not wish to displease them, they did not see a conflict between human creativity and godly displeasure brought about by self-expression. The Greeks believed that their ideas were gifts from their gods and that creative expression would please them.[2] Ancient Greek society likewise encouraged people to be self-sufficient and to perceive excellence as a readily attainable goal.

As the early Christians rose to power in the Roman Empire they generally enforced a strict code of behavior and beliefs, backed by the forces of the state. Hadas holds that creativity in early Christian medieval Europe suffered because of the society's fundamentalist orientation. It was not Christianity's restrictive teachings or its rejection of the temporal world that hampered creativity, but its claim to exclusive validity. In its struggle for acceptance, early Christianity rejected deviant ideas and labeled them heretical and harshly punished advocates of such thinking.[3]

With the fall of the Roman Empire and the repeated invasions of barbarian tribes, many early Christians recognized the value of ancient Greek knowledge and saved many priceless works of art and literature from destruction. Hadas contends that the saving and recreating of these treasures was one of the most important acts of human creativity. Monks preserved the writings of Christians as well as pagans, and painstakingly and artistically hand copied them. Despite hardships, the early and medieval Christian period produced some great works of creativity, including the writings of St. Augustine, Roman Boethius, Bede, and others.[4]

Historian Christopher Dawson believes that the general low creativity of early Christianity was not caused completely by its dogmatic approach to religion. He contends that Moslem cultures of the same period were just as dogmatic and rigid, but by contrast, these cultures were much more creative. Dawson holds that it was because medieval Europe was reduced to a rural, agrarian culture by invasions and widespread vandalism. Its population was politically destabilized and economically depressed. Dawson says that "the Church and its hold of the people was a consoling relief from fear of vandalism and starvation."[5]

Surprisingly, the Black Plague of the thirteenth century played a role in encouraging creativity in Europe. Because the plague had reduced the population by one-third, causing a labor shortage, the role of individuals became more important as clerical and feudal power waned. Artisans and craftspersons became more assertive, and guilds arose to trade privileges and to protect members from abuse. The desire to possess art of various kinds was no longer seen as a sin. The work of artists, poets, painters, musicians, and philosophers came to be appreciated as a part of human existence and as gifts from God.

At the beginning of the fourteenth century Europe's population was financially better off than at any time since the fall of Rome. Humanistic philosophy flourished, and long-neglected Greek texts were made available through contact with Moslem scholars. Long-held beliefs were being challenged, and inquiries were undertaken with a new sense of freedom. The following centuries brought scientific, artistic, philosophical, and political revolutions.[6]

By the beginning of the seventeenth century, the scientific method had taken firm hold, and with it the underlying belief that humans had the innate ability to solve their problems through their own mental efforts. This belief system, known as humanism, grew rapidly. The Bible was seen by some scholars as a work of literature rather than the word of God, and the right of individuals to reach their own religious and social conclusions gained wide acceptance.

It was during this century that the first scientifically based investigation of the creative process was undertaken. William Duff distinguished between original genius and talent. Talent was productive, but only genius broke new ground. Duff hypothesized that human creativity was influenced by heredity, social influences, biology, and psychology. He believed that genius was a product of imagination, judgment, and taste.[7] Each of these alone could not produce genius, but all were necessary in combination to produce genius. The work of Duff and others of this time produced a new concept of creativity, based on the following principles:

1. Genius is divorced from the supernatural.
2. Genius, although exceptional, is the potential of every individual.
3. Talent and genius are to be distinguished from each other.
4. Talent and genius are often dependent on the political atmosphere of the time.[8]

Scientific research in the nineteenth and twentieth centuries has gradually led to a wide acceptance of the biopsychosocial model of creativity suggested by Duff.[9] That is, creativity is seen as a product of an individual's biology—including brain chemistry and functions, psychological makeup—and of the society and political structure in which he or she lives. The creation of information products is simply a byproduct of these complicated and provocative elements of humanity.

CREATIVITY, INFORMATION, CULTURAL TRANSMISSION, AND REFORMATION

Societies and cultures induce creativity by permitting the development of environments that support the individual as well as ideas. Creativity is also induced by change, problems, issues, value conflicts, and social and political energies that propel intellectuals, teachers, statespersons, and artists to contemplate and reflect on challenges and problems facing society. It has often been said that great movements in literature, poetry, drama, and philosophy come at a time when a society is under stress and new ideas are needed for survival and redirection. For example, when populations face social, cultural, and political changes much like those the United States and other parts of the Western world faced in the 1960s, the stress and uncertainties that grow from such changes are often expressed in poetry, fiction, music, and other areas. The innovativeness and energy released may present new models for the society.[10]

Social and cultural information that presents conflict and diversity confronts all of society with challenges. In Western society in general this challenge is not new. Cultural transmission and the information that supports it have been one of the hallmarks of Western social education for many years. In school environments this often comes under the general term "citizenship education." In society at large and in the academic community there seems to be little agreement over what this means. Recent developments in North American culture underscore this lack of agreement concerning content and direction. Should citizenship education center only on history, biography, and geography, or should it focus more on issues and problems found in society and educate students to be critical thinkers? Should citizenship training now include subjects formerly considered taboo, such as sexual behaviors, sexual orientation, and dysfunctional elements in family and community life? Should decision making be a topic for focused attention? Should the formation of public policy, environmental issues and competencies, moral development, and adult social roles be integrated into citizenship education?[11]

Cultural transmission as a part of citizenship education is generally conservative in its approach. It promotes the teaching of values, content, and behaviors generally agreed upon by the dominant society. It values political stability and common standards of thought and behavior. On the other hand, the critical or reflective thinking approach sees curriculum and information products as means of promoting social transformation. This approach emphasizes content, behaviors, and values that question and challenge views accepted by the prevailing majority society. This approach supports diversity and social action that can reconstruct society.[12] Such diverse views naturally produce diverse information products and systems that must be evaluated and considered for inclusion in curricula as well as in school library media collections. Those who create information products—information workers—play key roles in this debate and struggle.

THE INFORMATION WORKER AND CULTURAL TRANSFORMATION

Through the creative process information workers both influence and are influenced by their societies and cultures. Today they play a major role in citizenship education and in defining social order.

In ancient times information production belonged largely to kings, priests, shamans, medicine men, and witch doctors. As society developed, lawyers, tutors, and professors made their appearance. The growing sophistication, diversification, and complexity of society over time produced new and different kinds of information workers.

The eighteenth century saw an increase in teachers, lawyers, writers, editors, and ministers in the West. The truly modern information worker arose in the period from 1840 to 1920. These workers included writers, novelists, and authors of children's and young people's books and materials. During this period many publishers established children's and youth literature divisions and appointed well-regarded children's book editors to manage them. Although often innovative in approach, during this time these products for children and youth continued to reflect and transmit the cultural values of the dominant majority, using acceptable didactic styles of the time.

James Cortada tells us that with historical progression, information and knowledge have generally come to be valued and respected.[13] As such, information and information products are powerful tools for the promotion and transmission of conservative cultural ideas as well as intellectual skills that challenge accepted beliefs.

Faced with an information-rich environment and the conflicts that often occur between cultural transmission and critical thinking theories, it is clear that school library media specialists must make wise decisions when building collections. This is no easy task because we face deep-seated issues and problems in society that invite conflict and division.

CREATING INFORMATION IN MODERN SOCIETY: SELECTED ISSUES AND PROBLEMS

Schools in North America have always been expected to support cultural transmission, but over time the specific skills and values to be transmitted have varied. Early instruction emphasized religious and moral values. Nationalism, middle-class standards of work and behavior and the role of the patriotic citizen were introduced early in the nineteenth century. Although in recent years this framework has been influenced by the role of power and politics and the growth of multiculturalism, the basic framework supporting cultural transmission remains very much a part of society and instruction today.

The remaining part of this chapter looks more closely at some of these issues through brief case reports on three issues: sex education, family and community life, and community information, culture, and social education. Chapter 9 continues this review of the creative process by addressing in summary form fiction and other forms of prose, folklore, biography and history, and science and technology.

CASE REPORT 1: SEX INFORMATION

Definitions and Background

When parents are asked about sex education for their children, almost all agree that it is needed. However, they often disagree about what values to present, techniques to employ, and materials to use in sex education programs.[14]

Sexual Information Interests of Children and Young Adults

Recent research indicates that adolescents want information about the following subjects:

- Birth control
- Homosexuality
- Abortion
- Sexually transmitted diseases (STDs)
- Relationships and intimacy
- Sexual anatomy
- Menstruation
- Fertility cycles
- Physical changes at puberty
- Basic romantic or relationship attraction dynamics
- Reproductive functions
- Establishing relationships and dating etiquette
- Refusal techniques
- Problem sexual behaviors (rape, violence, drugs)
- Language of sex (including street language)[15]

A basic understanding of these needs is useful in selecting suitable sex education materials for school library media collections. Historically, sex education trade books have not always met the information needs of youth.[16] Recent reviews of sex education books suggest that this situation may be improving for some age groups.[17] Cornog and Perper delve extensively into sexuality issues as they impact on library collection development in their book *For Sex Education, See Librarian: A Guide to Issues and Resources*. All school media center librarians involved in building a sex education collection are advised to become familiar with this excellent resource.[18]

Approaches to Sex Education

Modern-day approaches to sex education vary in terms of content, values, and pedagogy. The three major approaches in the United States today can be termed **comprehensive, abstinence-only**, and **abstinence-plus** sex education.

Values are important in each approach. Comprehensive programs stress building a sense of responsibility, positive attitudes about sex and sexual behavior and language, and concern for others, including sexual partners. Comprehensive program advocates suggest the use of age-appropriate materials about pregnancy, contraception, and STDs. Avoiding pregnancy and preparing for adult life are also covered.[19]

Abstinence-only programs typically emphasize family values. Character building and refusal skills are taught. Discussions of contraceptives or safer sex, are generally avoided, although adverse side effects and inadequacies of contraception methods may be covered.[20] Sexual activity outside of marriage is discouraged.

Abstinence-plus curricula include information on abstinence as well as on contraception. Although they teach that sexual abstinence until marriage is the best option, they recognize that an abstinence-only approach will not meet the needs of all adolescents.[21]

The Sexuality Information and Education Council of the United States (SIECUS, www.siecus.org) and the Sex Information Council of Canada (SIECCAN, www.sieccan.org) believe that the best sex educators of youth are parents. However, they recognize that not all parents are equipped to be good sex educators and that parents need help and community support. Support systems include such organizations as Planned Parenthood (http://www.plannedparenthood.org), National Mental Health Association (http://www.nmha.org), and Planned Parenthood Federation of Canada (http://www.ppfc.ca/). These national groups generally can provide contact to local affiliates and related agencies. They also provide publications and educational programs. Many local churches and government agencies offer sex information and guidance as well. Local directories and Web sites can provide access to these resources.

Government Policies and Sex Education

The U.S. government has formally approved the abstinence-only approach as official policy and has provided funding for states and other agencies to establish such programs under the Adolescent Family Act and the Federal Welfare Reform Act. Some $500 million in public funds is to be spent over a five-year period to support abstinence-only education.[22]

Although stressing the importance of abstinence and personal responsibility, the National Strategy to Prevent Teen Pregnancy program, administered by the U.S. Department of Health and Human Services, is more broadly based. This program centers on a mandate from the president and Congress to reduce teen pregnancy. The operating principles driving the program are as follows:

1. Parents and other adult mentors must play key roles in encouraging young adults to avoid early pregnancy and to stay in school.
2. Abstinence and personal responsibility must be the primary message of prevention programs.
3. Young people must be given clear connections and pathways to college or jobs that give them hope and a reason to stay in school and avoid pregnancy.

4. Public and private-sector partners throughout communities—including parents, schools, business, media, health and human service providers, and religious organizations—must work together to develop comprehensive strategies.

5. Real success requires a sustained commitment to the young person over a long period of time.[23]

A national 1999 representative sample survey of 825 U.S. school superintendents or their representatives revealed these trends in sex education programs:

- 69% of schools surveyed have a district-wide policy to teach sex education.
- 14% have a comprehensive policy that treats abstinence as one option for adolescents in a broader sexuality education program.
- 51% have an abstinence-plus approach and teach abstinence as the preferred option for adolescents, but also permit discussion about contraception as an effective means of protecting against unintended pregnancy and disease.
- 35% (or 23% of all U.S. schools) follow an abstinence-only policy and teach abstinence as the only option outside of marriage, with discussion of contraception either prohibited entirely or permitted only to emphasize its shortcomings.

Schools in the South were five times more likely to adhere to an abstinence-only policy than schools in the Northeast. Nationally, one district in three forbids dissemination of any positive information about contraception regardless of the level of sexual activity among the student population.[24]

The Canadian government's official guidelines accommodate a variety of approaches to sexuality education and attempt to address the needs of a wide segment of the population. The guidelines stress knowledge acquisition, motivational opportunities, and skill building experiences and supportive environments. The guidelines also address the development of critical thinking skills, gender roles and gender-role stereotyping, and sensitivity to others who might be different.[25]

School Policies and Materials in the School Library Media Center

Regardless of the emphasis of the school's instructional policies, comprehensive sex education materials should be available in the school library media center. Censorship questions may certainly arise, but well-constructed official materials selection policies should address such issues. School media center librarians, administrators, and parents should not forget that the U.S. Supreme Court in *Pico* offered school library media collections some degree of protection from having materials removed without sound educational reasons for doing so.

Evaluation of Materials

Comprehensive Materials Evaluation

Some authorities on sex education have claimed that, historically, materials on sex education have presented sex as a reproductive function only, separated from life as a whole, and have viewed sex from a rigid standard of morality. They see such an approach as ineffective, favoring instead an informational and nonjudgmental approach to sexual issues. These critics have also been concerned that traditional sex education materials have not addressed sex outside of marriage, including premarital relationships and homosexuality.

The issue of how homosexuality has historically been addressed has attracted particular attention in recent years. When homosexuality was mentioned at all in early books it was viewed as a sin. Later it was discussed in psychological terms as a mental illness. In recent years it has been presented as a freely chosen but erroneous lifestyle. Comprehensive sex educators today prefer that homosexuality be discussed as an innate human orientation. Such variations in interpretations and social values add to the controversy surrounding sex education discussions and information provided for youth.

The subject of premarital relationships has likewise proven problematic. Early sex education materials labeled premarital relations a sin. Today's more comprehensive sex education materials address it in terms of making correct decisions based on proper information and attitudes, a strong sense of self-understanding, and a commitment to responsible behavior.

Critics have also expressed concern about the selective nature of some types of information in traditional sex education materials for youth and the outright omission of other information. Topics such as abortion, birth control, and legal rights of minors were intentionally omitted to the detriment of young people. Illustrations have also been criticized for being unclear, uninformative, or distorted. Critics also felt that some information was sexist and gender stereotyped in approach.[26]

Within this context, the evaluation of sex information materials increases in importance. Librarian William S. Palmer has suggested a number of important criteria to use when evaluating comprehensive sex information materials. He based his evaluation standards on a growing consensus among sex educators that a holistic approach to the subject is most effective.

Palmer suggested that **physiological and related factors** need to be taken into account when evaluating sex education items. The body's maturing process and reproductive functions must be well understood. In addition, **sociological aspects** need to be considered. As society and culture change, sex education materials must reflect those changes. The **moral dimensions** of sex need to be addressed as well. Morality here is defined as responsible behavior and attitudes, and concern for others. Related problem behaviors also need to be covered. These include sex abuse, rape, incest, and other forms of sexual dysfunction that bring harm to self and others.

Age-appropriate information relating to life coping skills should be presented as well. Depending on the purpose of the item, this might include information on abortion and various forms of birth control. **Additional sources of information** outside the book or item should be provided. These might include suggested reading, as well as numbers and addresses of helplines, counseling centers, crisis centers, and social agencies that offer help to youth on sexual matters. Inexpensive and readily accessible information such as pamphlets should also be included as additional sources.

The book or item being evaluated must present reliable and current information. Its tone and style must be supportive, it must have an appealing format or production values, and it must be readable or visually appealing.[27]

Classroom Materials Evaluation

Organizations such as SIECUS, SIECCAN, and Planned Parenthood of America that support comprehensive sex education suggest that materials intended for group or class instruction meet strict criteria. Instructional objectives must be appropriate to the physical, intellectual, and social maturity of the audience. Like all comprehensive sex educational materials, curriculum materials must be accurate, current, honest, and complete. Although materials may certainly have a point of view and advocate a set of values, these values should be clearly labeled and they should support decision making based on information. Equality between males and females should be maintained and items must avoid sex role stereotyping. A teacher's guide should be provided for instructional materials, and it is generally agreed that parents should be involved in selection of materials.[28]

Abstinence-Only Materials Evaluation

Supporters of the abstinence-only approach to sex education contend that criteria for the evaluation of sex education materials must be based on the principles set out in the Federal Welfare Reform Act (P.L. 104–

193). According to the National Coalition for Abstinence Education, abstinence-only materials must be strictly evaluated according to the guidelines of the Title V of the Welfare Reform Act and must reflect the congressional intent of the new federal abstinence-only effort and policy. Specifically, materials and projects funded under this law must teach that abstinence from sex outside of marriage is the expected standard of society and that individual maturity or circumstances cannot offset this. Materials and projects must not promote the use of condoms; and materials also must not endorse "safe-sex" practices. Marriage must be presented in a favorable light.[29]

Availability of Sex Information Materials

Sex education materials are available through the publishing and film trade, but materials are not always accessible in school library media center collections. Often they are not selected simply because they may seem too controversial. Some materials may simply not be purchased because they are not considered of interest to the library's general users.

A study conducted in the mid-1970s in Colorado found that secondary schools with formal sex education programs had more sex education titles listed in their school library media center catalogs than schools with no formal programs, and that urban schools had more sex education titles listed in catalogs than did rural schools. Nevertheless, the study noted that even in schools that had materials listed publicly, titles were not always available. A surprising number were stored outside the library, and some titles simply could not be located. The author concluded that censorship did not appear to be occurring at the book review level, the book dealer level, or the school library purchasing level, but books were not generally available.[30] Apparently little or no field research has been conducted since that time to ascertain the actual availability of sex education materials on school library media center shelves. However, a study conducted in Great Britain indicated that adolescents valued reading as a way of learning about sex and sexuality as well as about substance abuse.[31] This again raises serious questions about whether school library media centers are meeting their responsibility in providing needed information to youth.

Some legal critics have suggested in recent years that a library's selection policy may be used in court as evidence of how content-neutral and viewpoint-nondiscriminatory a library has been in making selection decisions. In other words, by reading a school library media center's selection policy and then examining its acquisition practices, could a pattern of deliberate bias in the selection of materials be detected under the framework of court rulings and First Amendment principles?[32] This seems to imply that content neutrality and a nondiscriminatory approach to selection ought to be applied to sex education materials and to the various pedagogical and value theories that support them.

Programs and Services

School library media center specialists can facilitate sex education for students in a number of ways. They can select materials that will help parents build their own family sex education programs. Mary Calderone, the late founder and first executive director of SIECUS, suggested that librarians can involve themselves in the education of preadolescents and adolescents by providing reading and other materials that promote positive values and sound attitudes and options about sexuality.[33] The school media center librarian should provide materials that present the viewpoint of those who see sexual abstinence outside of marriage as the only proper path.

CASE REPORT 2: FAMILY AND COMMUNITY LIFE

Curriculum Contents

As mentioned earlier, formal citizenship education in schools often begins with self, home, family, and classroom. These components often make up the heart of the elementary social science curriculum. Among the areas covered are heritage, rules, roles, authority, customs, symbols and celebrations, and technology in the home, school, and workplace. Community education within the elementary social science curriculum generally includes a study of neighborhood, how people work, and how to build and successfully contribute to community. In secondary schools history and historic persons, civics, and economics are added to the standard social science curriculum.[34]

Public Libraries and Cooperative Programs

Like school library media centers, public libraries have also shown a great deal of interest in meeting the family and community needs of parents and their children. Public library programs have generally focused on literacy, parenting education, and home schooling needs. In many cases, public libraries have established special collections and services for parents and their children. School library media center specialists and public librarians can work together in establishing cooperative arrangements to serve the family and community information needs of both children and their parents.

For example, the Family Center in Pittsburgh is operated by both the Point Park College and the Carnegie Library of Pittsburgh. The center has identified a wide variety of topics of concern to both parents and their children that both school and public library collections must address, some of which are listed here:

- AIDS/HIV
- Adoptions
- Alcoholism
- Appreciating the elderly
- Biting
- Death
- Feelings
- Homosexuality
- Illness, hospitalization, and medical concerns
- Moving
- Self-esteem
- Security blankets
- Toilet training[35]

The National Parent Information Network (NPIN), a project of the ERIC Clearinghouse system, is an Internet-based information network for parents and for organizations and individuals who support parents. In a 1998 report it identified important components of parenting programs that should be available within a community. A selected listing of these programs follows:

- Sibling rivalry
- Divorce and custody issues
- Aggressive behavior
- Positive discipline
- Choosing a school
- Father involvement
- Home schooling
- Family communication and relationships
- Adolescent behavior
- Substance abuse
- Gifted children
- Family literacy[36]

Lisbeth Schorr has identified seven attributes of highly effective family education programs, all of which could serve as program objectives for public and school library media center programs. She observes that successful programs

- are comprehensive, flexible, responsive, and persevering.
- see children in the context of their families.
- deal with families as parts of neighborhoods and communities.
- have a long-term preventive orientation, a clear mission, and continue to evolve over time.
- are well managed by competent and committed individuals with clearly identifiable skills.
- have staff who are trained to provide high-quality, responsive services.
- operate in settings that encourage practitioners to build strong relationships based on mutual trust and respect.[37]

Many public libraries active in parenting information services have Web sites that include useful parenting information. For example, a "Parenting Page" maintained by the Tempe (Arizona) Public Library presents an extensive listing of Web sites that offer links to parenting information from various places and organizations.[38] Nonlibrary-based organizations and agencies such as the Children's Trust Fund organizations of various states (individual states have separate Web addresses), Family Resource Coalition (www.parenting-qa), the Parenting Project (www.parentingproject.org), Active Parenting Canada (www.cadvision.com/alreynar), and the National Council on Family Relationships (www.ncfr.com) offer useful Web sites.

Materials directed at the needs of teenage parents, including teen fathers, are also required in the modern school library media center. This is especially true in localities where laws require parents under eighteen to attend a school or training program in order to maintain certain support benefits such as food stamps and medical care. The TeenAge Parent Program (TAP) operated by the Brevard Public Schools System in Florida is one example of a program that has established resources and support systems for teenage parents (http://studentservices.brevard.k12.fl.us/tap.htm). TAP's goal is to provide educational programs for pregnant and parenting students that will help them finish school with a diploma or earn a high school equivalence certificate. The recognition that teenage fathers must assume a more involved role in the upbringing of their children also reinforces the need for diversified teen-focused materials. Publishers such as Annick Press (http://www.annickpress.com), Rosen Publishing (http://www.rosenpublishing.com), Lucent Books (www.

lucentbooks.com), and Morning Glory Press (www.morningglorypress. com) have produced useful titles in this area.

Materials in School Environments

Many school library media centers not only buy community life materials appropriate for youth, but also provide collections and materials for parents. Nevertheless, such materials are expensive, and for that reason some school library media programs may find collaboration with other agencies, especially other libraries, to be an option worth considering.

The Family Life Collection at the N. A. Walbran Elementary School Library Media Center in Oriskany, New York, a good example of such a school-based collection, consists of a large array of books, videos, books on tape, magazines, and pamphlets on topics of concern to all families. Parents may check out materials from the media center as well.[39]

Several other models of service are available for consideration. One option is to have loan collections supplied by public libraries or other agencies placed in school library media centers. Another is for the school library media center to operate a small-scale referral service whereby parents and other caregivers are referred to other agencies in the community that have suitable parenting materials. This model requires knowledge of community resources. Basic here is a willingness to canvas the community to locate relevant collections, to keep records of useful referral sources, and to locate and evaluate local communities' Web sites.

Communication technology systems such as the Internet and the World Wide Web have greatly influenced the nature of collection development in the school library media center. No longer are we reliant only on materials found in the building-level collection itself, but we can expect to find and use a variety of resources well beyond the school site. The United States Institute of Museum and Library Services (IMLS), soon after it was established by Congress in 1996, recognized the responsibility of libraries, museums, and archives to make their resources widely available. IMLS sponsored a series of grant programs designed to encourage cooperation among these various institutions in the development technology-based delivery systems allowing educational and cultural resources to be better developed and shared.

The program at the Children's Museum of Houston (CHM) is a good example of such a resource initiative. Supported through an IMLS grant and in cooperation with the Houston Public Library (HPL), the CMH established and maintains a parent resource library located in CMH quarters. The primary goals of the project are to disseminate "quality, relevant, and varied information on early childhood, parenting, and family learning and to provide a centralized location for parents to explore resources while their children are occupied with activities that promote literacy skills."[40] The Houston Public Library allows materials to be checked out from the CMH parenting collection using its Power Card to be returned to neighborhood branch libraries throughout the system. The HPL markets this service through its Web site, where it describes the service in detail for persons living in the greater Houston area.[41]

Family Information Problems and Issues

Inappropriate Parent and Family Behaviors

Although much about family life is good, parenting collections must also deal with problems caused by parent behaviors, which can range from inappropriate parenting based on lack of information about child development to intentional criminal behaviors such as incest and sexual and mental abuse. The following list, drawn from various parenting and Internet sites, suggests areas in which some parents and families need help and guidance.

- Child abuse—what it means and how and when it occurs
- Domestic violence prevention (including spousal abuse)
- Foster care training
- Expectant and new parents
- Punishments and punishment guidelines for children
- Understanding children's capabilities and limitations (child development)
- Nutrition and wellness
- Food quality and safety

This list, along with other research and commentaries on family life, can easily serve as a purchase checklist for items to be acquired for the school library media center collection.

Defining the Modern Family

In recent decades issues centering on how to define a family unit have arisen. Some define the family as consisting of a married father (male), mother (female), and their biological children.[42] Nevertheless, the family throughout history has taken on many definitions and contexts. Social historians tell us that the traditional view of the Western family dates from the middle of the nineteenth century and is closely associated with the rise of the middle class. Before that time, the family was seen largely as a political and economic unit in which all members followed well-defined personal and work roles. This type of family structure offered a great deal of protection from the ills of society.[43] As economic conditions improved, parents came to value their children as individuals and to give more attention to their growth and development.

The nature of the Western family is changing once again, and the middle-class family model is now under stress and is being reevaluated. Single-parent families, adoptive parents, stepfamilies, teen parents, and the gay and lesbian family are just a few examples of how this model is now being challenged. Such models present new ways of looking at family structures.[44] Publishers and producers of materials have responded to debates over these new family structures with a wide variety of materials. As a consequence, school library media collections have a great many resources to choose from in areas such as single parenting, stepfamilies, and teen parents. Publishers such as Annick Press, Rosen Publishing, and Morning Glory Press, mentioned earlier as sources for teen parenting, also have materials that address parenting in general. Currently one of the major issues society faces is whether to recognize the legitimacy of the gay and lesbian family unit.[45] This issue is very troubling for some, and legal challenges to library holdings on the subject have been made. Whether they become parents through adoption, artificial insemination, or divorce and child custody arrangements, gay and lesbian parents have been insisting that they be treated as legitimate parents. In some communities, gay and lesbian parents may insist that resources be made available in the school and the school library media center that reflect the legitimacy of their families and offer guidance and affirmation for their children. In other communities, homophobia may be so intense that gay or lesbian parents live in fear and make no demands on the school or the media center.

The controversy surrounding two books on gay and lesbian parenting indicates the volatile nature of this issue. *Daddy's Roommate* by Michael Willhoite (Alyson Wonderland Publications, 1990) and *Heather Has Two Mommies* by Leslea Newman (Alyson Wonderland Publications, 1989) present gay and lesbian parenting in a positive light and seek to convey the message that this type of family unit is acceptable and normal. The Alyson Wonderland Publications series itself includes books that are intended to support gay parenting and gay and lesbian interests in child rearing.

In Texas a dispute over *Heather Has Two Mommies* and *Daddy's Roommate* reached a federal district court when a Wichita Falls city ordinance known as the Altman Resolution, which was designed to restrict children's access to some books in the public library, was challenged by a citizen group. In issuing a restraining order against this ordinance, the court stated:

The Altman Resolution, and the City's removal of the two Books, constitutes impermissible content-based and viewpoint-based discrimination. From a review of the history of the Resolution it is clear that the ordinance was enacted specifically for the purpose of suppressing *Heather Has Two Mommies* and *Daddy's Roommate*. When opponents of the books failed to censor the books outright, they sought to accomplish indirectly what they could not do directly.[46]

The court further noted that opponents of these books had a "moral" agenda, had made no pretense about their objectives, and had circulated a petition in which they asked for a federal law that would deprive federal courts of jurisdiction "to make any decision, or issue any order concerning the matter of material *censored* . . . in any library"[47]

Despite this opposition, the education community has recognized a need to make available information suitable for youth, parents, and the community in general on gay and lesbian parenting. For example, the ERIC system, through its AskERIC Info Guides series, published a detailed guide to gay and lesbian parenting in 1995 and reissued it in 1998. It is currently available through the AskEric Web site.[48]

Organizations that are strongly opposed to gay and lesbian parenting and which have mounted campaigns against it include the American Family Association (www.afa.net), Family Policy Network (http://www.familypolicy.net), and others. Although these groups may not offer book reviews regarding parenting issues on a regular basis, they do highlight their positions explaining their opposition to gay and lesbian parenting. Other sources that generally take more reserved positions on gay and lesbian parenting as well as parenting in general include *Christian Librarian* published by the Association of Christian Librarians (www.acl.org). Journals such as *Religious Education* also provide information on this controversy as well as other social issues involving religious values and family life. In order to build balanced collections, the school library media specialist needs to be well informed regarding sources, especially publishers. Michale Farry's *The Directory of Publishers in Religion* (Scholars Press, 1997) provides a good overview of presses of all types, including conservative publishers. *Christian Fiction: A Guide to the Genre* by John Mort (Libraries Unlimited, 2002) is another helpful guide. It is a comprehensive readers' advisory guide to 1,900 titles based on readers' interests.

CASE REPORT 3: COMMUNITY INFORMATION, CULTURE, AND SOCIAL EDUCATION

Information collections that address social issues and citizenship and that support critical thinking must acquire and make available information about the local community.[49] The idea of community information has been discussed rather extensively since the 1960s and 1970s in professional literature, and a rather impressive literature now exists on how to select, organize, and present this information.

School libraries have traditionally media provided information about community resources. Shores, Rufsvold, Davies, and Van Orden all noted the importance of community resources.[50] Shores and Rufsvold wrote of community resources as early as 1949 and 1954.

Community Information in Schools

Beginning in the 1970s, Terence Brake researched for the British Library the question of how to equip students while in school with broad information handling skills in addition to traditional library knowledge, including community information in this expanded body of competencies. Based on research findings, Brake felt that the school library media center should play a more central role in disseminating community information. His summary suggestions follow.

- Collect community information within the school environment or neighborhood. Begin with the public library, but include other social agencies, clubs, local newspapers, magazines, and individuals.
- Organize a community information collection around these components: Provide a bulletin broad for quick access to timely information; a local community information index offering access to a wide range of resources; a literature file (e.g., information or vertical file) consisting of relevant pamphlets and leaflets; a small ready reference shelf consisting of local published directories, yellow pages, and other useful local reference items; a section of "give away" items.[51]

Of course, these recommendations were made before the advent of the desktop computer, and more up-to-date recommendations would take this technology into account, especially the feasibility of community information being listed through the public access catalog (PAC) and other electronic database file systems.

Problems and Issues

Until recently, community information resources have not been widely used or developed in school media library centers, although their importance to the curriculum have long been recognized. The increase in their use has been greatly enhanced by the Internet and its ability to make community information more accessible and affordable than previously. For example, most cities have Web sites that carry community directories and local or regional information sources. These are often hosted by city governments, chambers of commerce, newspapers, and television and radio stations. Such availability makes community information access easy and affordable for school library media centers. Nevertheless, problems and issues do exist and must be faced.

Generally, community Internet sources are not specific to school needs. Although useful, they are targeted for a general audience. To develop a community information resource program for a school media library center requires time and expense in terms of planning and ongoing management. Information policies must be established, and information located, evaluated, cataloged and organized, and mounted electronically on a system that is accessible within the school.

Much of the available information in the community consists of "life-coping" or information based on personal needs. This can include crisis intervention and counseling, sex and family planning information, and a host of other needs. Because of this, community information guidelines must be considered and built into the official selection policy. In addition to personal needs information, community information includes sports, the arts, recreation, and cultural institutions such as museums and libraries. A review of the New York Public Library's community information Web site provides an overview of the wealth of resources available in a community, and demonstrates how one of the great libraries of the world has responded to the need for community-based information (http://www.nypl.org/branch/services/cis.html).

Another problem that libraries have faced over the years is how to deliver community information because so much of it is personal and needs-centered. Public libraries, for the most part, have developed policies that direct the librarian away from the role of counselor or social worker and have emphasized the librarian's responsibility of facilitating access to information through directory preparation and use. School library media center personnel also need to consider what approaches to take when involved with personal problems and information. The school library media center specialist has a different role than that of a public librarian. In a school situation the specialist is considered part of the professional team charged with the care and development of students. In this role the specialist not only selects, acquires, and makes information available, but must be alert to information requests that may signal personal issues and problems that require intervention. In this capacity, the school library media specialist generally has the support of others on the professional staff such as counselors, who can assume a greater role when personal problems arise.

Following the emphasis given to directory preparation as opposed to direct counseling and guidance by librarians, many public libraries such as the Baltimore County Public Library (http://www.bcplonline.org/

info/comm) have responded by either creating their own community information system through their PACs or they have mounted links to community information on their Web sites. Numerous school districts such as the Austin (Texas) Independent School District (http://www.austin.isd.tenet.edu/community/resourceorgs/) also provide links to suitable community sources through their Web sites.

Community information and its proper use play an important role in information literacy. The importance given to information in such standards and guides as *Information Literacy Standards for Student Learning* (prepared by AASL and AECT, 1998); *A Planning Guide for Information Power: Building Partnerships for Learning with School Library Media Program Assessment Rubric for the 21st century* (1999), and *The Information-Powered School*, edited by Sandra Hughes-Hassell and Anne Wheelock, (ALA, 2001) underscores the growing importance of community information.

Within the school curriculum the proper use of community information can support the development of critical thinking skills. It presents intellectual challenges in terms of helping students understand social and community life, government policies, and access to information. Curriculum issues and the selection of resources that relate to social life and community are discussed further in Chapter 9.

Another important issue that community information presents is the need for networking. Libraries have long recognized that information exists well beyond their collections. Public libraries have especially realized that the only way to acquire this information and develop community information contacts is to "network" within the community. The Internet has reinforced this need. Stephen Bajjaly's *The Librarian's Community Network Handbook* (ALA, 1999) is a guide that describes how public libraries can become more involved in the life of their communities. This book supports earlier writings on community information that also emphasized community contacts such as *Information and Referral in Reference Services*, edited by Marcia S. Middleton and William Katz (Haworth Press, 1988), and Thomas Childers' *Information and Referral: Public Libraries* (Scarecrow Press, 1975). Apparently no recent guides specifically focused on community information within the school library media center have been published. Nevertheless, guides to Internet resources such as *The Internet and the School Library Media Specialist* by Randall M. MacDonald (Greenwood, 1997) and *School Libraries and the Electronic Community* by Laurel A. Clyde (Scarecrow Press, 1997) are helpful in building collections of community information resources.

CONCLUSION

Throughout history a great assortment of people have used their creative ability to produce information and information products. Along with individual effort, social and cultural factors play a huge role in how creativity is allowed to develop.

As the twenty-first century begins to unfold the world is awash in information.[52] Much of it comes from science, technology, and the arts. But much of it deals with the changing and conflicting social and cultural values in modern society. Sexuality, family and community life, and the role of citizenship are just a few areas where Western cultures face challenges involving fundamental values.

As cultural institutions, libraries are caught in this struggle. Libraries in an open society are both agents of cultural transmission for old, established values and instruments of change. They offer the collected knowledge of the past as well as information about new ways of thinking and behaving that may challenge prevailing ideas.

School library media centers are especially important agents for both change and stability because of their position within the educational system. They serve as repositories of culture and help to transmit established cultural values to the young. They also play an important role in helping students develop critical thinking skills. In an open society conflict is inevitable. School library media center librarians must strengthen their resolve to accept their role as mediators in society and culture by providing information with all of its many views and challenges.

NOTES

1. *Merriam-Webster's New Collegiate Dictionary*, 10th ed., p. 1358; Jonscher, *Evolution*, p. 61.

2. M. Hadas, "A Greek Paradigm of Self Control," in *The Quest for Self Control*, edited by R. Klausner (New York: Free Press, 1965), p. 201, quoted in John Dacey, "Concepts of Creativity: A History," in *Encyclopedia of Creativity*, edited by Mark A. Runco and Steven R. Pritzker (San Diego: Academic Press, 1999), p. 312.

3. Dacey "Concepts," p. 312.

4. Peter Kreeft and Ronald K. Tacelli, *Handbook of Christian Apologetics: Hundreds of Answers to Crucial Questions* (Downers Grove, IL: InterVarsity Press, 1994).

5. C. Dawson, *Medieval Essays* (New York: Image Books, 1954), pp. 246–47, quoted in Dacey, "Concepts," p. 314.

6. Dacey, "Concepts," p. 315.

7. Dacey, p. 316.

8. Robert Albert and Mark Runco, "A History of Research on Creativity," in *Handbook of Creativity*, edited by R. Sternberg (Cambridge: Cambridge University Press, 1999), p. 26, quoted in Dacey, "Concepts," p. 316.

9. Dacey, "Concepts," pp. 321–22.

10. Lawrence Lipton, "Beat Generation," in *The Encyclopedia Americana*, International ed. (Danbury, CT: Americana, 1990), vol. 3, p. 409.

11. E. Wayne Ross, "The Struggle for the Social Studies Curriculum," in *The*

Social Studies Curriculum: Purpose, Problems, and Possibilities, edited by E. Wayne Ross (Albany: State University of New York Press, 1997), p. 6.

12. Ross, "Struggle," p. 7.

13. James W. Cortada, *Rise of the Knowledge Worker* (Boston: Butterworth-Heinemann, 1998), chap. 1.

14. Susan N. Wilson, "Sexuality Education: Our Current Status, and an Agenda for 2010," *Family Planning Perspectives* 32 (September/October 2000), available at www.agi-usa.org/pubs/journals/3225200.html.

15. Kathy McCoy and Charles Wibbelsman, *The Teenage Body Book* (New York: Perigee, 1999); Michael J. Basso, *The Underground Guide to Teenage Sexuality* (Minneapolis: Fairview Press, 1997).

16. Hudith Selig Rubenstein, "A Comparison Between Student Interest and Book Information in Sex Education for Teenagers," dissertation, Harvard University, 1974, in *Dissertation Abstracts International* 35 (February 1975): 5153-A.

17. Martha Cornog and Timothy Perper, "For Sex: See Librarian: A Plague on Both Your Houses? The Other Sex Books," *Journal of Information Ethics* 6 (Spring 1997): 8–12; Christine M. Heppermann, "Laughing in the Face of Puberty: Books about Sex," *Horn Book Magazine* 76 (March–April 2000): 162–68; Lois Winkel, "Family Life and Sex Education," *School Library Media Activities Monthly* 15 (February 1999): 31–32.

18. Martha Cornog and Timothy Perper, *For Sex Education, See Librarian: A Guide to Issues and Resources* (Westport, CT: Greenwood Press, 1996).

19. Douglas J. Besharov and Karen N. Gardiner, "Sex Education and Abstinence: Programs and Evaluation," *Children and Youth Services Review* 19, no. 5/6 (1997): 327–26, available at www.aei.org/sw/swbesharov2.htm.

20. Ibid.

21. Ibid.

22. Ibid.

23. U.S. Department of Health and Human Services, *A National Strategy to Prevent Teen Pregnancy: Annual Report, 1999–2000* (Washington, D.C.: The Department, 2000), available at www.aspe.hhs.gov/hsp/teenp/ann-reptool.

24. David J. Landry and others, "Abstinence Promotion and the Provision of Information About Contraception in Public School District Sexuality Education Programs," *Family Planning Perspectives* 31 (November/December 1999): 280–86, available at http://www.agi-usa.org/pubs/journals/3128099.html.

25. Canada, Ministry of National Health and Welfare, "Canadian Guideline for Sexual Health Education," available at http://www.hc-gc.ca/lcdc/web/publicat.

26. Patricia J. Campbell, *Sex Education Books for Young Adults, 1892–1979* (New York: R. R. Bowker, 1979).

27. William S. Palmer, "Evolving Criteria for Evaluating Sex Education Books," *Voice of Youth Advocates* 5 (April 1982): 23–24.

28. Sex Information and Education Council of the United States, National Guidelines Task Force, *Guidelines for Comprehensive Sexuality Education, Kindergarten–12th Grade* (New York: Sex Information and Education Council of the U.S., 1992). "Family Life and Human Sexuality," available at http://www.ashaweb.org/resolutions1.html#familylife.

29. National Coalition for Abstinence Education, "ETR Associates Entry into

Abstinence Education Resources Is a Sham. Analysis April 15, 1998," available at http://www.abstinence.net/sub_pages/etrasham.html.

30. Keith Torke, "Sex Education Books, Censorship, and Colorado High School Libraries: A Survey," dissertation, University of Northern Colorado, 1975, in *Dissertation Abstracts International* 36 (May 1976): 7175-A.

31. K. Reynolds, "Reluctant Readers and Risk Taking," *British Library Research and Information Report* 14 (1996) 220–29.

32. Munic, "Education or Indoctrination," pp. 213–53.

33. Mary Calderone, "Young People, Sexuality and Librarians," *Top of the News* 34 (Winter 1978): 125–30.

34. Ross, "Struggle," pp. 10–11.

35. The Family Center Website of the Carnegie Library of Pittsburgh and the Point Park College, available at www.clpgh.org/clp/libctr/famctr/aboutfam. html.

36. Anne S. Robertson, "The Parenting Education Spectrum: A Look at the Scope of Parenting Programs that Should Be Available Within a Community," *Parent News*, June 1998, available at http://www.npin.org/html.

37. Lisbeth Schorr, *Common Purpose: Strengthening Families and Neighborhoods to Rebuild America* (New York: Doubleday, 1997), quoted in Anne S. Robertson, "Parenting Education," pp. 5–10.

38. Tempe Public Library, "Parenting Page," available at http://www.tempe. gov/library/youth/parent.htm.

39. N. A. Walbran Elementary School Library Center Website, available at www.cyhbervillage.com/ocs/mediaelm.htm.

40. Maureen White and others, "Great Things Come in Small Packages: A Parent Resource Library," *Journal of Youth Services in Libraries* 14 (Fall 2000): 8–11.

41. Houston Public Library, "About the Parent Resource Library," available at http://www.hpl.lib.tx.us/youth.prl_about.html.

42. Bridget Maher, "The State of the Family," available at http://www.frc. org/iss/mar/retrieve.cfm?get=1F00H3.

43. Priscella Robertson, "Home as Nest: Middle Class Childhood in Nineteenth-Century Europe," in *The History of Childhood*, edited by Lloyd de Mause (New York: Psychohistory Press, 1974), pp. 407–31.

44. Mary Ann Mason and others, eds., *All Our Families: New Policies for a New Century. A Report of the Berkeley Family Forum* (New York: Oxford University Press, 1998).

45. Valerie Lehr, *Queer Family Values: Debunking the Myth of the Nuclear Family* (Philadelphia: Temple University Press, 1999).

46. *Sund v. City of Wichita Falls*, 114 F Supp 2d 566 (2000), available at http:// www.lexis-nexis.com/universe (United States District Court for the Northern District of Texas, Wichita Falls Division, Civil Action No. 7:99-CV-155-R. "Amended Memorandum Opinion" at page 33.)

47. *Sund v. City of Wichita Falls*. Emphasis added by the court.

48. "Gay and Lesbian Parents," available at http://www.askeric.org/Virtual /infoGuides/alpha_list/Gay_and_Lesbian_Parents-5_98.html.

49. This section is a brief summary and updating of W. Bernard Lukenbill, "Community Information in Schools: An Operational Approach and Model," in

Information and Referral in References Services, edited by Marcia Middleton and Bill Katz (New York: Haworth Press, 1988), pp. 173–88.

50. RuthAnn Davies, *The School Library Media Center: A Force for Educational Excellence* (New York: R. R. Bowker, 1969); Margaret I. Rufsvold, *Audio-Visual School Library Service: A Handbook for Librarians* (Chicago: American Library Association, 1949); Louis Shores, *Basic Reference Sources* (Chicago: American Library Association, 1954); Van Orden, *Collection Program.*

51. Terence Brake, *The Need to Know: Teaching the Importance of Information: Final Report for the Period January 1978–March 1979* (London: British Library, 1980).

52. Peter V. Lyman and others, "How Much Information?" available at http://wwwsims.berkeley.edu/research/projects/how-much-info/.

Literature, Information, and the Creative Process

9

This chapter continues the discussion of the creative process begun in Chapter 8, focusing on literature and on a number aspects of social life. Major categories to be addressed include

imaginative literature, including drama and poetry
biography and personal narratives
folklore and the oral tradition
science, technology, and health
social science: history and events
music and art
religion and spirituality

AUTHORS AND THE CREATIVE PROCESS

Whether authors write imaginative literature or nonfiction, they are always influenced in some way by their environment. Good literature, whether it be fiction or nonfiction, not only presents a good story, but also reveals something about human life and the interpersonal relationships that bind individuals and societies together. In the various editions of *Literature for Today's Young Adults*, Nilsen and Donelson have profiled authors who have been popular with children and young adults, revealing much about how the creative process has influenced these successful authors. For example, Gary Soto says his writing has always been influenced by the Hispanic neighborhoods of his childhood in Fresno,

California. The late Robert Cormier favored a first-person narrative style because it allowed him and his characters to better interact with each other and the reader. Michael Cadnum tells of his love for animals and how they influence and give form to his writing. Gary Paulsen reflects on his beginnings as a writer and the many rejections he received from publishers and editors, and how he used those rejections and the comments that often came with them in a creative way to better shape the growth of his writing. In reflecting on her career as a nonfiction writer for youth, Ellen Levine says that she strives to help her readers develop a sense of social and ethical responsibility. Sharon Creech believes that she can lead her readers on a path of discovery through the kind of creative approach to journeys used in *Walk Two Moons* (HarperCollins, 1994). M. E. Kerr writes of how prejudice and her own sexuality have influenced her feelings about social and personal justice.[1]

All these personal reflections and stories attest to the power of the written word and further emphasize the importance of the school library media collection. Without question, the school library media collection plays an important role in the continuation of the cultural process by providing ready access to both classic and standard works of imaginative literature and nonfiction.

Each book and information item in a collection is the product of the creative mind and has a life of its own. The creation of literature and information products is influenced by many factors in society. An understanding of these creative processes and influences can help school library media specialists make better decisions about which items to acquire for their collections.

COLLECTION ISSUES—PROFILES FOR DEVELOPMENT

Building collections is a complicated process, and there is really no one perfect approach to it. Nevertheless, conventional wisdom and practice over the years provide some fundamental guidelines. The following brief profiles are designed to place these practices in perspective for those who are just beginning, and may serve as a review for those experienced in making selections for the school library media center.

PROFILE 1. IMAGINATIVE LITERATURE, DRAMA, AND POETRY

Standard Works and Classics

A major obligation of any collection of imaginative literature is to provide for the classics and standards works. Although perhaps not the most popular items in the collection, they are reflective of our culture and society and promote literary and aesthetic development. Works such as *Little Women* by Louisa May Alcott, Lewis Carroll's *Alice's Adventures in Wonderland* with original illustrations by Sir John Tenniel, Edward Lear's *A Book of Nonsense*, Walter Crane's *The Baby's Own Aesop*, and Howard Pyle's wonderful woodcut illustrations of Robin Hood and other medieval accounts are all important to any collection.

Critical guides and textbooks such as those by Charlotte S. Huck, Donna E. Norton, and Zena Sutherland offer background and guidance.[2] Selection aids described in Chapter 7, such as the *Children's Catalog, Standard Catalog for Middle and Junior High School Libraries*, and *Senior High School Library Catalog* likewise offer suggestions for standard and classic authors, titles, and editions worthy of inclusion in collections.

Current and New Materials

Selecting new materials is always a challenge. Publishers and producers constantly bring new materials to the market, many focused on meeting special needs, for example, high interest–low vocabulary materials suitable for the unskilled reader, or materials that avoid traditional stereotyping of minority groups and women. Likewise, reading interests change and reading fads come along which must also be accommodated. People have always read for enjoyment and pleasure, and good collection development procedures will honor that need as well. Numerous selection aids are available. *Booklist, School Library Journal*, and *Horn Book* help in acquisitions decisions for current materials. Award lists of books selected as favorites by children and students are excellent guides to what is popular and enjoyable. Current Newbery and Caldecott award lists also offer excellent guides to outstanding new materials. (See Chapter 7 for more suggestions.)

Drama and Poetry

Drama and poetry are an important part of imaginative literature and they surround us in our daily lives through the mass media. The school library media center collection can do a great deal to promote literary and social appreciation of both drama and poetry. Charlotte Huck and her colleagues suggest that drama is an excellent way to extend the enjoyment of literature and that both librarians and teachers need to work hard at promoting the natural relationship among books, characters, and drama. Dramatic play offers an excellent approach to the development of literary appreciation for children. Children as young as five can begin to identify with literary characters and situations. Often children of this age can take a simple folktale and enact the story without much adult supervision. Techniques to promote dramatic play and the appreciation of drama include pantomime, dramatizing stories, improvisation, readers' theater, and puppetry. All of these techniques rely upon an abundance of materials in a central school library media collection for support.

Children and youth already have wide exposure to theater through television and movies, and writers are now producing plays that reflect this interest in drama. Often themes that find their way into such dramas reflect the adolescent experience, such as fitting in with the group, popularity, sex, drugs, making choices, and taking chances. Writers such as Jerome McDonough have crafted plays that are practical to produce, provide for flexible casting, and have contemporary settings. Teachers and library media specialists need to encourage adolescents to both read and experience drama. Dramatic form is not easy for most adolescents. It is a visual experience, and students must be guided in dramatic reading and performance. Dramas also must be carefully selected to reflect the maturity and experience levels of adolescents. Well-selected subjects as well as age-appropriate themes are key to acceptance by youth.[3]

Poetry is also important to the full development of literary appreciation. Huck defines poetry as a "distillation of experience that captures the essence of an object, a feeling, or a thought. Such intensification requires a more highly structured patterning of words than prose does. Each word must be chosen with care for both sound and meaning, because poetry is language in its most connotative and concentrated form."[4] She further notes that poetry for youth does not differ significantly from that for adults except that it speaks about life in ways that are meaningful for youth. Its language, content, and subjects should appeal to youth. Its emotional appeal must reflect the emotions experienced in childhood and youth. Poetry for youth should not be didactic, moralizing, preachy, or sentimental. It can take many forms, including ballads, narrative poems, lyrical poetry, limericks, free verse, Haiku, and concrete poetry (e.g., poems in which the arrangement of words provide meanings and where meanings are further reinforced and often carried by the geometric shape of the poem).

Although poetry may have lost some of its former appeal for adolescents in this age of mass media, it still surrounds us. It is reflected in social and political movements, changes in lifestyles, street and urban life, rock and rap music, and ethnic experiences. Successful poetry for youth today reflects the sounds and stories of life. One of the most popular poetry movements today for youth is the free verse made popular by Mel Glenn, which reads like a novel, but tells its story through poetry.

Development of Literary Appreciation

One important responsibility of the school library media program is to promote the development of literary appreciation. Classics, standards, and popular reading can all contribute. Robert Carlsen outlines several stages of literary development:

Age	Major Characteristics
Elementary School	Unconscious delight and reading for enjoyment
Middle and Junior High School	Living vicariously through others and through literary characters
Junior High, Early High School	Seeing others and seeing what's happening in one's own life through literature
Upper Level High School	Philosophical speculations and interest in others and social relationships as reflected in literature
Late High School and Adulthood	Aesthetic delight. Critical awareness of literature and possessing the vocabulary necessary to describe literary elements.

Source: Sarah K. Herz and Donald R. Gallo, *From Hinton to Hamlet: Building Bridges Between Young Adult Literature and the Classics* (Westport, CT: Greenwood Publishing Group, 1996), p. 16.

Carlsen's list suggests that literature of all kinds is needed in school library collections to help realize the full development of literary appreciation in students.

PROFILE 2. BIOGRAPHY AND PERSONAL NARRATIVES

Biography is the branch of literature that is concerned with the lives of men and women. Some of the world's great literature has been in the form of biography, for example Lytton Strachey's biographies of great Victorians such as Queen Victoria. Biographies written especially for children such as those by Ingri and Edar d'Aulaire are also fine examples of age-appropriate literature.

Biography and personal narrative serve many purposes aside from providing interesting and informative reading. Biography is an excellent bridge between fiction and nonfiction. Students who are reluctant to leave fiction and to take up reading nonfiction can often be encouraged to move first to biography, as it contains elements of imagination as well as facts.

Biography also satisfies basic psychological needs for identification, stimulation, role modeling, and socialization. Since the publication of her diary, thousand of students have undoubtedly identified with Anne Frank. Probably the same can be said of Helen Keller. Biographies can be powerful statements about the human spirit and will to survive. Biographies and personal narratives encourage new ways of thinking and of seeing the world through different life perspectives and experiences, offering students great opportunities for stimulation and for moving beyond the limits of their own lives. Whether the biographies are about famous sports figures or unknown individuals who surmount great odds to survive and thrive, their accomplishments offer encouragement to readers.

Biography is an excellent source for both cultural and historical information and has traditionally been used to promote national pride and identity. National heroes and national values and expectations have been promoted and defined through biography. Biography is also an excellent source for commentary about contemporary life. Biography not only outlines what society perceives as important, but it offers insight and reflection on contemporary society.

Nonetheless the selection of biography presents certain challenges to collection development. Students are very much attuned to mass culture, and their interest in biography reflects that. Students want to read and hear about personalities in television and film, rock music, and sports. In addition, students like to read about contemporary individuals who do interesting and extraordinary things in their lives. They also like to read about little-known individuals who overcome the hardships of life.

Without encouragement, students may not willingly choose biographies of historical figures. Historically biographies have been used to promote nationalism, propaganda, and personality cults, to exalt rulers, and to encourage xenophobia. In contemporary times, we need only look to Nazi Germany and to the Stalinist Soviet Union for such examples. Archeological research provides ample evidence of how biography and the distortion of biography were used by ancient civilizations to promote personality cults and to glorify the achievements of rulers.

Although the situation is improving, school library media collection development for biography has traditionally suffered from a dearth of good ethnic materials and materials about women and their accomplishments. Good high interest, low vocabulary materials have been generally lacking. But, in recent years publishers such as Chelsea House (www.chelseahouse.com) have produced biographies that reflect a wide range of interests and that are easy to read. The Chelsea series ranges in coverage from well-known popular music entertainers and sports figures to historical and political figures. For example, *Jesse James* by T.J. Stiles (Chelsea House, 1994) would have wide appeal. It accurately reflects

James's murderous past and crimes, but it does not reveal much of him as a personality. Other publishers such as Three Rivers Press, Warner Books (www.twbookmark.com), and Ballantine Books (http://www.randomhouse.com) publish biographies that reflect popular mass-culture interests and attitudes and are easy to read. As with most forms of literature for youth, biography has generally avoided taboo topics, although such subjects may have been a driving force in an individual's life. For example, sexuality and the holding of unconventional opinions and beliefs have been underdeveloped. How many biographies of Thomas Jefferson for youth discuss his alleged African American mistress, Sally Hemings, the half-sister of his wife? Despite such caution, biographical materials are often subject to censorship. Censorship of biographical materials often involves charges of sexism, racism, and politics, values, religion, ideology, and lifestyles.

Mass media, including television, radio, print, and the Internet, provide a great deal of biographical information. Some is well researched and well presented, but much is focused on entertainment and sensationalism. This abundance of mass-media biography places even more responsibility on the school library media specialist to make balanced biographical materials available to students.

As with any type of literature, readers need to know how to approach biography. They need to be aware of an author's purpose, philosophy, and political alliances as well as what sources the author used. Learning to read biography is a process that must be started young and encouraged as students mature and develop the ability to apply critical judgment. Critical evaluation of film adaptations of biography is especially important. In films biographical information is often fictionalized and distorted for dramatic effect and interest, and youth need to understand the role that literary license plays in film adaptations. How is the life of Eva Peron to be critically evaluated? Some writers and film producers see her as a national heroine, while others paint her as a ruthless fascist. How are we to look at the evidence of her life as we read or view these various interpretations? According to film critic Kate Waites of Nova Southeastern University, the film adaptation of actress Frances Farmer's autobiography is a good example of how dramatic considerations compromised accuracy and violated Farmer's interpretation of her own life. Because biography and biographical information are pervasive in modern culture through the mass media, the careful consideration of biographical materials for a school library media center collection is crucial for the overall development of information literacy. Reference materials such as the authoritative *Dictionary of American Biography* (Scribner, 1996) and the more affordable *Concise Dictionary of American History* (Scribner, 1997) offer students excellent guides for objective biography writing and reporting.

PROFILE 3. FOLKLORE AND THE ORAL TRADITION

Traditional literature or folklore consists of all forms of narratives that can be written or oral. Three defining characteristics are that it must be anonymous, preserved in some way, and passed down by the people. Traditional literature consists of many forms including customs, tales, sayings, dances, riddles, fiddle tunes, ballads, folk speech, tall tales, beliefs and witchcraft, jokes (often obscene), rhymes, games, legends, epics, myths, stories from the Bible, hero tales, college stories, ghostly personas, armed forces folklore (G.I. stories), and art forms. It does not include fanciful stories written by known authors.

Traditional literature is important to a collection in many ways. Traditional literature is an important part of culture and society, as it helps explain the spiritual, communal, and psychological qualities of the human experience. Traditional literature also helps define our modern heritage through its place in literature, history, art, and other forms of modern social life.[5] Traditional literature is widely used within the modern-day curriculum. It is fundamental to literature study as it provides background and cultural appreciation. It can be used in social studies to examine social norms and group expectations and values. Art, drama, and music rely heavily upon the forms and sources of traditional literature or much of their content. Selecting traditional literature for a school library media collection requires knowledge of the forms and types of folklore as well as the many cultural communities that provide folklore.

In the United States this naturally includes the folklore of such communities and groups as the Pennsylvania Germans, and other immigrant groups, Ozark and Appalachian mountain people, the Spanish in New Mexico and Texas, Utah Mormons, Maine Coast Yankees, African Americans, Native Americans, Jews, and Eskimos. Other major sources of folklore include that from Britain, Germany, Scandinavia, France, Russia, and the Middle East, India, Asia, and Africa. In building folklore collections it is important to recognize the great collectors and compilers of folklore, such as Peter Asbjornsen and Jorgen E. Moe (Norway); Richard Chase (southern mountains, United States); Harold Courlander (West Africa, African Americans and Native Americans, United States); the brothers Grimm (Germany); Virginia Hamilton (African Americans, United States); Margaret Hodges (various nations); Julius Lester (African Americans, United States); Gerald McDermontt (West Africa, African Americans and Native Americans, United States); Charles Perrault (France); John Bierhorst (Native North Americans, United States and Canada); Padraic Colum (Ireland); Howard Pyle (Britian); and Richard F. Burton (Arabia). Other authorities whose writings or works written about them provide background and insight in folklore and mythology include Thomas Bullfinch, Joseph Campbell, Edith Hamilton, and John A. Lomax. The works of illustrators of folklore are also important to collections. Illustrations by Arthur Rackham, Barbara Cooney, Adroemme Adams, Marcia Brown, and Maurice Sendak will add value to all collections.

Authors who have taken traditional stories and rewritten them to appeal to modern readers need to be collected as well. Among others, these include Rosemary Sutcliff, Robert Nye, Virginia Hamilton, and Robin McKinley. Reconstructionist and feminist versions of famous folktales such as "Beauty and the Beast" and "Cinderella" are also needed. Regional folklore, especially state or provincial folklore, is also vital. Small presses and university presses located within the state or province are excellent sources for such publications.

Traditional literature has some problem areas that are subject to controversy. Folklore, being a product of society, often reflects its problems. Original folklore is often sexist, racist, xenophobic, violent, prejudicial, and sexual. It can also present cultural values and expectations that may not be well understood by those who come from other cultures. Careful consideration and the use of reliable selection aids and guides can alleviate many of the problems encountered in choosing a viable, inclusive, and well-rounded collection of traditional literature. Examples of titles include Sir Richard Burton's well-known translation of the Arabian Nights, *The Arabian Nights: Tales from a Thousand and One Nights* (Modern Library Classics, 2001) for mature readers. A recommended version more suitable for young children is Geraldine McCaughrean's *1001 Arabian Nights* (Oxford University Press, 2000), Richard Chase's delightful *Jack Tales* (Houghton Mifflin, 50th anniversary ed., 1993), and his *Grandfather Tales* (Houghton Mifflin, 1973) are wonderful resources for an American folklore collection. Collections such as *Cowboy Songs and Other Frontier Ballads* (Reprint Services, 1993) and *American Ballads and Folksongs* (Dover, 1994) developed by scholar John A. Lomax and his son Alan Lomax likewise add depth to a collection. Unfortunately, many of Harold Courlander's works are now out of print, but they are generally available in many older, well-established collections. His works reflect a wide variety of groups including *People of the Blue Corn: Tales and Legends of the Hopi Indians* (Harcourt Brace Jovanovich, 1970), and the scholarly but entertaining *A Treasury of Afro-American Folklore: The Oral Literature, Traditions, Recollections, Legends, Tales, Songs, Religious Beliefs, Customs, Sayings, and Humor of Peoples of African Descent in the Americas* with decorations by Enrico Arno (Crown, 1976).

Well-known European collections and adaptations of folktales include Joseph Jacobs's *English Fairy Tales* (Knopf, 1993) and *Celtic Fairy Tales* (Dover, 1972); Charles Perrault's *Puss in Boots* (Farrar, Straus and Giroux,

1998); Christen Asbjorsen and Jorgen Moe's *East Of the Sun and West Of the Moon: Fifty-Nine Norwegian Folk Tales from the Collection of Peter Chris- ten Asbjornsen and Jorgen Moe*, (Dover, 1970); *English Fairy Tales* by Flora Annie Steel (Macmillan, 1962) and Howard Pyle's *The Merry Adventures of Robin Hood of Great Renown in Nottinghamshire* (Scribner, 1954; New American Library, 1991). Padraic Colum's *Nordic Gods and Heroes* (Dover, 1996), as well as his works representing Irish folklore such as *The King of Ireland's Son* (Floris Books, 1997) are solid additions to collections. The Grimm Brothers' *Grimms' Fairy Tales* (Gossett and Dunlap, 1995) are stan- dard collections that should be represented. Extensive references and citations to collections of folklore are provided in *Children and Books by Zena Sutherland* (Addison-Wesley, 9th ed., 1996) as well as other text- books on youth literature. The *Standard Library Catalog Series* published by the H. W. Wilson Company is another excellent source for folklore collections recommendations.

PROFILE 4. SCIENCE, TECHNOLOGY, AND HEALTH

Scientific and technological ideas and advances have always been a part of social and cultural developments. For example, the Egyptians developed measurement systems for taxation and building purposes, and a mathematical system originated by the ancient Babylonians and further refined by the Hindus of India contributed to the development of algebra. The ancient Greeks advanced the development of geometry, so much so that Plato came to use it as a means to measure those who were worthy of education because of its perceived intellectual rigor.[6]

Nations and groups of people who have been able to develop within a scientific and technological framework have always experienced an advantage in protecting themselves and their values from challenge and in advancing their views of social order. In medieval times the Arabic countries and China contributed to scientific and technological devel- opment and became powerful. In modern times, within Western cultures we see how early advances made within the scientific and technological communities in Britain, Germany, and France contributed to coloniza- tion, imperialism, and nationalistic advances.

Contemporary society continues to face major challenges in science and technology. In developing school library media collections in these areas many problems must be faced. Although science and technology materials must be current and up-to-date, retrospective materials must also be considered. For example, Darwin's famous *Voyage of the Beagle* (or a good adaptation for younger readers) deserves a place in any col- lection.

Many problems involved in building science and technology collections can be overcome with determination and insight. These materials are expensive and often have very short shelf lives. In schools that offer advanced science and technology curriculums, the local school library media collection may not be able to meet the demands placed upon it. In such situations the library media specialist may need to consider document delivery systems such as cooperative arrangements with local libraries and networking, interlibrary loan, copy reproduction, and even contract document delivery services.

Criteria for evaluation include accuracy and authenticity, currency, inclusiveness as to significant facts, and avoidance of stereotypes. In works for small children anthropomorphism should be avoided, although in some cases this can be effective if handled well. An important concept to promote in scientific literacy is the ability to distinguish among fact, hypothesis, and theory. Works selected should present the scientific method in understandable and age-appropriate ways.

Works are also needed that show interrelationships among science, technology, and social issues and policy. Science and technology play major roles in public policy debates centered around issues that are political and value-laden, and have far-reaching consequences. Conservation and use of natural resources, drug use and abuse theories, access to health care and supporting technologies, genetic engineering, and creationism and evolution are just a few examples of highly controversial issues fueling social debate that must be covered in school library media collections.

Scientific and technological concepts are often complicated, and authors who cover these areas must have a special gift for transmitting difficult concepts to a variety of youthful readers. Good scientific and technological writing for youth requires clear and direct style that invites reader involvement. Vivid language is always needed.

The design and structure of books, media, and Internet Web sites require an understanding of information architecture. Information architecture is based on the psychology of how people learn and process information. A good book, piece of media, or web page will reflect these elements through selection of type fonts, colors, arrangement of figures, learning cues, and an understanding of how people perceive the world around them and how they retain and remember information. Art and illustrations are very much a part of information architecture, playing a major role in conveying information to the reader or user. Illustrations must both clarify and extend the text or message.[7]

Reference materials, lab manuals, motor repair manuals, and guides for student-based experiments are especially needed in science and technology. Print-based reference materials as well as well selected Internet resources are vital to any collection. Because of the demand for currency, the school library media center must have adequate financial resources to devote to periodical and journal subscriptions. In some cases, resources must be set aside for specially selected report literature produced by laboratories and universities.

Health and access to medical care are important aspects of science and technology. Health encompasses many diverse subject areas, among them physiology, sexuality, mental health, drug use, safety, psychology, care of the sick and aged, and specific illnesses such as cancer. Information on these topics is required for a better understanding of health issues. Health concerns also involve provocative social policy issues such as how environmental pollution and other factors may be related to disease.

Changes in the health care delivery system may also affect the role of the school library media center specialist. For example, schools often provide parenting classes that include information on consumer and family health. School-based community health clinics are being rapidly established around the country. Both of these developments place some responsibility on the school library media collection to provide consumer health information for parents and age-appropriate health information for students.

PROFILE 5. SOCIAL STUDIES: HISTORY AND EVENTS

Although social studies has a relatively brief history as a part of the school curriculum, it is one that has been filled with turbulence. Social studies can be broadly defined as the study of human enterprise across space and time. The concept as generally understood today was introduced in 1916 as a part of a broad-based American educational reform movement. It was heavily influenced by the introduction of the academic study of history as a core element of the secondary curriculum and by the need for citizenship education.[8]

The content and pedagogical approach to social studies continue to be debated. Over the years several approaches have won favor with educators and with the public. These include the life adjustment movement, progressive education principles, social reconstructionism, and nationalistic history study. Today the argument seems to be between those who favor a social problems approach and those who support a disciplined and academic study of history and geography.[9] The school library media specialist may indeed take part in this debate, but the professional challenge is to see that the school media center collection includes materials that support all sides in the continuing debate. As has been stressed throughout this book, the development of a balanced and inclusive school library media collection is a social and cultural responsibility. Many issues in social studies are controversial, and views and opinions differ on many issues. Information on all of the major political ideologies, including communism, socialism, and democracy, is needed in the collection. The school library media specialist has a moral obligation to present a balanced collection that includes various points of view and to support intellectual freedom as defined by law, court interpretations, and constitutional rights. In this area school media specialists need to be especially aware of how their personal biases might influence the development of the collection. In addition to meeting the usual evaluation criteria of authority, accuracy, clear points of view, truthfulness, stimulating style, and good organization and design, items should also offer readers or users opportunities to extend their knowledge and experience.

The social studies collection must present both standard and/or definitive age and grade appropriate works that have influenced history and other relevant fields of study. Under this guideline works by or about Hitler, Stalin, Lenin, and Gandhi can be justified. Current issues and events such as immigration policies and patterns and the treatment of the environment as both a social and political issue need to be included.

Historical revisionism and reinterpretation are unpopular in many traditional quarters because they often challenge long-held beliefs and value systems. Revisionist works can be inaccurate as well as is the case with many works of Holocaust revisionism. Ben S. Austin sees historical revisionism as

a perfectly legitimate, respectable and necessary approach to historical analysis. Each new generation has at its disposal new information, new facts and new methods not available to its predecessors. Contemporary historians, armed with new documentary, archaeological and anthropological data, are in a much better position to assess the slavery era in the American south than were historians writing during slavery or in the decades immediately following Emancipation. Similarly, we are in a much better position today to assess the Vietnam War than we were in the 60s or the 70s. Our understanding of the role of women in U.S. and world history is largely the product of historical revisionists who dared to challenge the historical invisibility of women. African American historians are now doing the same thing with regard to important contributions of African Americans. The canons of scholarship and academic integrity make it incumbent upon historians to involve themselves in the on-going re-evaluation of historical events and issues. Even if they have an ideological "axe to grind," revisionist historians render a valuable service by bringing the issues into public discussion and clarification.[10]

Works on the development of the modern industrial state, the roles African Americans and native peoples have played in the historical fabric of nations, and the women's rights movement add both depth and perspective to a collection, and they are important in promoting students' critical thinking skills.[11]

The preservation of history though documents, artifacts, and the encouragement of historic memory at the local, national, and international level needs further discussion. The role of public history and how to best serve the information needs for public history is also open for discussion. Public history is a movement within the history profession that seeks to bring history to the people. Public historians attempt to transfer their insights and understandings of history to a non-academic public. Public history can play a vital role in helping students to not only understand history, but to appreciate their unique place in its unfolding. School projects in which students go into the community for information is a form of public history. Often, societies that have their origin in the recognition of history—one such is the National Society of Colonial Dames in America (http://www.tatehouse.org/damesright.html)—have as one of their goals to stimulate interest in history. For example, the local society in Austin, Texas, prepared curriculum guide for use in the local schools to help students understand the significance of one of the historical homes that the society owns. Public history also serves as another example of the expanding role of collection development. No longer can we rely only on what is in the building-level collection, but we must consider resources outside the collection as vital to the educational process. Resources offered by museums, zoos, archives, and concert halls offer students opportunities to broaden their understanding of the world in which they live. For more information on public history and public history resources that support school curriculums consult the National Council on Public History (http://ncph.org).

Young people have an intense interest in many aspects of history and current society, and collection development policy should reflect those interests. World War II, the Vietnam War, and the Gulf War are popular topics. Firsthand accounts of those who experienced the Holocaust and other injustices remain popular. Materials that deal with current events such as social unrest, wilderness and catastrophe survival themes, AIDS/HIV, socially dysfunctional behavior caused by drugs and alcohol, child abuse, and other forms of violence are popular. Personal safety and gun control issues are also of concern to youth.

PROFILE 6. MUSIC AND ART

Music, including rock, rap, soul, country, and classical, is one of the major interests of youth. Collection development policies need to address both what is popular with youth and what is appropriate within a curricular and cultural framework. While it may not be feasible to purchase examples of every popular music fad, it is possible to build a collection that recognizes the many and varied forms of music. School library media center collections need to present a balanced view of music and include the popular as well as the classic. Examples of regional music and the music of minority groups are also important. The collection will need to be developed around use, recreation, curriculum needs, research, and study, and should include trade books, reference materials, mass market paperbacks when appropriate, and nonbook items such as video recordings and CDs. Well-reviewed Web sites on music information will also prove valuable. Standard works in music and music biography as well as the history of various music forms should not be neglected. Teen magazines and popular music periodicals such as *Rolling Stone, Down Beat*, the *Journal of Country Music*, and *Opera News* are filled with information about music, and a careful selection of these will be welcomed by users of the collection.

Art is also an important area in the collection. Classic and standard works as well as current materials are needed. Artists' biographies and art history works are particularly valuable. Reference materials are needed to help answer specific questions, as are materials that describe the history and development of art movements or styles. Works that help identify specific works of art are always in demand. Perhaps not always affordable, *The Dictionary of Art* (Grove 1996, www.macmillanonline.net /art/indexgrove.htm) is one of the great reference works of the world, and any school library media center would benefit greatly by its acquisition. Catalogs on exhibits published by art museums likewise are excellent sources on the background and history of significant artists and art movements. Art book dealers can be of great assistance in locating these as well as other art books.

In addition to background materials, an art collection should include portfolios of works by artists such as Ansel Adams, John James Audubon, and others. Regional artwork should also be reflected in the collection. Works explaining art styles and techniques are also needed. The art collection should be wide-ranging, including works on architecture, home and industrial design, and visual arts, including cinema and photography. When building an art collection, school library media specialists should also remember that art is both a visual and an emotional experience. One of the major uses of an art collection is to build appreciation for and knowledge of art so that students can become discriminating critics. Observation skills and an appreciation for how an artist uses line shape, color, and point of view or perspective are just a few of the many aspects of visual literacy an art collection can promote in students.[12]

PROFILE 7. RELIGION AND SPIRITUALITY

Religion and spirituality materials have a place in school library media collections. Traditionally collections have included items on religion because it is part of the human cultural heritage. Under this guideline materials on religious thought and practice can be included. Materials that are decidedly doctrinal and treat other religions in a derogatory manner have generally been rejected by public school library collections. A current question is whether religious fiction has a place in the school media library collection. Simply because the characters and setting reflect religion is no reason to reject such works. The novel *The Bronze Bow* by Elizabeth George Speare (Houghton Mifflin, 1961), set in ancient Israel, concerns the conflict of religion, friendship, and patriotism and is most suitable for a school collection. Fran Arrick, in her novel *God's Radar* (Bradbury Press, 1983), attacks the abusive methods of extreme religious Christian fundamentalists as they seek to enforce conformity on new converts. It is clear that the author is opposed to the pervasive influence of this type of fundamentalism in the community. This novel has been well reviewed and recommended for youth collections largely because of the social and cultural issues it raises. Doctrinal fiction that supports a particular style of religious expression remains problematic. *Library Journal* now reviews Christian fiction—which is often fundamentalist in its approach—for public libraries, and many public libraries now purchase this fiction for their users. Some, if not most, American public school library collections would find such fiction hard to defend based on the separation of church and state provisions of the First Amendment to the Constitution. School library media specialists have rarely objected to religious or spiritual themes being present in fiction and information books for youth. Numerous examples can be found in collections. For example, *One God, How We Worship Him* by Mary F. Fitch (Lothrop, Lee & Shepard, 1944) is an overview of how one God is worshipped by three peoples—Jews, Christians, and Muslins. The Newbery Award winner, . . . *And Now Miguel* by Joseph Krumgold (Crowell, 1953) has a scene where the young Miguel prays to the Virgin Mary asking for forgiveness for a transgression that he believes he has committed against his brother. Rumer Godden's *The Kitchen Madonna* (Viking, 1967) uses religious symbolism as a way to formulate friendship and self-discovery. Some school library media center specialists believe that more direct theologically based religious fiction and non-fiction may be justified in a school media library collection provided they meet the general selection guidelines established for all items. Based on good selection criteria they contend that the school library media specialist can justify books and media that contain controversial theological concepts such as The Rapture and the theological message found in the best-selling Left Behind series (http://www.leftbehind.com/).

On the other hand, the argument can be made that specific religious theology that is exclusionary, such as the concept of The Rapture, where some people are taken directly to heaven by Jesus because of their faith in him as savior while others are left behind to suffer pain and torment for their sin of disbelief cannot easily be justified in a collection meant to serve youth from various backgrounds. Once again, collection guidelines about selection can greatly help when such decisions have to be made.

Materials that explain atheistic and agnostic ideas and New Age religious belief systems also reflect society and culture and multiculturalism, and they have a place in a collection providing they meet appropriate review standards. The complaint is often heard that religions other than Christianity are not well represented in school library collections. The school library media specialist should investigate such complaints and, if necessary, take steps to remedy the situation. Standard selection aids such as those mentioned in Chapter 7 and *Children's Books About Religion* by Patricia Pearl Dole (Libraries Unlimited, 1999) are available to help make good and defensible decisions on religious and spiritual materials.

CONCLUSION

The art and science of collection building require a great deal of knowledge about those who will use the collection, whether they are students, staff, faculty, or parents. In addition, building collections is a social and cultural process, reflecting the values and expectations of society. Fundamental to developing viable collections that will meet a variety of needs is an understanding of society, its laws and expectations, and the demands it places on the educational system. Also helpful in making selection decisions is the ability to recognize the many creative processes that go into making an information or literary product. Although not all of these products will be suitable for individual collections, the knowledge, expertise, insight, and creativity authors and producers bring to their work in an open, democratic society can only enrich libraries helping them to contribute to the intellectual, social, and cognitive development of youth.

NOTES

1. Nilsen and Donelson, *Literature*, 6th ed., pp. 67, 116–17, 149, 159, 180–81, 263, 292–93.

2. Charlotte S. Huck and others, *Children's Literature in the Elementary School*, 7th ed. (Dubuque, IA: McGraw-Hill, 2001); Donna E. Norton, *Multicultural Children's Literature: Through the Eyes of Many Children* (Upper Saddle River, NJ: Merrill Prentice-Hall, 2001); Zena Sutherland and Trina Schart Hyman, *Children and Books*, 9th ed. (New York: Longman, 1997).

3. Nilsen and Donelson, *Literature*, 6th ed., pp. 304–7.

4. Charlotte S. Huck and others, *Children's Literature in the Elementary School*, 6th ed. (Madison, WI: Brown and Benchmark, 1997), p. 390.

5. Ibid., pp. 266–68.

6. Joseph Schwartz and Michael McGuinness, *Einstein for Beginners* (New York: Pantheon Books, 1979), pp. 121–31.

7. Huck and others, *Children's Literature*, 6th ed., pp. 577–93.

8. E. Wayne Ross, ed., *The Social Studies Curriculum: Purposes, Problems, and Possibilities* (Albany: State University of New York Press, 1997), p. xi.

9. Ibid., p. xii.

10. Ben S. Austin, "Deniers in Revisionists Clothing," available at http://www.mtsu.edu/~baustin/revision.htm.

11. Oliver Arnold, "Historicism," in *Dictionary of Cultural and Critical Theory*, edited by Michael Payne and others (Oxford: Blackwell, 1996), pp. 245–46; R. De Keyser, "History: Educational Programs," in *The International Encyclopedia of Education*, 2d ed., vol. 8, edited by Torsten Husén and T. Neville Postlethwaite (London: Pergamon, 1994); Stuart Shapiro, "Teaching of Social History," in *Encyclopedia of Social History*, edited by Peter N. Stearns (New York: Garland, 1994), pp. 740–46.

12. Janet Moor Gaylord, *The Many Ways of Seeing* (Cleveland: World Publishing, 1968).

Selected Bibliography

Albrecth, M. C. "The Relationship of Literature and Society." *American Journal of Sociology* 59 (March 1954): 425–26, 431–32.

American Association of School Librarians. *Media Programs: District and School.* Chicago: American Library Association; Washington, DC: Association for Educational Communication and Technology, 1975.

———. *Standards for School Library Programs.* Chicago: American Library Association, 1960.

———. *A Planning Guide for Information Power: Building Partnerships for Learning with School Library Media Program Assessment Rubric for the 21st Century.* Chicago: American Library Association, 1999.

———. "Statements on Filtering." Available at http://www.ala.org/alaorg/oif/filtersandfiltering.html.

American Association of School Librarians and Association for Educational Communications and Technology. *Information Literacy Standards for Student Learning.* Chicago: American Library Association, 1998.

———. *Information Power: Building Partnerships for Learning.* Chicago: American Library Association; Washington, DC: Association for Educational Communications and Technology, 1998.

———. *Information Power: Guidelines for School Library Media Programs.* Chicago: American Library Association; Washington, DC: Association for Educational Communications and Technology, 1988.

———. *Standards for School Media Programs.* Chicago: American Library Association; Washington, DC: National Education Association, 1969.

American Library Association. *ALA's Guide to Best Reading in 2001.* Chicago: American Library Association, 2001.

———. *Banned Books Resource Guide.* Chicago: American Library Association, 2000.

————. *Intellectual Freedom Manual.* 5th ed. Chicago: American Library Association, 1996.

————. *Libraries and the Internet Toolkit.* Chicago: American Library Association, 2000.

————. *Guide for Written Collection Policy Statements.* 2d ed. Chicago: American Library Association, 1996.

————. *Guide to the Evaluation of Library Collections.* Chicago: American Library Association, 1989.

American Library Association. Committee on Post-War Planning. *School Libraries for Today and Tomorrow.* Chicago: American Library Association, 1945.

Anderson, Joanne S. *Guide for Written Collection Policy Statements.* Chicago: American Library Association, 1996.

Ang, Susan. *The Widening World of Children's Literature.* New York: St. Martin's Press, 2000.

Aronson, Marc. *Exploding the Myths: The Truth about Teenagers and Reading.* Lanham, MD: Scarecrow Press, 2001.

————. "Not a Necessary Purchase: The Journals Judged: Reviewing Children's Literature in General Interest Publications." *The Horn Book* 73 (July/August 1997): 427–31.

Association for Library Service to Children. *Intellectual Freedom for Children: The Censor is Coming.* Chicago: American Library Association, 2000.

Avery, Gillian. *Beyond the Child: American Children and Their Books, 1621–1922.* Baltimore, MD: Johns Hopkins University Press, 1994.

Bajjaly, Stephen. *The Librarian's Community Network Handbook.* Chicago: American Library Association, 1999.

Baldwin, James A. "Putting Your Trust in Reviews: The Ethics of Book Reviewing." *Library Collection Acquisition and Technical Services* 23 (Summer 1999): 202–3.

Bazerman, Max. *Judgment in Managerial Decision Making.* 4th ed. New York: John Wiley and Sons, 1998.

Bearne, Eve, and Victor Watson, eds. *Where Texts and Child Meet.* New York: Routledge, 2000.

Beckett, Sandra, ed. *Transcending Boundaries: Writing for a Dual Audience of Children and Adults.* New York: Garland Publishing, 1999.

Besharov, Douglas J., and Karen N. Gardiner. "Sex Education and Abstinence: Programs and Evaluation." *Children and Youth Services Review* 19, no. 5/6 (1997): 327–39.

Beyer, Bonnie M., and Connie Ruhl-Smith. "Leadership Styles for Total Quality Schools." In *Creating High Functioning Schools: Practice and Research*, edited by Yvonne Cano and others. Springfield, IL: Charles C Thomas, 1998, pp. 9–19.

Bielefield, Arlene, and Lawrence Cheeseman. *Interpreting and Negotiating Licensing Agreements: A Guide for Library Research and Teaching Professions.* New York: Neal-Schuman, 1999.

Bishop, Kay, and Phyllis J. Van Orden. "Reviewing Children's Books: A Content Analysis of Book Reviews in Six Major Journals." *Library Quarterly* 68 (April 1998): 145–82.

Boaz, Martha. "Censorship." In *Encyclopedia of Library and Information Science*, edited by Allen Kent and Harold Lancour. New York: Marcel Dekker, 1970, Vol. 4, pp. 328–38.

Bonime, Andrew, and Ken C. Pohlman. *Writing for New Media: The Essential Guide for Writing for Interactive Media, CD-ROMs, and the Web.* New York: John Wiley and Sons, 1998.

Bowman, Cynthia Ann, ed. *Using Literature to Help Troubled Teenagers Cope with Health Issues.* Westport, CT: Greenwood Publishing Group, 2000.

Bradburn, Bryant. *Output Measures for School Library Media Programs.* New York: Neal-Schuman, 1999.

Brake, Terence. *The Need to Know: Teaching the Importance of Information: Final Report for the Period January 1978–March 1979.* London: British Library, 1980.

Braverman, Miriam. *Youth, Society, and the Public Library.* Chicago: American Library Association, 1979.

Breivik, Patricia Senn. *Student Learning in an Information Age.* Phoenix: Oryx Press, 1997.

Burden, Paul R. "The Key to Intellectual Freedom Is Universal Access to Information." *American Libraries* 31 (September 2000): 46–49.

Busha, Charles H. *Freedom Versus Suppression and Censorship; With a Study of Attitudes of Midwestern Public Librarians and a Bibliography of Censorship.* Littleton, CO: Libraries Unlimited, 1972.

Caiden, Gerald E. "Excessive Bureaucratization: The J-Curve of Bureaucracy and Max Weber Through the Looking Glass." In *Handbook of Bureaucracy*, edited by Ali Farazmand. New York: Marcel Dekker, 1994, pp. 31–32.

Calderone, Mary. "Young People, Sexuality and Librarians." *Top of the News* 34 (Winter 1978): 125–30.

Campbell, Patricia J. *Sex Education Books for Young Adults, 1892–1979.* New York: R. R. Bowker, 1979.

Canada. Ministry of National Health and Welfare. "Canadian Guideline for Sexual Health Education." Available at http://www.hc-gc.ca/lcdc/web/publicat.

Cano, Yvonne, and others, eds. *Creating High Functioning Schools: Practice and Research.* Springfield, IL: Charles C Thomas, 1998.

Carlton, Eric. *Values and the Social Sciences: An Introduction.* London: Gerald Duckworth, 1995.

Carol, Ann Doll. "Quality and Elementary School Library Collections." *School Library Media Quarterly* 25 (Winter 1997): 95–102.

Carpenter, Humphrey, and Mari Pichard. *The Oxford Companion to Children's Literature.* New York: Oxford University Press, 1999.

Cart, Michael. *From Romance to Realism: Fifty Years of Growth and Change in Young Adult Literature.* 1st ed. New York: HarperCollins, 1996.

Castro, Rafaela G., and others, eds. *What Do I Read Next? Multicultural Literature.* Detroit: Gale Group, 1997.

Champion, Sandra G. "The Adolescent Quest for Meaning Through Multicultural Readings: A Case Study." *Library Trends* 41 (Winter 1993): 462–92.

Cheeseman, Jennifer Day. *Population Projections of the United States, by Age, Sex, Race, and Hispanic Origin, 1995 to 2050. Current Population Reports.* Washington, DC: U.S. Bureau of the Census, U.S. Government Printing Office, 1996.

Children and the Internet: Guidelines for Developing Public Library Policy. Chicago: American Library Association, 1998.

Children's Literature: Annual of the Modern Language Association on Children's Literature and the Children's Literature Association, vol. 19, edited by Francelia Butler and others. New Haven, CT: Yale University Press, 1994.

Cianciolo, Patricia J. *Informational Books for Children.* Chicago: American Library Association, 2000.

Clark, Beverly Lyon. *Regendering the School Story: Sassy Sissies and Tattling Tomboys.* New York: Garland Publishing, 2001.

Clark, Beverly Lyon, and Janice M. Alberghene, eds. *"Little Women" and the Feminist Imagination: Criticism, Controversy, Personal Essays.* New York: Garland Publishing, 1999.

Clark, Beverly Lyon, and Margaret R. Higonnet, eds. *Girls, Boys, Books, Toys: Gender in Children's Literature and Culture.* Baltimore, MD: Johns Hopkins University Press, 1999.

Clyde, Laurel A. *Managing InfoTech in School Library Media Centers.* Englewood, CO: Libraries Unlimited, 1999.

Cooke, Alison. *Neal-Schuman Authoritative Guide to Evaluating Information on the Internet.* New York: Neal-Schuman, 1999.

Cornog, Martha, and Timothy Perper. *For Sex Education, See Librarian: A Guide to Issues and Resources.* Westport, CT: Greenwood Press, 1996.

Cortada, James W. *Rise of the Knowledge Worker.* Boston: Butterworth-Heinemann, 1998.

Craver, Kathleen W. *School Library Media Centers in the 21st Century: Changes and Challenges.* Westport, CT: Greenwood Press, 1994.

Crew, Hilary S. *Is It Really Mommie Dearest? Daughter-Mother Narratives in Young Adult Fiction.* Lanham, MD: Scarecrow Press, 2000.

Cullinan, Bernice E., and Diane Goetz Person, eds. *The Continuum Encyclopedia of Children's Literature.* New York: Continuum, 2001.

Cullingford, Cedric. *Children's Literature and Its Effects: The Formative Years.* Washington, DC: Cassell Academic, 1998.

D'Andrade, Roy. "Culture." In *The Social Science Encyclopedia,* 2d ed., edited by Adam Kuper and Jessica Kuper. London: Routledge, 1996, pp. 161–62.

Day, Frances Ann. *Lesbian and Gay Voices: An Annotated Bibliography and Guide to Literature for Children and Young Adults.* Westport, CT: Greenwood Press, 2000.

Deeds, Sharon, and Catherine Chastain, eds. *The New Books Kids Like.* Prepared for Association for Library Service to Children. Chicago: American Library Association, 2001.

De Vos, Gail, and Anna E. Altmann. *New Tales for Old: Folktales as Literary Fictions for Young Adults.* Englewood, CO: Libraries Unlimited, 1999.

Doggett, Sandra L. *Beyond the Book: Technology Integration into the Elementary School Library Media Curriculum.* Edited by Paula K. Montgomery. Englewood, CO: Libraries Unlimited, 2000.

Doiron, Connie, and Cathie May. "Book Power: The Role of Collection Development in Library Power." *Louisiana Library Association Bulletin* 57 (Winter 1995): 173–75.

Donham, Jean. *Enhancing Teaching and Learning: A Leadership Guide for School Media Specialists.* New York: Neal-Schuman, 1998.

Dresang, Eliza T. *Radical Change: Books for Youth in a Digital Age.* New York: H.W. Wilson, 1999.

Eaglen, Audrey. *Buying Books: A How-to-Do-It Manual for Librarians.* 2d ed. New York: Neal-Schuman, 2000.

Egoff, Sheila A., and others, eds. *Only Connect: Readings on Children's Literature.* 3d ed. New York: Oxford University Press, 1996.

Eisenberg, Michael B., and Robert Berkowitz. *Curriculum Initiative: An Agenda and Strategy for Library Media Programs.* Norwood, NJ: Ablex, 1988.

Eisenberg, Michael B., and others. *Teaching Information and Technology Skills: The Big 6 in Elementary Schools.* Worthington, OH: Linworth, 1999.

England, Clare, and Adele M. Fasick. *ChildView: Evaluating and Reviewing Materials for Children.* Littleton, CO: Libraries Unlimited, 1987.

Erikson, Rolf, and Carolyn Markuson. *Designing a School Media Center for the Future.* Chicago: American Library Association, 2001.

Evans, G. Edward, and Margaret R. Zarnosky. *Developing Library and Information Center Collections.* 4th ed. Englewood, CO: Libraries Unlimited, 2000.

Everhart, Nancy. *Evaluating the School Media Center: Analysis Techniques and Research Practices.* Englewood, CO: Libraries Unlimited, 1998.

Farmer, Lesley S. J., and Will Fowler. *More than Information: The Role of the Library Media Center in the Multimedia Classroom.* Worthington, OH: Linworth, 1999.

Fitzgerald, Mary Ann. "Critical Thinking 101: The Basics of Evaluating Information." *Knowledge Quest* 29 (November/December 2000): 13–20, 22–24.

Flood, Susan, ed. *Guide to Managing Approval Plans.* Chicago: American Library Association, 1998.

Freeman, Evelyn B., and Barbara A. Lehman. *Global Perspectives in Children's Literature.* Boston: Allyn and Bacon, 2001.

French, Martha M. *Starting with Assessment: A Developmental Approach to Deaf Children's Literacy.* Washington, DC: Gallaudet University, 1999.

Gillespie, John T., and Ralph J. Folcarelli. *Guide to Library Collection Development.* Englewood, CO: Libraries Unlimited, 1994.

Glazer, Joan I. *Literature for Young Children.* 4th ed. Upper Saddle River, NJ: Prentice-Hall, 1999.

Glennan, Thomas K., and Arthur Melmed. *Fostering the Use of Educational Technology: Elements of National Strategy.* RAND MR-682-OSTP. Santa Monica, CA: RAND, 1996.

Gorman, G. E., and Ruth H. Miller, eds. *Collection Management for the 21st Century: A Handbook for Librarians.* Westport, CT: Greenwood Press, 1997.

Gorman, Michael. *Our Enduring Values: Librarianship in the 21st Century.* Chicago: American Library Association, 2000.

Graham, Lisa. *The Principles of Interactive Design.* Albany, NY: Delmar, 1998.

Gregory, Vicki L. *Selecting and Managing Electronic Resources.* New York: Neal-Schuman, 2000.

Gregory, Vicki L., and others. *Multicultural Resources on the Internet: The United States and Canada*. Englewood, CO: Libraries Unlimited, 1999.

Guroian, Vigen. *Tending the Heart of Virtue: How Classic Stories Awaken a Child's Moral Imagination*. New York: Oxford University Press, 1998.

Gwinnett County (Georgia) Public Library Staff, comp. *Weeding Guidelines*. Distributed by the Public Library Association. Chicago: American Library Association, 1999.

Haffner, Debra Wynne, and William L. Yarber. *Guidelines for Comprehensive Sexuality Education: Kindergarten–12th Grade*. 2d ed. New York: Sexuality Information and Education Council of the United States, National Guidelines Task Force, 1996.

Harrington, Janice N. *Multiculturalism in Library Programming for Children*. Chicago: American Library Association, 1994.

Hauptman, Robert, and others. "Pragmatic Capitulation: Why the Information Specialist Censors." *Library Talk* 12 (May–June 1999): 20–21.

Haycock, Ken, ed. *Foundations for Effective School Library Media Programs*. Englewood, CO: Libraries Unlimited, 1999.

Hearne, Betsy Gould, and Deborah Stevenson. *Choosing Books for Children: A Commonsense Guide*. 3d ed. Urbana: University of Illinois Press, 1999.

Heinich, Robert, and others. *Instructional Media and Technologies for Learning*. 7th ed. Upper Saddle River, NJ: Merrill, 2002.

Helmer, Dona J., comp. *Selecting Materials for School Library Media Centers*. 2d ed. Chicago: American Library Association, 1993.

Herald, Diana Tixier. *Fluent in Fantasy: A Guide to Reading Interests*. Englewood, CO: Libraries Unlimited, 1999.

———. *Genreflecting: A Guide to Reading Interest in Genre Fiction*. 5th ed. Englewood, CO: Libraries Unlimited, 2000.

———. *Teen Genreflecting*. Englewood, CO: Libraries Unlimited, 1997.

Herz, Sarah K., and Donald R. Gallo. *From Hinton to Hamlet*. Westport, CT: Greenwood Publishing Group, 1996.

Himmelfarb, Gertrude. *One Nation, Two Cultures*. New York: Alfred A. Knopf, 1999.

Horning, Kathleen T. *From Cover to Cover: Evaluating and Reviewing Children's Books*. New York: HarperCollins, 1997.

Huck, Charlotte S., and others. *Children's Literature in the Elementary School, with Free Children's Literature CD-ROM*. 7th ed. Dubuque, IA: McGraw-Hill, 2001.

Hughes-Hassell, Sandra, and Anne Wheelock, eds. *The Information-Powered School*. Chicago: American Library Association, 2001.

Hull, Mary. *Censorship in America: A Reference Handbook*. Santa Barbara, CA: ABC-CLIO, 1999.

Hunt, Peter. *Children's Literature*. Malden, MA: Blackwell, 2001.

———. *An Introduction to Children's Literature*. Oxford: Oxford University Press, 1994.

Illinois Library Association. *The Internet and Our Children: A Community Partnership*. Chicago: Illinois Library Association, 2000.

Immroth, Barbara, Kathleen McCook de la Peña, and others. *Library Services to Youth of Hispanic Heritage*. Jefferson, NC: McFarland, 2000.

Isaac, R. G. "Organization Culture: Some New Perspectives." In *Handbook of Organizational Behavior*, edited by T. Y. Golembiewski. New York: Marcel Dekker, 1992, pp. 92–93.

Januszewski, Alan. *Educational Technology: The Development of a Concept*. Englewood, CO: Libraries Unlimited, 2001.

Johnson, Peggy, and Bonnie MacEwan, eds. *Virtually Yours: Models for Managing Electronic Resources and Services*. Chicago: American Library Association, 1998.

Jones, Dolores Blythe. *Building a Special Collection of Children's Literature in Your Library: A Guide to Identifying, Maintaining, and Sharing Rare or Collectible Items*. Chicago: American Library Association, 1998.

———. *Special Collections in Children's Literature: An International Directory*. 3d ed. Chicago: American Library Association, 1995.

Jones, Dudley, and others, eds. *A Necessary Fantasy? The Heroic Figure in Children's Popular Culture*. New York: Garland Publishing, 2000.

Jonscher, Charles. *The Evolution of Wired Life*. New York: John Wiley and Sons, 1999.

Jweid, Rosann, and Margaret Rizzo. *Building Character through Literature*. Lanham, MD: Scarecrow Press, 2001.

Karolides, Nicholas J., and others. *100 Banned Books: Censorship Histories of World Literature*. New York: Facts on File, 1999.

Katz, Bill, ed. *New Technologies and Reference Services*. New York: Haworth Press, 2000.

Kearney, Carol A. *Curriculum Partner: Redefining the Role of the Library Media Specialist*. Westport, CT: Greenwood Press, 2000.

Kennemer, Phyllis Kay. "An Analysis of Reviews of Books of Fiction for Children and Adolescents Published in Major Selection Aids in the United States in 1979." Dissertation, University of Colorado at Boulder, 1980. *Dissertation Abstracts International-A* 42 (July 1981): 81.

Kohl, Herbert R. *Should We Burn Babar? Essays on Children's Literature and the Power of Stories*. New York: New Press, Distributed by W. W. Norton, 1995.

Kouki, Rafa, and David Wright. *Telelearning via the Internet*. Hershey, PA: Idea Group Pub., 1999.

Kristin, Ramsdell. *Romance Fiction*. Englewood, CO: Libraries Unlimited, 1999.

Kuhlthau, Carol Collier. "Information Search Process: A Summary of Research and Implications for School Media Programs." *School Library Media Quarterly* 18 (Fall 1989): 19–25.

———. *Seeking Meaning: A Process Approach to Library and Information Services*. Norwood, NJ: Ablex, 1994.

Kuhlthau, Carol Collier, ed. *Assessment and the School Library Media Center*. Englewood, CO: Libraries Unlimited, 1994.

Kuhlthau, Carol Collier, and others, eds. *The Virtual School Library: Gateway to the Information Superhighway*. Englewood, CO: Libraries Unlimited, 1999.

Kuhn, Thomas S. *The Structure of Scientific Revolutions*. 2d ed., enl. Chicago: University of Chicago Press, 1970.

Kunzel, Bonnie, and Suzanne Manczuk. *First Contact: Reader's Selection of Science Fiction and Fantasy*. Lanham, MD: Scarecrow Press, 2001.

Kutzer, Daphne, and Emmanuel S. Nelson, eds. *Writers of Multicultural Fiction for Young Adults.* Westport, CT: Greenwood Publishing Group, 1996.

Lance, Keith Curry, and others. *How School Librarians Help Kids Achieve Standards: The Second Colorado Study.* San Jose, CA: Hi Willow Research and Publishing, 2000.

Landry, David J., and others. "Abstinence Promotion and the Provision of Information About Contraception in Public School District Sexuality Education Programs." *Family Planning Perspectives* 31 (November/December 1999): 280–86.

Lehn, Susan S., ed. *Beauty, Brains, and Brawn: The Construction of Gender in Children's Literature.* Portsmouth, NH: Heinemann, 2001.

Lehr, Valerie. *Queer Family Values: Debunking the Myth of the Nuclear Family.* Philadelphia: Temple University Press, 1999.

Lewis, Marjorie, ed. *Outstanding Books for the College Bound: Choices for a Generation.* Chicago: American Library Association, 1996.

Loertscher, David V. *Collection Mapping in the LMC: Building Access in a World of Technology.* Castle Rock, CO: Hi Willow Research and Publishing, 1996.

Loertscher, David V., and Blanche Woolls. *Information Literacy: A Review of the Research.* San Jose: Hi Willow Research and Publishing, 1999.

Loertscher, David V., and others. *Building a School Library Collection Plan: A Beginning Handbook with Internet Assist.* San Jose, CA: Hi Willow Research and Publishing, 1999.

Lowell, Martin A. *Enrichment: A History of the Public Library in the United States in the Twentieth Century.* Lanham, MD: Scarecrow Press, 1998.

Lukenbill, W. Bernard. "Community Information in Schools: An Operational Approach and Model." In *Information and Referral in Reference Services*, edited by Marcia Middleton and Bill Katz. New York: Haworth Press, 1988, pp. 173–88.

———. "Erotized, AIDS-HIV Information on Public-Access Television: A Study in Obscenity, State Censorship and Cultural Resistance." *AIDS Education and Prevention* 10 (June 1998): 229–44.

———. "Learning Resources and Interactive Learning Principles." *Drexel Library Quarterly* 19 (Spring 1983).

Lukens, Rebecca J. *A Critical Handbook of Children's Literature.* 6th ed. New York: Longman, 1999.

Lundin, Anne H. "Victorian Horizons: The Reception of Children's Books in England and America, 1880–1900." *Library Quarterly* 64 (January 1994): 30–59.

MacLeod, Ann Scott. *American Childhood: Essays on Children's Literature of the Nineteenth and Twentieth Centuries.* Athens: University of Georgia Press, 1994.

———. *A Moral Tale: Children's Fiction and American Culture, 1820–1860.* Hamden, CT: Archon, 1990.

MacNee, Marie J. *Science Fiction, Fantasy, and Horror Writers.* New York: UXL, 1995.

Makowski, Silk. *Serious About Series: Evaluation and Annotations of Teen Fiction in Paperback Series.* Edited by Dorothy Broderick. Lanham, MD: Scarecrow Press, 1998.

Mandel, Mimi. *Teen Resources on the Web: A Guide for Librarians, Parents, and Teachers*. Fort Atkinson, WI: Alleyside Press/Highsmith Press, 2000.

Mason, Mary Ann, and others, eds. *All Our Families: New Policies for a New Century. A Report of the Berkeley Family Forum*. New York: Oxford University Press, 1998.

Mass, Wendy, ed. *Children's Literature*. San Diego, CA: Greenhaven Press, 2001.

McCaffery, Laura Hibbets. *Building an ESL Collection for Young Adults: A Bibliography of Recommended Fiction and Nonfiction for Schools and Public Libraries*. Westport, CT: Greenwood Press, 1998.

McCallum, Elizabeth, and Jane Scott. *The Book Tree: A Christian Reference for Children's Literature*. Moscow, ID: Canon Press, 2000.

McCallum, Robyn, and Jack Zipes, eds. *Ideologies of Identity in Adolescent Fiction: The Dialogic Construction of Subjectivity*. New York: Garland Publishing, 1999.

McGillis, Roderick, ed. *Voices of the Other: Children's Literature and the Postcolonial Context*. New York: Garland Publishing, 1999.

Miller, Marilyn L., and Marilyn L. Shontz. "Small Change: Expenditures for Resources in School Library Media Centers, FY 1995–96." *School Library Journal* 43 (October 1997): 28–37.

Monaghan, Jennifer. *A Common Heritage: Noah Webster's Blue-Back Speller*. Hamden, CT: Archon Books, 1983.

Munic, Martin D. "Education or Indoctrination—Removal of Books from Public School Libraries: *Board of Education, Island Trees Union Free School District No. 26 v. Pico*." *Minnesota Law Review* 68 (October 1983): 213–53.

Murray, Gail Schmunk, and Warren French. *American Children's Literature and the Construction of Childhood*. New York: Prentice-Hall, 1998.

Napier, Rodney W., and Matti I. Gershenfeld. *Groups: Theory and Experience*. 6th ed. Boston: Houghton Mifflin, 1999.

National Center for Education Statistics. *Highlights of U.S. Results from the International IEA Civic Education Study (CivEd)*. Washington, DC: U.S. Department of Education, 2001, available at http://nces.ed.gov.

National Education Association and North Central Association of Colleges and Secondary Schools. Committee on Library Organization and Equipment. *Standard Library Organization and Equipment for Secondary Schools of Different Sizes*, C.C. Certain, chairman. Chicago: American Library Association, 1920.

National Education Association of the United States. Department of Elementary School Principals. "Report of the Joint Committee on Elementary School Library Standards." In *Fourth Yearbook: The Elementary School Principalship: A Study of Its Instructional and Administrative Aspects*, edited by Arthur Gist. Washington, DC: National Education Association, 1925, pp. 326–59.

Nebraska Educational Media Association. *Guide for Developing and Evaluating School Library Media Programs 2000*. 6th ed. Englewood, CO: Libraries Unlimited, 2000.

The Newbery and Caldecott Medal Books, 1986–2000: A Comprehensive Guide to the Winners. Chicago: American Library Association, 2001.

Nikolajeva, Naria, and Carole Scott. *How Picturebooks Work*. New York: Garland Publishing, 2000.

Nilsen, Alleen Pace, and Kenneth L. Donelson. *Literature for Today's Young Adults.* 6th ed. New York: Longman, 2001.

Norfolk, Bobby, and Sherry Norfolk. *The Moral of the Story: Folktales for Character Development.* Little Rock, AR: August House, 1999.

Norton, Donna E. *Multicultural Children's Literature: Through the Eyes of Many Children.* Upper Saddle River, NJ: Merrill Prentice-Hall, 2001.

O'Brien, Michael. *A Landscape with Dragons: The Battle for Your Child's Mind.* 2d ed. San Francisco: Ignatius Press, 1998.

O'Keefe, Deborah. *Good Girl Messages: How Young Women Were Misled by Their Favorite Books.* New York: Continuum, 2000.

Olson, Joan Blodgett Peterson. "An Interpretive History of the *Horn Book Magazine*, 1924–1973." Ph.D. dissertation, Stanford University, 1976, cited in *Dissertations Abstracts International*, vol. 37-A, p. 2875.

Orna, Elizabeth. *Practical Information Policies.* 2d ed. Brookfield, VT: Gower, 1999.

Overstreet, Deborah Wilson. *Unencumbered by History: The Vietnam Experience in Young Adult Fiction.* Lanham, MD: Scarecrow Press, 1998.

Palmer, William S. "Evolving Criteria for Evaluating Sex Education Books." *Voice of Youth Advocates* 5 (April 1982): 23–24.

Peck, Robert S. *Libraries, the First Amendment and Cyberspace. What You Need to Know.* Chicago: American Library Association, 2000.

Pratt, Linda, and others. *Transcultural Children's Literature.* Upper Saddle River, NJ: Merrill, 1999.

Public Library Association. *Guidelines for Establishing Community Information and Referral Services in Public Libraries.* 4th ed. Chicago: American Library Association, 1997.

Rankin, Virginia. *The Thoughtful Researcher: Teaching the Research Process to Middle School Students.* Englewood, CO: Libraries Unlimited, 1999.

Reed, Arthea J.S. *Reaching Adolescents: The Young Adult Book and the School.* New York: Merrill, 1994.

Reese, William J. *The Origins of the American High School.* New Haven: Yale University Press, 1995.

Reid, Susanne Elizabeth. *Presenting Young Adult Science Fiction.* New York: Twayne, 1998.

Rice, Philip F. *The Adolescent: Development, Relationships, and Culture.* 9th ed. Boston: Allyn and Bacon, 1999.

Robertson, Anne S. "The Parenting Education Spectrum: A Look at the Scope of Parenting Programs that Should Be Available Within a Community." *Parent News*, June 1998. Available at http://www.npin.org/pnew698/pbew698b.html.

Robertson, Priscella. "Home as Nest: Middle Class Childhood in Nineteenth-Century Europe." In *The History of Childhood*, edited by Lloyd de Mause. New York: Psychohistory Press, 1974, pp. 407–31.

Rochman, Hazel. *Against Borders: Promoting Books for a Multicultural World.* Chicago: American Library Association, 1993.

Roderic, Ogley. "Theories of Conflict." In *Encyclopedia of Violence, Peace, and Conflict*, Vol. 1, edited by Lester Kurtz and Jennifer Turpin. San Diego: Academic Press, 1999, pp. 401–12.

Ross, E. Wayne, ed. *The Social Studies Curriculum: Purpose, Problems, and Possibilities*. Albany: State University of New York Press, 1997.

Russell, David L. *Literature for Children: A Short Introduction*. 3d ed. New York: Longman, 2000.

Ryan, Jenny and Steph Capra. *Information Literacy Toolkit. Grades 7 and Up*. Chicago: American Library Association, 2001.

Saettler, Paul. *The Evolution of American Educational Technology*. Englewood, CO: Libraries Unlimited, 1990.

Samoriski, J. H., and others. "Indecency, the Federal Communications Commission, the Post-Siker Era: A Framework for Regulations." *Journal of Broadcasting and Electronic Media* 39 (Winter 1995): 51–57.

Sands, Karen, and Marietta Frank. *Back in the Spaceship Again: Juvenile Science Fiction Series Since 1945*. Westport, CT: Greenwood Publishing Group, 1999.

Schmidt, Karen, ed. *Understanding the Business of Library Acquisitions*. 2d ed. Chicago: American Library Association, 1998.

Schon, Isabel. *Recommended Books in Spanish for Children and Young Adults, 1996– Through 1999*. Lanham, MD: Scarecrow Press, 2000.

Schorr, Lisbeth. *Common Purpose: Strengthening Families and Neighborhoods to Rebuild America*. New York: Doubleday, 1997.

Seibel, Dieter. *The Dynamics of Achievement: A Radical Perspective*. Indianapolis: Bobbs-Merrill, 1974.

Seidman, Steven. *Embattled Eros: Sexual Politics and Ethics in Contemporary America*. New York: Routledge, 1992.

Semenza, Jenny Lynne. *The Librarian's Quick Guide to Internet Resources*. Fort Atkinson, WI: Highsmith Press, 1999.

Sex Information and Education Council of the United States. National Guidelines Task Force. *Guidelines for Comprehensive Sexuality Education, Kindergarten– 12th Grade*. New York: Sex Information and Education Council of the U.S., 1992.

Shapiro, Stuart. "Teaching of Social History." In *Encyclopedia of Social History*, edited by Peter N. Stearns. New York: Garland Publishing, 1994, pp. 740– 46.

Sherman, Gale W., and Bette D. Ammon. *Handbook for the Newbery Medal and Honor Books, 1990–1999*. Hagerstown, MD: Alleyside Press, 2000.

Silvey, Anita. *Children's Books and Their Creators*. Boston: Houghton Mifflin, 1995.

Spitzer, Kathleen L. *Information Literacy: Essential Skills for the Information Age*. Syracuse, NY: ERIC Clearinghouse on Information and Technology/Syracuse University Press, 1998.

Slote, Stanley J. *Weeding Library Collections: Library Weeding Methods*. 4th ed. Englewood, CO: Libraries Unlimited, 1997.

Smith, Mark. *Neal-Schuman Internet Policy Handbook for Librarians*. New York: Neal-Schuman, 1999.

Spenser, Pam. *What Do Young Adults Read Next? A Reader's Guide to Fiction for Young Adults*. Vol. 1. Detroit: Gale Group, 1994–.

Stripling, Barbara J. *Learning and Libraries in an Information Age: Principles and Practices*. Englewood, CO: Libraries Unlimited, 1999.

Strohl, Bonnie, ed. *Collection Evaluation Techniques: A Short, Selective, Practical,*

Current, Annotated Bibliography. Chicago: American Library Association, 1999.

Stueart, Robert D., and Barbara B. Moran. *Library and Information Center Management*. 5th ed. Littleton, CO: Libraries Unlimited, 1998.

Sutherland, Zena. *Children and Books*. 9th ed. New York: Longman, 1997.

Sydie, Rosalind. *Natural Women, Cultured Men: A Feminist Perspective on Sociological Theory*. Toronto: Methuen, 1987.

Symons, Ann K., and Sally Gardner Reed, eds. *Speaking Out! Voices in Celebration of Intellectual Freedom*. Chicago: American Library Association, 1999.

Tarbox, Gwen Athene. *The Clubwomen's Daughters: Collectivist Impulses in Progressive-Era Girl's Fiction, 1890–1940*. New York: Garland Publishing, 2000.

Texas Library Association. *Intellectual Freedom Handbook*. 5th ed. Austin: Texas Library Association, 1996. Available at http://www.txla.org/doc/ifhbk.html.

Thompson, Helen M., and Susan A. Henley. *Fostering Information Literacy: Connecting National Standards, Goals 2000, and the SCANS Report*. Englewood, CO: Libraries Unlimited, 2000.

Townsend, John Rowe. *Written for Children: An Outline of English-Language Children's Literature*. 6th American ed. Lanham, MD: Scarecrow Press, 1966.

Traw, Jeri L., comp. *Library Web Site Policies*. Chicago: American Library Association, 2000.

U.S. Department of Health and Human Services. *A National Strategy to Prevent Teen Pregnancy: Annual Report, 1999–2000*. Washington, DC: The Department, 2000. Available at www.aspe.hhs.gov/hsp/teenp/ann-rpt00/.

User Interface Engineering. *Eye for Design* (bimonthly periodical). [The User Interface Engineering items are available at 800 Turnpike Street, Suite 101, North Andover, MA, 01845, e-mail, uie@uie.com.]

———. *Web Site Usability: A Designer's Guide*. North Andover, MA: User Interface Engineering, 1999.

Vandergrift, Kay E. "Journey or Destination: Female Voices in Youth Literature." In *Mosaics of Meaning: Enhancing the Intellectual Life of Young Adults Through Story*, edited by Kay E. Vandergrift. Lanham, MD: Scarecrow Press, 1996), pp. 17–46.

Van Geel, Tyll. "The Search for Constitutional Limits on Government Authority to Inculcate Youth." *Texas Law Review* 62 (October 1983): 197–297.

Van Orden, Phyllis J., and Kay Bishop. *The Collection Program in Schools: Concepts, Practices and Information Sources*. 3d ed. Englewood, CO: Libraries Unlimited, 2001.

———. *Selecting Books for the Elementary School Library Media Center: A Complete Guide*. New York: Neal-Schuman, 2000.

Volz, Bridget Dealy, and others. *Junior Genreflecting: A Guide to Good Reads and Series Fiction for Children*. Englewood, CO: Libraries Unlimited, 2000.

Wadham, Tim. *Programming with Latino Children's Materials: A How-to-Do-It Manual for Librarians*. New York: Neal-Schuman, 1999.

Walker, Barbara J. *Developing Christian Fiction Collections for Children and Adults: Selection Criteria and a Core Collection*. New York: Neal-Schuman, 1998.

Walter, Virginia. A. *Children and Libraries: Getting It Right*. Chicago: American Library Association, 2001.

Watkins, Kevin. *Education Now: Break the Cycle of Poverty. A Report*. Washington, DC: Oxfam, 1999. Available at http://www.caa.org.au/oxfam/advocacy/education/report/html.

Watson, Victor. *Reading Series Fiction: From Arthur Ransome to Gene Kemp*. New York: Routledge, 2000.

Watson, Victor, and others, eds. *The Cambridge Guide to Children's Books in English*. New York: Cambridge University Press, 2001.

What Do Children & Young Adults Read? Vol. 1. Detroit: Gale Group, 1998–.

What Do Children Read Next: A Reader's Guide for Children. 3 vols. Detroit: Gale Group, 1994–1999.

What Do I Read Next? A Reader's Guide to Current Genre Fiction. Vol. 1. Detroit: Gale Group, 1990–.

White, Maureen, and others. "Great Things Come in Small Packages: A Parent Resource Library." *Journal of Youth Services in Libraries*. 14 (Fall 2000): 8–11.

Whitlatch, Jo Bell. *Evaluating Reference Services: A Practical Guide*. Chicago: American Library Association, 2000.

Willcoxon, Wanda Odom. "Collection Evaluation in a Georgia Elementary School." *Knowledge Quest* 29 (May/June 2001): 23–29.

Wilson, Margo, and Kay Bishop. "Criteria for Reviewing Children's Books Applied to Four Professional Journals." *Library Resources and Technical Services* 43 (January 1999): 3–13.

Wood, M. Sandra, ed. *Health Care Resources on the Internet: A Guide for Librarians and Health Care Consumers*. New York: Haworth Press, 2000.

Wright, Keith C., and Judith F. Davie. *Forecasting the Future: School Media Programs in an Age of Change*. Lanham, MD: Scarecrow Press, 1999.

Yesner, Bernice L., and Hilda L. Jay. *Operating and Evaluating School Library Media Programs: A Handbook for Administrators and Librarians*. New York: Neal-Schuman, 1998.

Yolen, Jane. *Touch Magic: Fantasy, Faerie, and Folklore in the Literature of Childhood*. Little Rock, AK: August House, 2000.

Young Adult Library Services Association. *Hit List: Frequently Challenged Books for Young Adults*. Chicago: American Library Association, 1994.

Zipes, Jack David. *Happily Ever After: Fairy Tales, Children, and the Culture Industry*. New York: Routledge, 1997.

———. *Sticks and Stones: The Troublesome Success of Children's Literature from Slovenly Peter to Harry Potter*. New York: Routledge, 2000.

Zornado, Joseph L. *Inventing the Child: Culture, Ideology, and the Story of Childhood*. New York: Garland Publishing, 2000.

Index

About the Author

W. BERNARD LUKENBILL is a professor in the graduate program of Library and Information Science at the University of Texas, Austin.